Get the eBooks FREE!

(PDF, ePub, and Kindle all included)

We believe that once you buy a book from us, you should be able to read it in any format we have available. To get electronic versions of this book at no additional cost to you, purchase and then register this book at the Manning website following the instructions inside this insert.

That's it!
Thanks from Manning!

D1225781

To register this book and download your free ebook:

1. Go to http://www.manning.com/ebookoffer
2. Enter the codes from this table when prompted
3. Download ebook using link emailed to you

	A	B	C	D	E	F	G	H	I
1	NJ 498 7620	JJ 756 4432	RP 362 1842	NJ 498 7620	MB 893 2715	WQ 869 3415	SO 972 3005	FF 906 8663	YK 952 5364
2	RD 736 5739	UN 578 8961	ML 340 9212	BV 909 4960	KX 185 1511	NF 890 7314	VS 499 6370	QF 141 8846	RX 518 3956
3	MM 841 1424	AA 454 9482	MQ 261 5909	AR 743 1904	UA 453 9538	MI 878 9199	MQ 224 7464	DC 475 4133	QB 428 0846
4	QI 128 9421	AV 692 5782	XW 261 9590	IT 916 9987	OP 399 9710	QO 923 8883	WF 640 7342	TK 517 9296	RK 404 8084
5	NS 637 9265	EE 414 4003	IB 972 8177	WR 407 0129	GI 987 6635	LR 200 1936	YP 320 3896	MK 249 9186	IS 392 8234
6	RR 415 9047	NQ 672 0608	KF 264 2695	TY 292 0679	UB 322 0002	CF 857 4735	RH 540 0436	LJ 560 9210	XV 269 5034

	A	B	C	D	E	F	G	H	I
7	HL 417 9972	WS 192 6192	PX 868 5657	WG 621 6584	TP 464 3907	WD 238 7720	KS 280 8607	RK 842 8321	NR 366 0642
8	WM 757 5254	RC 793 4748	KV 930 9218	WU 556 6671	EF 245 0280	NQ 785 4587	VB 501 3420	VX 609 9344	SN 475 3101
9	VU 205 5668	DQ 971 4718	SG 780 2619	XX 810 7321	AW 314 3021	XS 293 3319	KC 397 8322	OL 266 8164	HG 650 5315
10	VA 977 8020	YB 323 2242	WU 425 9045	YS 373 2652	EG 544 8698	MO 650 7217	RK 744 9595	AA 294 5514	MT 194 4588
11	HM 128 6678	GO 527 5629	TJ 934 7780	PO 500 8435	OC 383 4273	JS 698 4213	CO 355 1629	LL 469 7958	UJ 950 6922
12	YP 872 6516	XP 502 9481	TU 561 7700	KR 546 3273	WX 939 8601	LM 389 0960	NN 872 2433	CB 298 6777	BO 380 7686
13	WS 553 3684	RT 693 4845	LE 955 8187	BL 185 0780	YI 998 9585	GW 502 8358	BK 398 4797	MI 962 9727	LI 753 2403
14	LW 846 7100	AC 211 8469	GG 949 0788	RE 733 0491	RK 732 1781	NL 331 3885	HQ 578 1203	QS 530 2618	GJ 548 7355
15	HE 884 8541	DG 915 1190	GI 781 5549	AW 482 3953	QB 451 0813	VR 280 5122	QB 518 9138	GW 549 4289	UV 622 3520
16	RM 205 0099	NR 219 0831	SB 178 2914	OW 996 2645	BK 719 3183	WJ 423 7686	VG 213 8312	FX 574 1324	MW 880 3894
17	QX 800 5208	RD 204 8508	RK 986 9591	RK 401 3901	PT 383 1070	YD 533 7592	LP 919 6514	HJ 133 3702	XG 911 5103
18	YB 742 5608	MM 818 3965	GQ 897 8171	VB 871 2454	MC 196 0641	JA 244 3174	WW 496 8920	MV 413 8000	KY 460 1690
19	EX 764 7826	KX 608 5667	HW 516 4522	YH 552 9072	SY 869 9710	BY 312 0095	BX 808 6241	GC 341 6615	VO 890 9027
20	YV 499 8578	PP 811 9356	EA 370 5728	SO 338 2751	WB 492 6062	YI 911 6932	PF 102 1422	AT 112 5972	TH 839 2578

Irresistible APIs

DESIGNING WEB APIS
THAT DEVELOPERS WILL LOVE

KIRSTEN L. HUNTER

MANNING
SHELTER ISLAND

For online information and ordering of this and other Manning books, please visit
www.manning.com. The publisher offers discounts on this book when ordered in quantity.
For more information, please contact

Special Sales Department
Manning Publications Co.
20 Baldwin Road
PO Box 761
Shelter Island, NY 11964
Email: orders@manning.com

Manning Publications Co.
20 Baldwin Road
PO Box 761
Shelter Island, NY 11964

Development editor:	Lesley Trites
Technical development editor:	Nick Watts
Copyeditor:	Elizabeth Welch
Proofreader:	Corbin Collins
Technical proofreader:	David Fombella Pombal
Typesetter:	Dottie Marsico
Illustrator:	Viseslav Radovic
Cover designer:	Leslie Haimes

ISBN 9781617292552
Printed in the United States of America
1 2 3 4 5 6 7 8 9 10 – EBM – 21 20 19 18 17 16

brief contents

contents

foreword

Building an irresistible API doesn't only make good business sense—it also makes developers happy and productive rather than grumpy and frustrated. I'm very happy to see Kirsten write this book, which explains how to build well-engineered APIs and explores what makes a developer actively want to use that API.

I'll begin with a story. It's September 2008, and Netflix is running a "hack day." This is a day on which anyone at Netflix can build anything they want. It starts at noon one day and finishes at noon the next. You can work through the night if you need to. The Netflix API team was about to release the initial version of a public API for Netflix and had scheduled the hack day as a way to get extra testing time before the release. The Apple iPhone had been released earlier that year, and the first software developer toolkit for the iPhone had been released that summer. I was a manager at Netflix at that time, but I had started to build an iPhone app in my spare time and decided to build the first ever Netflix mobile app for the hack day.

The odds weren't looking good. I barely knew the Objective-C language that iPhone apps are written in, and no one else at Netflix had ever used it. The authentication protocol was new and buggy, and I had to improvise some iPhone code to connect to Netflix. I recruited an engineer to help. We spent several hours understanding and debugging the OAuth security protocol. Finally, I got the iPhone to connect successfully and started trying to make sense of the responses from API queries. The API was based on an XML-based standard called AtomPub, and generating the requests was awkward. Parsing them was even more awkward. It was really intended to be used from a web browser, not to support a mobile app. After a late night of coding and a lot of grumbling, I finally had a working prototype. In the afternoon, we all showed our hacks to a panel of judges, and I won a prize. I put it on the App Store, and it was the first public Netflix mobile app. It wasn't until 2010 that Netflix released official iPad and iPhone apps.

Netflix created a developer program around the public API, and Kirsten was one of the engineers hired to help run the program. In 2010 we both attended an iPad Dev Camp, run like an extended public hack day, and worked together on a Netflix-related iPad app. We were using the Netflix API despite its shortcomings, and I think there was a missed opportunity. Ultimately, the public API was a failure for Netflix, and the company shut it down. Kirsten tells the rest of this story in chapter 1 of this book.

I learned a lot from this experience—and from Kirsten herself. In 2016 this is a very important topic. Many companies need an API to do business. Many are even actively competing with other companies that have alternative APIs. In the past, software products were bought as prebuilt packages and were hand configured. Today software is often chosen by rummaging around on GitHub, trying to figure out which project has the most developer traction, and installation and deployment is automated via APIs. The lack of friction in web service and open source–based business models is there to be exploited by the viral spread of irresistible APIs.

Thank you, Kirsten, for this contribution to making the world a better place.

ADRIAN COCKCROFT
TECHNOLOGY FELLOW
AT BATTERY VENTURES

preface

From the time I started working with REST APIs at Socialtext in 2005, I've been fascinated by web services platforms. At Socialtext, we created a solid, consistent REST API, but it was only truly usable by our own team because the developer experience was immature. The documentation didn't have great tutorials, and our outreach was limited. I learned to love the idea of a platform built on a solid protocol like HTTP and the extensibility of REST APIs.

Ever since getting struck by the bug, I've been an enthusiastic advocate for the design and usability of web APIs. I've spent many a weekend creating mashups with Twitter, Facebook, Freebase (RIP), LinkedIn, Netflix, and tens of other web services. As I used these APIs, I started to develop an overall definition for platforms with irresistible APIs—platforms that offered amazing developer experiences. I came to realize that an irresistible API needs more than excellent, consistent interfaces. It's hard to succeed without great documentation, fantastic sample code, and an enthusiastic support structure.

As I worked in the industry, I was repeatedly employed in great positions to support developers and understand their needs. I came to realize that great developers who are trying to implement integrations with APIs don't automatically understand web services, so I integrated this information into my ideas about irresistible APIs: don't make assumptions about what your developers know. I started speaking at conferences and writing articles to help client developers understand and create amazing applications using web APIs.

I realized that educating the API creators was a more efficient way to improve the industry, and I began by speaking at the API Strategy and Practice conferences about developer experience to the companies developing and providing APIs. I started meeting and brainstorming with individuals in the API industry about best practices for web APIs. Over time I worked on ideas around creating APIs: treating your API as a first-class product, rather than shunting it off to the side of your main application. Despite the importance and visibility of web services, many companies hadn't given any thought to designing for use cases and business value.

After integrating the lessons I'd learned, I started proposing a talk on "Irresistible APIs," covering the entire spectrum of what I'd learned on the topic. Manning approached me to write a book with the information, and I jumped at the chance to share my ideas with people and companies across the globe. We are now on the cusp of a new stage of maturity for web services, and I hope my book can help move the industry in the right direction so that the use and integration of APIs will be easy for developers and profitable for companies.

I chose Node.js for this book because it's the most straightforward language for creating web platforms. I have also created a GitHub repository with multiple language examples, listed in the "About the code" section.

I hope you enjoy reading the book as much as I did writing it. Go forth and be excellent to your developers!

acknowledgments

First of all, thanks to Chris Dent and Matt Liggett for teaching me about REST APIs lo these 10 years ago. I'd never have gotten inspired to wave this flag if I hadn't been infected with their enthusiasm. Kin Lane, Steve Willmott, and Mike Admunsen, rock stars of the API industry, have helped me develop and advocate for best practices in the platform world. I'd also like to thank all the developer customers who have inspired me to make APIs more usable and friendly.

My appreciation also goes out to reviewers Heather Tooill, James Higginbotham, Jason Harmon, Manoj Agarwal, Adrian Cockcroft, Robert Walsh, Stephen Byrne, Joel Kotarski, Nickie Buckner, Kumar Unnikrishnan, Lourens Steyn, Karsten Strobaek, Marco Imperatore, Satadru Roy, Andrew Meredith, Aseem Anand, Chad Johnston, and all the MEAP purchasers for helping me to make the book the best it can be. My thanks go out to Michael Coury and my cats, Orange and Blue, for their help and patience while I spent weekends with my face buried in my computer. And a huge debt of gratitude is owed to Michael Aglietti and Corey Scobie and the whole team at Akamai for their support while I created the book.

Thanks also to the Manning team for all their support and guidance throughout the process of writing this, my first book. And of course, huge appreciation goes out to Adrian Cockcroft for his guidance early in my career and for writing my foreword.

about this book

Irresistible APIs provides all the information needed to plan and manage creation of a REST API. The book starts out with basic information about the technologies involved in web APIs—specifically REST APIs—to help make sure that readers have a great basic understanding of API functionality. Industry best practices are covered, informing the reader about how to think about creating a new platform. The book then describes a comprehensive process for planning, designing, and managing development of web APIs, from business value through developer support.

Who should read this book

This book is intended to be accessible to anyone interested on the topic of creating APIs—spanning from an individual developer or technical lead, through product and project managers, and up to executives directing engineering organizations. With that in mind, here are some thoughts on qualifications: the reader should understand, at least at a rudimentary level, the processes surrounding software development—planning, development, testing, and releasing. The reader should be able to follow somewhat technical discussions about software process, including the associated vocabulary. There are chapters that are introductions to specific topics and technologies. Where this occurs, there will be links out to the best supplemental material.

How this book is organized

The first part of the book covers the technologies and best practices for API creation and design. Topics include a discussion of the overall goals and ideals for an excellent API program and the notion of developer experience, the main focus for any web platform that is successful and engaging. A high-level description of the technologies and techniques used for web APIs is presented, as well as best practices for excellent APIs.

Part 2 features an overall strategy for API design and creation. Topics include the steps you need to follow before starting API creation. This covers determining business value, creating powerful metrics, and understanding use cases. Once these details are covered, the book moves on to techniques for designing, developing and supporting your web services to ensure they begin and remain as A-list destinations for your customers.

About the code

Code samples are provided in Node.js, and a Docker image is additionally provided for working with the API code directly. Examples of JSON and HTTP are provided to help understand these fundamental concepts. Developer-level understanding of code is not needed in order to understand the concepts in the book.

The code repository is at https://github.com/synedra/irresistible.

Author Online

Purchase of *Irresistible APIs* includes free access to a private web forum run by Manning Publications, where you can make comments about the book, ask technical questions, and receive help from the author and from other users. To access the forum and subscribe to it, point your web browser at www.manning.com/books/irresistible-apis. This page provides information on how to get on the forum once you are registered, what kind of help is available, and the rules of conduct on the forum.

Manning's commitment to our readers is to provide a venue where a meaningful dialogue between individual readers and between readers and the author can take place. It is not a commitment to any specific amount of participation on the part of the author, whose contribution to the Author Online remains voluntary (and unpaid). We suggest you try asking the author some challenging questions, lest her interest stray! The Author Online forum and the archives of previous discussions will be accessible from the publisher's website as long as the book is in print.

About the author

Kirsten Hunter is a passionate advocate for the development community. Her technical interests range from graph databases to cloud services, and her 10 years of experience using, supporting, and evangelizing REST APIs have given her a unique perspective on developer success. In her copious free time she's a gamer, fantasy reader, and all around rabble-rouser. Code samples, recipes, and philosophical musings can be found on her website at www.princesspolymath.com.

about the cover illustration

The figure on the cover of *Irresistible APIs* is captioned "The Conservatory Student." The illustration is taken from a nineteenth-century edition of Sylvain Maréchal's four-volume compendium of regional dress customs published in France. Each illustration is finely drawn and colored by hand. The rich variety of Maréchal's collection reminds us vividly of how culturally apart the world's towns and regions were just 200 years ago. Isolated from each other, people spoke different dialects and languages. In the streets or in the countryside, it was easy to identify where they lived and what their trade or station in life was just by their dress.

Dress codes have changed since then and the diversity by region, so rich at the time, has faded away. It is now hard to tell apart the inhabitants of different continents, let alone different towns or regions. Perhaps we have traded cultural diversity for a more varied personal life—certainly for a more varied and fast-paced technological life.

At a time when it is hard to tell one computer book from another, Manning celebrates the inventiveness and initiative of the computer business with book covers based on the rich diversity of regional life of two centuries ago, brought back to life by Maréchal's pictures.

Part 1

Understanding web APIs

This part covers the basic technologies involved in web APIs to help readers understand the context of this type of platform. Starting with a discussion of what makes an API irresistible, the chapters in part 1 drill down into the user experience for APIs, the ideal API infrastructure (API First), and an explanation of the technologies used for web APIs.

What makes an
API irresistible?

1

This chapter covers

- Defining a web API and what it can do
- Ensuring a great developer experience
- Avoiding common pitfalls

An API is an interface into a computer system—an application programming inter-face. Historically APIs started out as highly coupled interfaces between computer systems. Web APIs, which are much freer and less tied together, have been evolving for quite some time, but recently developers have seen a huge explosion in the web APIs available to them. Many of these APIs were developed without the end user (in this case, a developer using the API) in mind, resulting in a frustrating developer experience and a less successful web API.

An *irresistible API* is straightforward to use, well documented, and well supported, and the supported use cases are communicated and demonstrated well. Using your API should be a joyful and engaging experience, not a slog through a frustrating and never-ending series of challenges.

This book will help you understand how to create web APIs that are loved by developers, that are engaging and purposeful, and that will experience success. It also discusses the factors you should consider to determine whether you should have a platform at all. The guidelines included in this book are meaningful for any kind of web API, no matter the technology or audience.

When you've finished reading the book, you'll have a strong understanding of the process needed to create excellent web APIs—APIs that enchant customer engineers and extend the platform's reach naturally as those developers share their experiences with their colleagues. Although many different types of APIs are in use in the industry, each with its own advantages, this book focuses on the development of RESTful web APIs. Web APIs decouple the functionality of the server from the client's logic and features, encouraging client developers to use the data in whatever way works best for their application. Non-web APIs that tie the server and the client together tightly work to implement specific integrations between the client and the server. For instance, SQL, an interface language tied into many databases, represents an API, but the interaction is focused on specific actions. Exposing the data in a more free-form way wouldn't work for many of the uses people have for databases or other closely coupled systems.

In addition, you'll develop a good basic understanding of the technologies involved in creating a RESTful API. *REST* stands for Representational State Transfer and refers to APIs that are resource based—where the clients interact with the servers by requesting things rather than actions. The creation of web APIs is technologically simple: a skilled developer can use Flask, Django, Ruby on Rails, or Node.js to put together a basic REST API in a few minutes. Without a clear plan, design, and goal, that API is unlikely to be excellent, usable, or successful. *How* you use those technologies makes all the difference between a successful, irresistible API and one that lies fallow in the ecosystem with no users. The book is made for you, whether you're a product manager, technical lead, engineering manager, API developer, or even a developer who wants to assess APIs you've created or ones you're looking to use.

This chapter is focused on helping you understand the overall ecosystem of web APIs—what the terms mean, what things you want to accomplish (and avoid!) in creating your own API, and how to decide whether you need an API.

1.1 Integrating social APIs into web content

You likely use products that are incorporating APIs all the time. The share button you see on news sites and blogs uses the APIs for those social sites, like Twitter, Facebook, or LinkedIn. If you can "Sign in with Twitter," the site you're visiting is using Twitter's API to identify you. This makes for a much better user experience, because you don't need to remember more usernames and passwords and you can jump right into enjoying the system. Figure 1.1 demonstrates a website displaying several share buttons, enabling the reader to add the page to their feed in the social network. Figure 1.2 shows how an API can propagate changes to the clients so they can update their application's guidelines.

Figure 1.1   A blog incorporating a Twitter feed as well as API functionality for sharing to multiple social networks. A widget provides buttons for each of the social networks—Google+, Twitter, LinkedIn, and Facebook—and this widget incorporates that network's API into the site in a manner that's easy to implement.

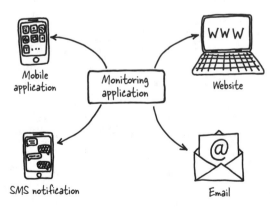

Figure 1.2   Example API interactions with a monitoring application. When the monitoring application detects a change, it can propagate it to a website, mobile application, SMS notification, or email.

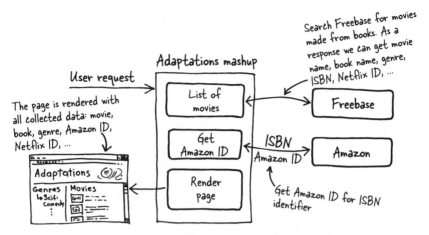

Figure 1.3   This chart describes an adaptations mashup using Freebase, Amazon, and Netflix. The user is presented with a grid of book-based movies matching a specific genre, and for each of the movies, the user is given the opportunity to watch the movie on Netflix or purchase the book on Amazon. This is an example of a mashup combining multiple APIs to create an integrated experience for the user.

A RESTful API is a platform that exposes data as resources on which to operate. For instance, a contact records management application might make it possible for you to interact with users, contacts, and locations. Each of these would be exposed as a resource, or object, you can interact with, whether reading or writing changes. When you create a well-designed RESTful API, developer users can create applications commonly referred to as mashups. A *mashup* combines multiple APIs together to create a new user experience (see figure 1.3).

As you can see, in figure 1.3 I created a mashup using Freebase (think of this as a database of the world's information), Amazon, and Netflix. The mashup allows users to find books that have been made into movies and then buy the book at Amazon or add it to their Netflix queue. I used information from Freebase to add genre information for the movies so users can browse around and find the movies that interest them most. This is a simple example of mashing up three different APIs to create a new way for users to explore a data space. Frequently, websites or applications are also leveraging the APIs of social networks for logins, sharing, and showing your user feed.

This is a great place to emphasize one of the main concepts of this book. The developer experience for your customers is the most important factor in the success of your API. If you're trying to encourage creativity and engagement with a larger community, or inspire developers to help you reimagine your main product via the APIs, REST might be your best bet. On the other hand, if your API needs action-based methods that do a small number of things in a specific manner, you may well want to make a non-REST API, using SOAP (Simple Object Access Protocol) or another technology designed for more tightly coupled clients and servers. Either way, the most important things to take into account are what your customers want and how you want them to use your API. Remember, developers are people too.

1.2 What is a web API?

The term *API* has been used for most of the history of computing to refer to the interfaces between computer systems, or between different programs on an existing system. Frequently these systems were *peers*, where neither of the systems was specifically a server or a client. For instance, a mail server might have used a database to store information, but the systems were inherently designed together, tightly coupled to work together seamlessly. More recently the term has been expanded to include web APIs, systems where a client—which could be anything from a web browser to a mobile application—contacts a web server and operates on the data on that server. The main difference here is that the developers who are writing the clients aren't the same as the developers writing the interface—the system is truly decoupled.

To understand the idea of a web API, it's useful to understand the *protocol*—the way the systems talk to each other. Think about the switchboard phone system from days long past. Your phone only knew how to do two things: connect to the switchboard and make noise. If you wanted to call your Aunt Mae, you'd pick up the handset and make noise with the ringer. After the operator answered, you'd give her Aunt Mae's phone number, and she would cause Aunt Mae's phone to make noise itself, and then she'd connect up your two phone lines. In this case, you contacted the switchboard (acting in this case as the "server") and gave a specific identifier to the operator, and that person connected your phones. The protocol for this was well known, and the users of the telephone were able to interact with each other long before auto-switching was technically possible. Figure 1.4 shows how an API interacts with front-end clients and the back-end server.

Similarly, HTTP is a well-known protocol used to drive the web traffic browsers generate. A web API is a system where clients use a defined interface to interact with a web server via the HTTP protocol; this can be an internal or an external system. To understand how this works in the context of a browser, when you type an address into the browser's address bar, you're asking that browser to retrieve a unique resource, like reaching a phone number. The browser asks the server for the information associated with that identifier, and it's returned and formatted for you to view in the window. Web API clients make similar calls to read and write to the system, but the responses are formatted for programs to process instead of for browsers to display. One of the best-known APIs is Twitter, whose APIs are open to third-party developers, allowing those developers to create applications that integrate directly with Twitter. I discuss HTTP in detail in chapter 4.

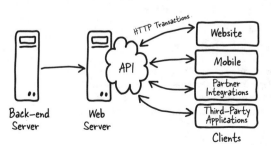

Figure 1.4 The basic interactions with an API are direct connections with the back-end server or servers, and a well-defined interaction with clients on the front end. This allows for countless front-end applications, whether mobile, website desktop, or system integrations, without changes to the back-end servers.

Figure 1.5 This example shows how common terms map to API concepts. Resources are unique names, the methods are easy to understand, and options and context allow the client to express specific concepts via the API transaction.

Once you're using a protocol, it's important to have a well-described format for the messages that are sent through that protocol. What does a request look like? What response can be expected? To help you understand what needs to be communicated via the transactions between client and server, the requests and responses being sent over HTTP, I'll bring these questions back into the real world. To support the needs of a computer system, a RESTful web API must support creating, reading, updating, and deleting items on the platform. Figure 1.5 describes how a web API works, comparing it to a real-world resource (an iced tea ordered at a coffee shop).

To understand how this works, think about what it looks like when you order a drink at a coffee shop (figure 1.6).

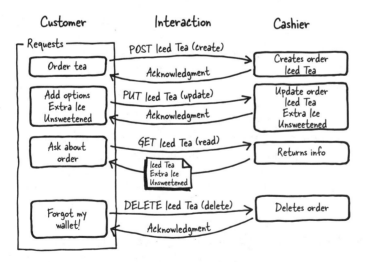

Figure 1.6 A customer interaction at a coffee shop. Though this diagram seems complicated, realize that the interaction represents exchanges you've had multiple times with service providers. An acknowledgment can be as simple as a nod from the cashier, and each of the requests made by the customer is a simple request.

When you request an iced tea, you've created a new item: an order. Adding options to this order, such as extra ice, updates that item. When you ask the cashier to tell you what you've ordered, you've performed a read of that item. And if you've accidentally left your wallet at home and have to cancel the order, that item is deleted. More complex factors are involved in the system, but this is the essence of a web API transaction.

You'll find several advantages to using a RESTful web API, which exposes the data in the system as objects for interactions between the client application and the platform. When two systems are tightly tied together at a deep level, it's hard to make a change on either side without breaking the other. This reduces productivity and creates a vulnerability to unexpected behavior, especially when the applications become out of sync. Writing code where the systems are separated by a documented interface protects both from unexpected changes. It's easier to test an API and easier to document the interface while protecting your internal methods from unexpected use.

So, what kinds of things can an API enable for you? We'll dive deeper into business goals later in the book. Grasping the various ways that you can leverage an API also depends on an understanding of what can be done with an API (see figure 1.7).

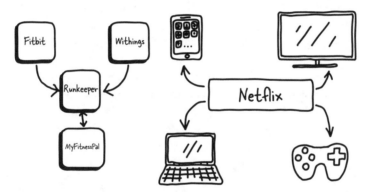

Figure 1.7   This diagram shows multiple systems integrated together. On the left, you can see Fitbit, MyFitnessPal, and Withings feeding into the Runkeeper system, which can aggregate all of your fitness data in one place. The picture on the right shows Netflix and all of the various types of devices it has integrated with, cementing its leadership in the video industry.

Figure 1.7 demonstrates a small number of the types of integrations that are possible with web APIs. Mobile devices are the main driving force between APIs; in almost all cases, the need for an API is driven by the requirement to have a responsive mobile application. Mobile is an almost universal use case for companies developing APIs. For this reason, it's frequently the main use case. Allowing your customer developers to integrate their system with your platform saves you the development resources needed to create custom implementations for each separate partner.

1.2.1   Do you need an API?

One of the first questions you'll want to answer is whether you have to create a web API at all. Creating an API without any purpose is destined to fail, as with any other product. This question should be clear once you go through the process of determining the business value for your API. Whether you're trying to improve engagement, support a mobile strategy, or integrate with other systems, an API takes time and resources to create correctly.

APIs can improve velocity, engage partners, and enable mobile devices, but if your business does not (and will not) need these things, a web API may not be right for you. But it's still worth going through the exercise to determine at what point an API may be needed.

1.2.2   Choosing REST APIs

When deciding whether to use REST for your API, take into account your customers' needs and the systems you have to interface with. Over the last several years, REST-style APIs have become the most popular type of web API. The main difference between previous API structures and REST is that REST APIs are designed around the idea of "nouns" in the system instead of "verbs."

REST APIs are designed to encourage creativity and innovation by allowing developer consumers to decide how to use the data available. As with open source, this openness can cause concern for large enterprise companies that are focused on protecting their proprietary information, but security and privacy can be retained in both open and internal RESTful APIs when mindfully designed. Another term for an API of this sort is *platform*, describing the underlying system as a foundation for developers to use to build their integration or application.

1.2.3   JSON

The most popular response format for a REST API is currently JavaScript Object Notation (JSON), which is an efficient way to represent data passed between the server and the client.

Listing 1.1   JSON sample

```
{
    "glossary": {                                    ◁── The top-level item of a JSON
        "title": "example glossary",                      item is usually an object
        "GlossDiv": {                                     (designated with curly braces).
            "title": "S",
            "GlossList": {
                "GlossEntry": {                      ◁── These objects can be objects contained
                    "ID":        "SGML",                  within the main object. Nesting of
                    "SortAs":    "SGML",                  objects is supported at every level.
                    "GlossTerm": "Standard Generalized Markup Language",
                    "Acronym":   "SGML",
                    "Abbrev": "ISO 8879:1986",
                    "GlossDef": {
```

Objects within objects are name :value.

```
            "para": "A meta-markup language, used to create
                    markup languages such as DocBook.",
            "GlossSeeAlso": ["GML", "XML"]
          },
          "GlossSee": "markup"
        }
      }
    }
  }
}
```

The JSON format is compact and easy to transmit on a slow network. For this reason, it's manageable on devices with questionable network connectivity (such as mobile devices). Interpreted languages such as JavaScript, PHP, Perl, and Python work with JSON quite easily —in fact, the objects look familiar to developers working in those languages, which is one reason it has become so popular. At this point, if you're creating a new API and must choose one format, you'll likely want to use JSON. Adding a second output type adds more overhead and duplication, so unless your customers explicitly require some other format (such as XML) for some reason, it's best to stick with one. Choosing to support two different formats will incur a reasonably large amount of technical debt—creating the need to do extra work as you develop your product, because you have to double your use case testing and increase development time.

1.3 *Developer experience*

The experience of the developers using your API is the most critical factor in the success of your APIs. An API that's open to external developers and that has a poor developer experience may well drive third-party developers to your competitors. You must create even an internal API with developer experience in mind. Creating internal APIs without excellent documentation and tutorials will result in a huge support burden as your consumers struggle to write their implementation and flounder without understanding how best to use your APIs.

A great developer experience begins with understanding your goals for your API and communicating those to the developers you want to engage. The more information you can share with them, the better able they will be to decide whether they want to use your APIs. Remember, when a developer comes to use your API, whether it be an internal, partner, or open API, that developer is giving you the only thing he or she can never get more of: time. Demonstrating that you recognize this is critical to developing a trusting and mutually beneficial relationship with those users.

Once you've determined the business value, metrics, and use cases for your API, communicate this information to your developers. A trusting relationship can most easily be accomplished by practicing transparency wherever you can. As you work through each section in this book, consider carefully whether you have a strong reason not to share information about your business values, metrics, and use cases with your developers. If not, share it! You may not think that developers will want to understand your business value or use cases, but giving them this information communicates to them clearly that you're serious about your API. Allowing your customers to view your design documents before the API is complete gives you the opportunity to get valuable feedback during the development process. Telling developers exactly how you're going to measure the success of your API—whether it's user engagement, number of end users, or some other factor—gives them the opportunity to work on your team, improving those metrics you've identified as critical to the success of the API.

Providing tools, example code, and tutorials is also crucial to the developer experience. Twilio, a company that provides APIs for voice calls and SMS messages, has a goal that any developer entering its site should be able to make a successful call from its system within five minutes. Having this kind of exercise available grabs your potential developers and engages them in your system. Although they may have only planned to browse your site for 5–10 minutes, making that call will encourage them to invest more time in understanding what they can do.

1.3.1 Versioning

Versioning is one of the hardest facets of API management. It may seem like a newly created API can be "pretty decent," assuming that you can fix it up later. Unfortunately, the choice of which version to use is in the hands of developers—developers you likely don't control. Once developers have made an integration or application with your system, they're not likely to be motivated to move to a new, incompatible version unless there's new functionality that's critical to them. You need to take your first version seriously, knowing that you may be supporting that version for a long time.

Compatible versions that don't change or delete existing functionality are generally well received, but as soon as you need to make a change that breaks existing implementations, you're going to be facing resistance from your developer community, especially if you deprecate a version that they've stuck with. Even if you give them a long warning period to migrate, they may not want to redo the work they've done. On the flip side, maintaining older versions creates duplicate code and requires that you make fixes to the earlier code as well as the existing code. Troubleshooting and support become much more difficult when you have developers on multiple versions. This means that your first version needs to be a solid contender, something you intend to use for a long time. The website model of releasing a new version every week or two doesn't work for an API. Although the API does provide a decoupled world, developers will still rely on the version they started with, so you need to be aware of the price of new versions.

1.3.2 Marketing to developers

Finally, make sure that your marketing is targeted appropriately to developers. A developer will have one main question when coming to your portal: "Why do I care?" This usually can be broken down into "What can I do?" and "How do I do X?" Unfortunately, documentation is frequently stuck in the realm of "What does each piece do?" which doesn't meet the needs of these questions. Developers don't tend to be inspired by pretty pictures or taglines—they want to play with toys. Give them example code and applications, the building blocks they need to get started making magic with your platform.

All of these ideas will be revisited throughout the book—developer experience should drive most of the decisions you make. (The specific topic of developer support is covered in more detail in chapter 9.) Following these guidelines will help you to avoid some of the commonly encountered problems with the first generation of APIs.

1.4 Common pitfalls of organic APIs

Though it may seem as if APIs are a new thing, REST APIs have been out in the world for over 10 years. At this point the industry is moving from innovators who are blazing the trail to more stable and mindful API creators who can leverage the learnings of previous platforms. This means that you have the advantage of learning from the mistakes made by the first APIs, which were created without a view toward how the APIs would be used and measured. Twitter, Netflix, and Flickr have well-known APIs that are very heavily used, but you may not realize that tens of thousands of APIs have been created, and as APIs become more common, that number will rise into the hundreds of thousands. Many of these APIs have been left by the wayside, and even more are struggling to achieve success in a relatively crowded marketplace. Distinguishing your platform from your competitors by having a usable API with a fantastic developer experience will help you rise to the top of the stack.

I'm going to discuss a few specific examples that illustrate common mistakes made by platform companies. Remember that the APIs I'm using as examples have attained success in the long run, but the early stumbles cost them money, resources, and credibility, and in some cases have prevented them from making design changes to improve their API.

1.4.1 Lack of vision

When the Netflix API was first released, it was open to the developer community at large. The goal of this product was to "let a thousand flowers bloom," to enable third-party developers to create amazing applications that would bring in new subscribers and make money for the applications while increasing Netflix's subscriber base. Guidance for developers on how to use the API was minimal and focused on what the API did rather than providing tutorials and use cases. Developers were attracted to the platform and created many applications, but the revenue benefit never occurred. Because the company's goal for the API was unfocused, developers didn't know what the company wanted them to accomplish with the API. As a result, many clients re-created the functionality of Netflix's website without adding new functionality. Netflix employed a large team to support the open API and encouraged developers to jump in with both feet and create applications and integrations into the system. But a somewhat restrictive Terms of Use, limiting the way that third-party developers could integrate with the system, muted the innovation they were hoping for. The main issues in this case were that Netflix required attribution, disallowed the ability to combine information with other vendors, and, most critically, required that advertisements were not associated with Netflix content.

Through partner use of its APIs—using the APIs to integrate Netflix into various video devices—Netflix discovered that the API was an excellent way to establish market dominance by creating efficient integrations into devices (such as the Xbox, Blu-ray players, and smart TVs) and partner products (such as Windows). This business decision was a great one for Netflix, but its API was now focused on a specific market segment. The existence of third-party developers, though, meant Netflix needed to continue to use resources to enable and support alternative use cases. This turned out to be a costly use of resources, for little business value. As time went on, Netflix focused the API more on the device market and less on the open version of the API. Support for open developers declined, new features were offered only to partners and device manufacturers, and the open API was eventually decommissioned entirely.

This is an excellent example of an innovator creating a product that had a strong negative developer experience but that turned out to have an excellent value for the business. That business value wasn't defined at the beginning—communication with developers encouraged them to innovate and create, and those developers trusted that the resource would continue to be available to them. This situation soured many developers on platforms in general, because they had spent a great deal of time and money implementing applications that eventually failed entirely.

1.4.2 *Prioritizing the developer experience*

Twitter started with a single web page where you typed your message, and you could follow people or send messages—that was the extent of the features. There was no image management, no lists, and none of the other features social systems feature now. Developers loved the API; though the developer experience was a little awkward at first, it was easy to imagine what you could do with such a system. Many Twitter features were initially created by external developers as part of their products, and Twitter adopted the new features because users liked them. This was a decent setup, although developers were somewhat unhappy with the feeling that their ideas were being "stolen" by Twitter.

Eventually, that situation changed for the worse. Twitter rewrote its Terms of Use so that developers couldn't create applications that competed directly with its product, and existing applications of that type needed to be killed. This meant that when Twitter adopted a new feature, any existing applications that relied on that feature to distinguish themselves from Twitter could no longer exist. Twitter wanted users to integrate sharing and social media into their own applications rather than creating applications based directly on Twitter. Unfortunately, because this message wasn't shared until after several missteps, the developer community was, by and large, quite unhappy with Twitter, and the company's credibility suffered as a result. Luckily, with its enormous user base, Twitter wasn't seriously affected by the fallout.

Twitter eventually realized that there were aspects of its API that were costing it time and resources without being used by the majority of its developer customers. For instance, all of Twitter's calls could be retrieved using JSON or XML—a more expansive structure preferred by some customers. The XML version, though, was used by fewer than 5 percent of the developers, so Twitter created a new incompatible version, which refined the API into something matching more closely with what most of its developers were using. As I mentioned, the creation of backward-incompatible version changes has a high cost. Twitter took a long time to "sunset" the older API, and many developers remained unhappy as a result of this change.

As an innovator, Twitter was bound to experience some growing pains as it developed its API. At this point, it has one of the best developer portals around, with excellent tutorials, support in the form of forums, and a well-documented API that's straightforward and consistent. If Twitter had known at the beginning what it's since learned about how users would use the platform—or had another API on which it could model its platform—it would've been able to create the right API at the start. On the other hand, Twitter learned valuable lessons from the developers, watching them use the API and seeing what they did. Sometimes you need to break the rules to figure out the right answer—but knowing what the right plan is can help you avoid unnecessary mistakes and help you achieve the success you want.

1.4.3 *Bad API design*

Flickr, one of the first photo-sharing services, was also one of the first APIs. Although it was attempting to create a RESTful API, instead it created an API that worked with actions instead of objects (verbs instead of nouns). Flickr has since made improvements in its API, but many developers had already implemented the old API, so it was difficult for them to create a new, better version. The original design choices are helpful examples to understand some of the problems that come with a lack of understanding of the basic technology to create RESTful APIs.

To help you see this, I'll describe an example of the non-RESTful choices made by Flickr. To delete a photo from Flickr, a consumer must make a request to the `delete_photo` resource related to the photo in question. Originally, this photo would be deleted by sending a `GET` request to the `delete_photo` resource. The RESTful way to make a change to the server is to use the appropriate HTTP verb Flickr—in this case, `DELETE` is the right way to delete a resource, where `GET` should be used only to read the existing value of a resource. The distinction may seem minor, but when you break these rules you create a situation where your API behaves in an unexpected way for the developers consuming that API. As with designing for the end users of a product, you don't want to create a situation where the behavior of the system is a surprise to the developer.

REST
```
DELETE /photos/1234
```

Flickr
```
GET /photos/1234/delete_photo
```

The specifics of this are covered in chapter 4, but for now I'll point out some issues with the Flickr implementation.

First, in REST APIs, a request using the GET method should never change the data on the server. One reason why this is important is that if your API doesn't follow this rule, a web crawler or other automated system could accidentally change or delete all the items in your system. Since the development of strong authentication, this has become less of an issue, but it's important to realize that this rule is known by most application and website developers, so making this kind of design choice creates a situation where the behavior of the API is not what the developer expects. HTTP provides a set of "verbs" that are well defined. In this case, there is a DELETE method that deletes the resource from the system, so that's the right way to accomplish this task—a DELETE on the resource rather than a GET to the action.

Another problem here is that by exposing actions instead of objects, developers are constrained in their use of the API. Exposing nouns instead of verbs means that a developer is free to imagine new and creative uses for that data. Additionally, operations on the same object are at the same address, which matches much better with object-oriented design and helps enforce consistency in the developer's experience. If a particular API object doesn't support a particular method (like DELETE), the system can send back an error code that's consistent with the HTTP specification, and the developer will know how to handle that error.

It may not seem terribly important to follow the REST specification for your API. It's your system; you can choose how to implement it. But remember that your developer customers may be familiar with how REST APIs tend to work, and whenever you change the way things work, they may well get confused or make incorrect assumptions. Wherever possible, follow the general principles laid out in chapter 4. The more similar your API is to other existing APIs, the better the developer experience will be. Once you've worked through these prerequisites, you're ready to create your API.

1.5   *API creation process*

Chapter 7 is where it all comes together; you'll learn the steps you need in order to create a successful and engaging web API. These steps, as shown in figure 1.8, include:

- Determining your business value
- Choosing your metrics
- Defining your use cases
- Designing your API and creating a schema model

Many times it's tempting to skip the steps I'm covering in this book, but like your main product, your web API should be a first-class citizen, with the same effort given to designing, implementing, and supporting your platform as you give to your website or

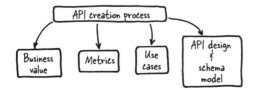

Figure 1.8   The process must contain all of these factors in order to be successful. Treat your platform like a first-class product and watch it thrive.

application. Treating your API like a real product will help you immensely in getting your platform right the first time.

1.5.1 *Determine your business value*

Many of the first platform products had vague goals. Third-party developers experienced a world where they had to struggle to understand what the company wanted them to do with the API, and even worse, the platforms they were relying on underwent drastic changes or were deprecated altogether. This could have been avoided had they clearly determined their business goals from the outset.

When thinking about business value, think of the elevator pitch so commonly targeted by new startups. If you get in the elevator with the CEO of your company and he asks why you have an API, you need to be able to succinctly answer the question in a way that convinces him that it's a valuable product. "Developer engagement" or "API use" is not a great goal. You need a tangible goal related to the larger business such as "Increase user engagement," "Establish industry leadership," "Move activity off the main product to the API," or "Engage and retain partners." Monetization is a nice aim, but unless your API is your main product, you need to see it as a supporting product, enhancing the value of your product.

Another compelling reason to have a great handle on your business value is resource contention. Your company can only afford to pay a certain number of engineers, and usually those engineers are divided into revenue-producing products and support engineers. An API is an awkward sort of product—a great API can exist that doesn't add directly to the bottom line. If you can't consistently and succinctly explain why your API is valuable to the company, and how it's supporting and enhancing the existing revenue-producing products, your API may well suffer. When the leaders of the company don't understand the value of an API, it may be relegated to the back burner to get updated "when the engineers have time," or worse yet, decommissioned entirely.

As you go through this book, keep thinking about what you want to accomplish with your API, and what you want your developers to do, so you can mindfully create your API to achieve success.

1.5.2 *Choose your metrics*

Whatever the business value of your platform, your CEO is going to want to know whether you're achieving it, and getting buy-in from other teams is much easier if you can demonstrate how your API is doing. You need this information so you can quickly evaluate the API you're creating, or the effectiveness of changes you make. Figure 1.9 demonstrates some common business values and the metrics you can use to track your progress toward achieving these goals.

Frequently you'll see API metrics such as "Number of developer keys in use" or "Number of applications developed," but that's an internal type of metric, unlikely to be meaningful to the business value of the platform itself. Developers have to get keys

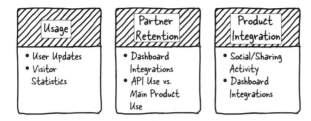

Figure 1.9   These are examples of different business values with the associated metrics. The most important concept to understand is that you want to have a business value that's meaningful to people outside of the API team, and metrics should support that value in a way that's meaningful to your overall organization or company.

in order to try out your system, and 90% of those keys may be completely inactive and meaningless. Instead, wouldn't it be great to know which actions your platform is providing for your customers? Or how many users are interacting via the API? Or how many times a day users interact with your system? Or how many of your partners have created integrations into their systems? Increasing engagement with your system is a great goal and relatively easy to measure, though you need to make sure that the actions that are happening are good for your business. Try to think about how your API is enhancing the goals of the company as a whole rather than determining how many people have begun to integrate with your system.

1.5.3   *Define your use cases*

Once you've identified your business value and how you're going to measure it, it's time to figure out what use cases you want to support. Your main product is frequently a great use case to target, whether it's the entire product or a subset. For instance, if there's a sharing component to your API, you may want to highlight and improve engagement for that feature through your platform. Thinking of your main product in terms of API features that might be useful is an effective way to start thinking about what use cases you want to support.

   If you want to engage mobile developers—and you probably do, because people spend an inordinate amount of time on their smartphones and have become conditioned to expect an excellent user experience on the smaller screen—you need to understand the needs of mobile developers and address them. This use case is important enough that I strongly suggest you consider it even if mobile isn't in your immediate future. This use case will have a strong effect on choices you make when designing your system. Mobile developers need the API to be performant and robust, and they aren't likely to use an API that can't deliver all the information they need from the system for a single screen in one call—ideally, with all the relevant information and no extra data. Your user could walk into a tunnel or elevator and lose connectivity, and the developer will want the application to be quick and robust enough to handle these cases. Unless the API is designed with these developers as a use case, it's easy to create an API that's not usable for mobile cases.

Partner integration is also a strong candidate for use cases. When designing an API, partner engagement is frequently a great business goal; these partnerships bring in consistent and reliable income, and you want to make it as easy as possible for partners to integrate your API into the systems they use. If your main product is a service they rely on, you may expose the metrics on those systems so they can integrate with your dashboard. If you have a social or communication element, they may want to display news streams within their employee portals. Whatever the case, these use cases are important to evaluate. Partner engagement is generally a key goal for the company, and supporting that will make your product central to that end.

1.5.4 *Design your API*

Developers are generally champing at the bit to create the API as soon as the topic comes up. Their aversion to taking the time to create designs stems from the fact that web APIs, and in particular REST APIs, are easy to implement, and it's hard to dampen their enthusiasm for the idea of creating a product they can code so quickly. Figure 1.10 shows what an organically grown API looks like when several different APIs are created separately, without any eye to consistency.

Unfortunately, APIs that are created without a deliberate design frequently end up looking a little bit like a potato you left in the garage for a couple of months, with sprouts coming out at weird angles, completely unrelated to each other, unattractive, with no clear goal or consistency. I frequently refer to the created APIs as the Wild Wild REST, because it's so easy to create a system that's functionally complete but unusable. Back-end architects tend to think of development in terms of reliability, scalability, and efficiency. But a web API is a form of user interface, so it's critical that you take the time to define how the API will be used and what it should look like, and defer prototyping or development until this task is complete.

The process of designing an API can be challenging unless you have some kind of system available to describe what the API will look like when it's done. Unlike earlier API structures, REST doesn't require any documentation about what an API does or how to use it. Historically this has meant that REST APIs are created without an explicit

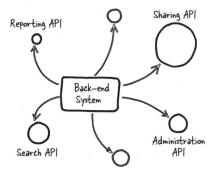

Figure 1.10 Organically grown APIs are unrelated to each other. This results in duplicate (and sometimes inconsistent) code, different interfaces to the same information, and extra work for the consumers of the various APIs to implement integrations with applications.

overall design, but that creates a variety of issues. First, the product manager for the API is generally the person most knowledgeable about the use cases for the API itself, but if no tangible description can be discussed, those product managers may be unable to weigh in on the appropriateness of the proposed API.

The answer to this problem lies in schema modeling systems. These products allow you to describe the interface for the API before any development starts. Deliberate design before starting development encourages open communication and prevents the frustration of duplicating development work and misunderstood requirements. When a model is created and used to drive the development process, use cases can be closely mapped to specific sets of endpoints (each named API resource is referred to as an endpoint), and work can be prioritized in a meaningful manner. The API can be reviewed to make sure that the endpoints are consistent and that there aren't any obvious holes or feature mismatches. A mock server can be deployed for customers or tests to determine if the use cases will be easy, and tests and example clients can use this structured documentation to stay current with new API functions and features.

Modeling schemas for REST APIs isn't necessarily an easy task; making sure that different products are presenting the same information in the same way is something that takes time and work. For instance, an endpoint associated with accounting and reporting might present a "user" and his or her accounting information differently than the document management system, which would show ownership and editorial information. This process helps you to avoid those clashes during development and meet your deadlines with a minimum of difficulty. Back-end systems usually keep all this information segregated, but when designing an API you should think of your data as items within a cohesive system rather than distinctive items within separate systems. This is one of the main guidelines that is frequently missed when API design is left to back-end architects, who are generally focused on scalability, performance, and precision as opposed to usability. Your API design should include a human-readable definition for each endpoint; the methods, fields, and formatting for the response; and any other metadata that's important within your system.

Chapter 7 discusses modeling schemas, and we'll explore two of the three main schema modeling languages: RAML and OpenAPI (previously Swagger). Each of them uses Markdown or JSON to define the behavior of API endpoints, and they all enable communication, documentation, and testing. Each one is an open standard, but each is championed by the company that originally created it, and if you're using one of the associated systems for API management, design, or documentation, you'll be best served by using the matching modeling language. What follows here are examples of the schema modeling languages to give you an idea of what information is maintained in each one. Figure 1.11 describes a Blueprint schema model.

Apiary is a company that provides API design tooling and support. Blueprint, the schema modeling language championed by Apiary, uses Markdown. This system focuses on the entire development cycle as described in this book. In addition to providing a structured language to describe the API, Apiary makes it easy to run a mock

```
FORMAT: 1A

# Polls

Polls is a simple API allowing consumers to view polls and vote in them.

## Questions Collection [/questions]

### List All Questions [GET]

+ Response 200 (application/json)

        {
            "question": "Favourite programming language?",
            "choices": [
                {
                    "choice": "Swift",
                    "votes": 2048
                }, {
                    "choice": "Python",
                    "votes": 1024
                }
            ]
        }
```

Figure 1.11 Blueprint definition for a simple "notes" API. Blueprint uses Markdown for the formatting, and as you can see this is a human-readable document. As long as someone understands the basics of HTTP interactions, they'll be able to parse this document—which means that your product manager, customers, and the other development teams you interact with will be able to understand your API long before you even start coding.

server and allow customers to comment on upcoming API changes. Apiary provides intuitive design tooling to make it easy for anyone to describe the API, and has a handy starter template to play around with when you're getting started.

Figure 1.12 demonstrates a schema modeled in OpenAPI (previously known as Swagger), one of the most popular and vibrant schema modeling languages. This is the only schema modeling language using JSON rather than Markdown, and it additionally supports YAML, a third markup language (YAML stands for Yet Another

```
{
    "title": "Swagger Sample App",
    "description": "This is a sample Petstore server",
    "termsOfService": "http://swagger.io/terms/",
    "contact": {
        "name": "API Support",
        "url": "http://www.swagger.io/support",
        "email": "support@swagger.io"
    },
    "license": {
        "name": "Apache 2.0",
        "url": "http://www.apache.org/licenses/LICENSE-2.0.html"
    },
    "version": "1.0.1"
}
```

Figure 1.12 OpenAPI sample markup. Unlike Blueprint, OpenAPI (previously Swagger) supports JSON and YAML as its markup languages and features the ability to include abstractions for objects in the system (such as a "user" or a "contact"), which encourages readers to consider the resources of the API in an object-oriented way.

Markup Language). The functionality of this system matches that of the other two, but there aren't any easy tools you can use to create OpenAPI documents, and no readily apparent templates to help you get started. This leads to a much steeper learning curve for new users and can discourage you from using the system.

Finally, figure 1.13 shows an example of a RAML schema model. MuleSoft is an API management system, and RAML is its schema modeling language. This language is designed to encourage reuse of best practices among API providers. Additionally, the language and tooling are designed to make API discovery and exploration easier. As with Apiary, templates and tooling are provided by MuleSoft to soften the learning curve.

```
/books:
  /{bookTitle}:
    get:
      description: Retrieve a specific book title
      responses:
        200:
          body:
            application/json:
            example: |
              {
                "data": {
                  "id": "SbBGk",
                  "title": "Stiff: The Curious Lives of Human Cadavers",
                  "description": null,
                  "datetime": 1341533193,
                  "genre": "science",
                  "author": "Mary Roach",
                  "link": "http://e-bookmobile.com/books/Stiff",
                },
                "success": true,
                "status": 200
              }
```

Figure 1.13   RAML from MuleSoft. RAML supports Markdown, as Blueprint does, but the schema that's created is more expressive than Blueprint. Additionally, like the OpenAPI framework, they support abstract objects more natively than Blueprint, making it easier to implement and maintain consistent APIs across a complex system.

None of these options is necessarily better than the others, and they each have different features and focus. Chapter 7 walks through two of the main schema modeling languages, RAML and OpenAPI. Whatever system you use, having a schema model will create an artifact representing the design choices you have made for your API.

1.5.5   *Industry standards*

As you design your API, one thing to keep in mind is that an open API, unlike a website or application, will be public once released. You won't be able to hide the schema from your competitors. This is not a problem—many companies believe that the model for their API is their competitive advantage, but those companies are wrong. The data you're presenting and the algorithms you use to make it more engaging are the things that separate your API from the other companies in your industry. The strong notion that your API should be secret until released has resulted in a huge disparity in schemas between companies in the same industry. This has created a situation where developers have to work much harder than they should to integrate similar APIs together to create a better client, because each API requires that they start anew with the development, and the task of combining data that's structured differently falls to the developer.

If you think of your API as a public interface, it becomes obvious that you should strive to learn from other companies in your industry and work toward best practices with them. This approach will help the entire API ecosystem to mature much more rapidly and will encourage more developers to try out your API. If you consider an industry such as fitness, for example, it's easy to see that body weight and number of steps per day are items that are quite simple. Creating different ways to access, manage, and interact with those items between Fitbit and Runkeeper increases the difficulty that a developer will encounter in integrating these systems.

Figure 1.14 introduces the concept of API Commons, where organizations can upload their schema models for re-use by other API producers. This sort of functionality will help the API industry to move toward best practices, improving the experience for developers using those APIs.

Figure 1.14 API Commons was designed for companies to define and store their schema models so that other companies with similar APIs can leverage these existing schemas when building their own APIs. This allows the developers consuming these APIs to interact with similar systems, rather than needing to translate between numerous different representations of the same object.

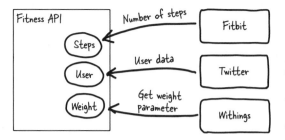

Figure 1.15   Building an API from other companies' schemas can allow you to use the schemas generated by different API providers when designing your own API, while still making it easy for developers who have already implemented these other APIs to integrate with your platform.

In keeping with this idea, API Commons was created as a place to store and share design schemas. The idea of this project is that companies with design schemas can check them into a shared repository, and other companies and organizations can use shared schemas to bootstrap their own schemas. Figure 1.15 illustrates the use of API Commons to create a new API by using other organizations' APIs as a basis.

A company could choose to use the "user" definition as described by Twitter, along with the "weight" model used by Withings and the "steps" description used by Fitbit, to create an application monitoring weight loss. In fact, several integrations already use these types of information, and normalizing the API interaction would make it significantly easier for developers to create these applications.

This approach has several advantages. Companies considering releasing a new platform can look to see what others in their industry have done. Web APIs with similar purposes can migrate to a compatible structure, easing the learning curve for developers looking to create integrations. Finally, as more and more companies place their schemas into the system, best practices will evolve, and newer APIs can present a more consistent interface and improve the developer experience. Without this kind of system, the evolution of APIs into a mature ecosystem will be a long and painful process.

1.5.6   *Design-driven development*

When you're developing a full application, you need to deploy the entire application at the same time, and new versions should be as complete as possible, because updating applications puts a burden on the user. On the other end of the spectrum are websites. A website can push out a new version on a daily basis, and broken functionality can generally be fixed quickly. New features can be added or removed as needed, and users don't need to do anything in order to take advantage of the newer version (on the other hand, users rarely have the option to go back to an earlier version if they're not happy with the new one).

APIs live somewhere in the middle of this spectrum. As mentioned earlier, breaking changes—changes that cause existing implementations to break—are expensive in terms of time, resources, and credibility, but new functionality can be added within an existing version. Although an application would need to "upgrade" in order to grab those new features, a well-designed API can add new functionality or new information within the existing data structure without breaking developers' existing applications.

For this reason, it's possible to create a targeted API and then build on it. Figure out the most important use case—for instance, mobile—and figure out what the minimum viable product (MVP) would be for that use case. (An MVP is a product that would perform the base functions for the product without any extra bells and whistles.) Perhaps you only want people to be able to look at your product line or see the activity feed of their friends. Make sure you know what the API will need to do in order to support this use case and develop your API for that. APIs lend themselves quite well to an agile development process, where short iterations allow for frequent review of changes and additions in order to stay on track.

Frequently, when design isn't determined ahead of time, the resulting product doesn't meet the use cases of the customers. This issue can be caught during testing or review of the API, but even when that happens you have to send the product back to development to try again. Nobody—not developers, marketers, or management— likes missed deadlines, so making sure that the requirements are well understood helps make sure that the development work is targeted exactly where it should be.

Because you'll have created a schema model for your API, it will be easy to make sure that there's documentation for each endpoint and tests that ensure that the coded product meets the expected behavior. Additionally, the existence of use cases makes it easy to test the integrated product to make sure that those use cases are, in fact, easy. A design-first methodology brings much of the contention to the front of the process and allows for much more streamlined development.

1.5.7 *Support your developers*

In a book focused on optimizing the developer experience for your API consumers, I'd be remiss not to discuss the support piece of your API. Sometimes APIs are released without a solid support system in place, which can cause a great deal of frustration within your developer community.

Rather than think of the developers in your community as interlopers whom you have to deal with, consider them valued partners and support them as such. Developer support includes a developer portal that includes documentation, example code, and a well-communicated process for finding help. Your documentation should include your use cases, presented as tutorials, your business value, and the metrics you're planning to use. Providing this information will make it possible for your developer users to help you succeed. The first step to a great developer experience is the trust developers feel when you demonstrate that you're committed to success for the API and for them as well.

Engaging developers means performing a lot of the support work up front. Although consumers of mainstream products respond well to illustrations and catchphrases, developers want to get started right away. They like building blocks to play with, in the form of example code. When the developer can make an API call in the shortest possible amount of time, it creates engagement and interest and is invaluable for the success of your platform.

The best portal to study for developer experience is Twitter. The company has put a great deal of effort into making sure that its got clear documentation and excellent tutorials. Twitter also makes sure that in the community there's a huge amount of sample code that developers can leverage in order to write their own applications.

Another great example is Twilio. It has a goal of making it possible for any new developer to be able to make a call to its API in less than five minutes. Although this isn't possible for every API, it's a great goal to strive for when creating your "getting started" documentation.

1.6 *Summary*

This chapter has covered the topic of creating APIs at an extremely high level. At this point you should understand what an API is and what you can do with one. I shared some cautionary tales to explain why a deliberate design process is so critical. The topics covered in this first chapter were as follows:

- What is a web API? A web API is distinct from other API systems in that it's designed to decouple the systems from each other, allowing for new and different integrations.
- What can a web API do? A web API can add an interface to your system—an integration point that your internal customers, partner developers, and external third-party engineers can use to integrate your system with theirs, using well-known and mature technology.
- Developer experience is the most important facet of this process. Focusing on the usability of the platform you're creating will lead to a more successful product.
- Most common pitfalls occur because a part of the first-class API process outlined in this chapter is skipped. If there are no use cases, there's no way to check and make sure that the resulting API meets the originally stated goals.

Chapter 2 walks you through a "live" API, which you can interact with as a client and see how it works. Advanced developers will have the opportunity to install the system themselves, but everyone will have the chance to see what the interface looks like for a basic REST web API.

Working with web APIs 2

This chapter covers

- Structure of a simple API
- Ways to inspect calls to an API
- Interaction between an API and a client application
- Deployment of the sample API and application on your system

The next few chapters cover the server-client interaction in detail, but this chapter helps you understand the concepts with a simple example of an API and sample application. Most basic API examples use a to-do list, but that's kind of overused. I decided to go a different way: I've selected a list application with pizza toppings. Note that this particular application is simple by design; the goal is to show you how to interact with the API, and how an application interacts with an API. If this were a production application it would have a full pizza, or pizzas, and the database wouldn't be shared, but for the goals here I've taken out as much complexity as possible to make the basic principles clear.

Looking at an API is interesting, but it doesn't necessarily help you to understand how it can drive an application. Additionally, performing actions such as create and delete in a browser is challenging, so in addition to the API I've included a simple application using this API with JavaScript. This application exercises all the functionality in the API so you can see how an application interacts with a web API.

To get an idea of how this works in practice, I've created a basic API using Node.js, a JavaScript-based web server framework. (You can learn more about this framework at www.nodejs.org.) The API supports all the needed actions to represent a complete system: create, read, update, and delete. The first task will be to explore the API in a browser using the read functionality.

This application runs on a web host at www.irresistibleapis.com/demo. You can check out the application there and follow along with the concepts in this chapter. If you're a developer and want to explore the code more intimately, use the exercises at the end of the chapter to get the example running on your own system, including both the Node.js application and the HTML/JavaScript web application. Section 2.6 also describes the various moving parts to this API and application so you can play with it as you like.

2.1   HTTP basics

To understand the transactions between the client and the server in API interactions, you'll need a basic grasp of how HTTP works. Chapter 4 covers this topic in more detail, but for now I'll give you some high-level information about the protocol.

You're probably most familiar with HTTP as the way web browsers get information from web servers. An HTTP transaction is composed of a request from the client to the server (like a browser asking for a web page), and a response from the server back to the client (the web page from the server, for a browser). First, I'll describe the elements in an HTTP request. You're familiar with the URL, the address that you type into the address box on a browser, but that address is only one portion of the information sent from your browser to the server in order to process a web request.

2.1.1   HTTP request

Figure 2.1 illustrates the elements that make up an HTTP request, along with examples of how these sections are used. The HTTP request is usually sent with headers, setting the context for the transaction. An HTTP request always has a method; methods are the verbs of the HTTP protocol. To understand what your browser does, imagine that you're visiting my main website. Here are the pieces of the request that are sent by your browser:

- *Headers: Accept: text/html*—This tells the server that the browser wants to get an HTML-formatted page back. It's the most readable format for humans, so it makes sense that your browser would request it.
- *Method:* GET—This is the read method in HTTP and is generally the method used by browsers when reading web pages.
- *URL: http://irresistibleapis.com*—This is the only piece you indicated for the browser.
- *Body: none*—A GET request doesn't need a body, because you're not changing anything on the server—you're reading what's there.

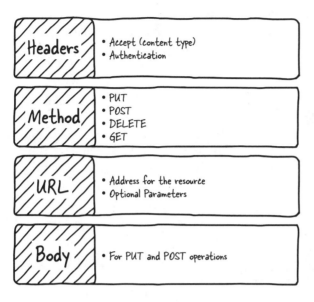

Figure 2.1   An HTTP request will always have a method and will be sent to a specific URL, or resource. Depending on the specific call, headers may be sent to specify information about the request. If the call is designed to write new information to the system, a body will be sent to convey that information.

All the actions of CRUD (create, read, update, and delete) are represented by methods within HTTP:

- Create: POST
- Read: GET
- Update: PUT
- Delete: DELETE

The URL is the unique identifier for the resource. It's like any other URL on the internet, except in this case it's used to describe the resource in an application system. If parameters are needed for the request, such as a keyword for search, they're included in the parameters of the request. To see how parameters would look, here's an example search request:

```
http://www.example.com/api/v1.0/search?keyword=flintstone&sort=alphabetical
```

In this example, the resource being called is http://www.example.com/api/v1.0/search. The question mark and everything following it are parameters giving more information about what the client wants in the response. A body section is only sent for create (POST) and update (PUT) transactions.

Next, I'll describe the sections of an HTTP response.

2.1.2   *HTTP response*

Figure 2.2 shows the elements of a typical HTTP server response. The server is likely to send back several headers giving information about the system and the response. All requests have a method, and all responses have a status code. These status codes are described in more detail in chapter 4, but for now it's sufficient to know that 2XX means that the request was successful, 3XX is a redirect to another location, 4XX is an error in the request from the client, and 5XX means the server had a problem. In the earlier example, calling my website, the server would've responded with the following:

- *Status code: 200*—Everything worked correctly.
- *Headers:*
  - *Content-Type: text/html*—as requested by the client
  - Date: <date of response>
  - Content-Length: <size of response>
- *Body*—The content of the page. This is what you see if you "view source" within the browser—the HTML page that tells the browser how to render the page and what content to display.

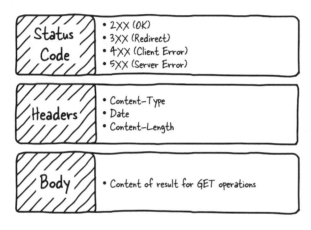

Figure 2.2   **A response will always have a status code, and a well-designed platform will send headers to provide information about the response (such as size or the content type). For most requests, a body will be sent back from the server to provide information about the current status of the resource.**

2.1.3   HTTP interactions

Every HTTP transaction between a client and server is composed of a request, sent from the client to the server, and a response, sent from the server back to the client. There's no higher level interaction; each request/response is stateless and starts again from scratch. To help you understand this better, I'll move on to a discussion of a specific API.

2.2   The Toppings API

Many different styles of API are available, but the one I'm going to be using and talking most about here is a Representational State Transfer (REST)-style API, the most common type of web API.

As discussed in chapter 1, REST APIs are designed to work with each resource as a noun. A specific resource within a system has a unique identifier, which is a URL, like the ones you visit in the browser. This URL identifies the resource in the system and is designed to be understandable when viewed. For example, with a REST API you could view the list of existing toppings with the following request:

```
http://irresistibleapis.com/api/v1.0/toppings
```

These are the actual URLs, retrieved with a GET (read) operation. If you put the preceding URL in a browser, you'll see the results displayed in figure 2.3.

You can visit this URL in your browser right now and get the information about a single topping or a list of toppings. Figure 2.3 shows what this call will look like in a web browser. Go ahead and try both of these calls in your own web browser to see how easy it is to retrieve information from this kind of service. Again, this is like any other web request, only formatted for a computer to work with.

Now, to view a single topping, you'd take the id field from the list you retrieved and append it to the URL. Basically, you're saying, "Give me the toppings list" and then, "but just the one with the ID of 1." Almost all APIs work this way. The parent level is a list of items, and adding an ID will retrieve a single member of the list.

```
http://irresistibleapis.com/api/v1.0/toppings/1
```

The same resource is accessed to update, view, or delete a particular item, using different HTTP methods (as described in section 2.1) to tell the server what you want to do. You can add new items by sending a POST to the list itself (so in the earlier case, the /toppings endpoint would be used to add a new topping). This type of API encourages engagement and innovation by the developers, and consistency across multiple API providers makes it easier to get up and going writing clients.

```
{
  "toppings": [
    {
      "title": "pepperoni",
      "id": 1
    },
    {
      "title": "peppers",
      "id": 2
    },
    {
      "title": "pickles",
      "id": 3
    }
  ]
}
```

Figure 2.3 Example result of a web call in a browser. The response is JSON, a common markup language for web APIs. As you can see, the formatting makes it easy to understand the content of the response.

2.3   *Designing the API*

To go through the steps, imagine an online website for a pizza parlor. Users are having trouble interfacing with the pizza ordering system and want to be able to customize their pizzas. The company wants to increase customer satisfaction. This represents the business value for this platform. Figure 2.4 illustrates each call to the system and how it would be formatted.

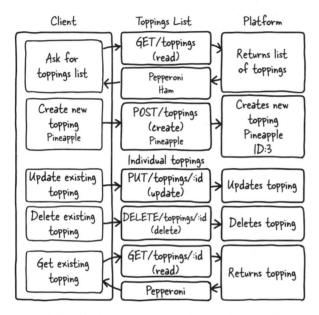

Figure 2.4   This diagram represents the complete set of interactions with the API system. The GET request reads the current value of the resource, whether it's a list or an individual item. POST is only allowed at the list level, and creates a new resource in the system. PUT updates and DELETE deletes an existing resource. All four of the needed methods, Create, Read, Update, and Delete, are represented in this diagram.

To provide this, they need to create a system that consistently allows users to pick different pizza toppings and keep them in a list (use case). The company decides to measure success by determining the increase in people finishing up started orders (measurements). Fortunately for this example, it's relatively easy to figure out how an API can meet these needs.

Because I'm creating a resource-based API, each request will be a unique URL describing one piece of the back-end structure with a method describing what the client wants to do with that resource. In this case, I have only two different types of resources: individual toppings and lists of toppings. Individual topping resources such as /api/v1.0/toppings/1 are used for viewing, editing, and deleting a single topping. The list resource /api/v1.0/toppings is used for viewing all toppings or for adding a new topping to the list. Table 2.1 shows each call to the API and a description of what it does.

Table 2.1 API calls

API call	Description
`GET /api/v1.0/toppings`	List current toppings
`GET /api/v1.0/toppings/1`	View a single topping
`POST /api/v1.0/toppings`	Create a new topping
`PUT /api/v1.0/toppings/1`	Update an existing topping
`DELETE /api/v1.0/toppings/1`	Delete an existing topping

And that's it. The platform features create, read, update, and delete operations available to you by combining the HTTP methods with the URLs for your resources. But what do you get when you make these calls? When you GET the resource for a single topping, you get information about that topping. Try this now in your browser: http://irresistibleapis.com/api/v1.0/toppings/1.

Listing 2.1 Retrieving a single topping

```
GET /api/v1.0/toppings/1
{                                  ⟵——— Curly braces indicate an object.
  "topping": {
    "id": 1,
    "title": "Pepperoni"
  }
}
```

This response is represented in JavaScript Object Notation (JSON), a formatting syntax first described in chapter 1. JSON is covered in more detail in chapter 4, but for now you can see how the data is structured. (If you want more information about JSON, you can find it at http://json.org.) The curly braces indicate an object, which is a group of pairings of names and values. What's represented here is a JSON structure describing a single object—a "topping," which has an ID of 1 and a title of Pepperoni. This is the same resource address a client can access to view, delete, or update an existing topping. This means that the URL for the single topping is the toppings list of http://irresistibleapis.com/api/v1.0/toppings followed by the ID of the topping from within this structure—so it's http://irresistibleapis.com/api/v1.0/toppings/1.

If you GET the resource for the list of toppings directly, the returned information includes a list instead of a single object. Call this URL in your browser to see the list: http://irresistibleapis.com/api/v1.0/toppings.

Listing 2.2 Retrieving a list of all toppings

```
GET /api/v1.0/toppings
{                                  ⟵——— Curly braces indicate dictionaries.
  "toppings": [                    ⟵——— Square braces indicate lists.
    {
```

```
      "id": 1,
      "title": "Pepperoni"
    },
    {
      "id": 2,
      "title": "Pineapple"
    }
  ]
}
```

In this case, because the request was for a list of objects, square brackets demonstrate that the returned object contains a *list* of toppings. Each individual topping looks the same as listing 2.1. Again, this is how information is represented in JSON. To understand these calls and responses, remember that an *object* (with keys and values) is represented by curly braces, and a *list* (an unnamed collection of items) is represented with square brackets. In some programming languages these are referred to as *hashes* and *arrays*.

Both of these calls can be made from a standard web browser. If other people have added items to the list, you'll see those included in the list view as well; this is a live call into the API system and returns the appropriate information. In this case, the API is generated by node. If you're a developer who's interested in learning more about the back end of the system, Exercise 3 at the end of the chapter will give you information about how to run this system on your own, as well as the application running on top of the API.

This simple API interaction gives you the opportunity to start understanding some of the topics covered in chapter 4.

2.4   Using a web API

You can interact with this API in various ways, as you'll learn in this section. Feel free to try any or all of these approaches to see how the interaction works.

2.4.1   Browser

A browser can make GET calls to specific resources easily. Note that this is easy in the case of my demo API because there's no authentication to worry about. The challenge is that the browser doesn't have any way to easily update, delete, or create new items. Using the developer tools or web inspector in your browser can give you more information about the call as well.

For instance, the Chrome web browser has developer tools that allow you to inspect the traffic it's processing. Figure 2.5 shows what these tools look like in the browser. I'll break down what you're seeing here in terms of what I described earlier. Note that the Chrome tools are showing the request and response combined together in the tab.

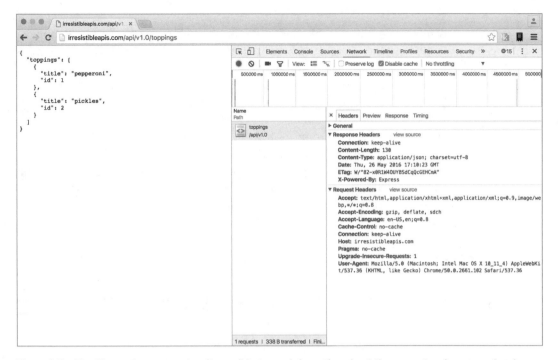

Figure 2.5 The Chrome browser makes it possible to see information about the request and response headers, the body of the request or response, and other useful information about the transaction. Although browsers aren't designed to send PUT or DELETE responses, the information provided here can go a long way in helping you to understand the interactions with the platform.

For the request:

- *Headers*—Accept: text/html,application/xhtml+xml,application/xml;q=0.9,image/webp;*/*;q=0.8—This is the list of accepted formats for this browser request, in order of preference. Because it includes */* (meaning "any content type") late in the list, the browser will accept any type of response and do the best it can with it. Many other headers are shown in figure 2.5. Take a look at them and run the same request on your system to see how they change and what stays the same in each request/response transaction.
- *Method*—GET
- *URL*—http://irresistibleapis.com/api/v1.0/toppings
- *Request body*—none
- *Status code*—200 OK

2.4.2   *Command line (curl)*

If you're comfortable with the command line, you can use the `curl` command to make calls to the API as well. This tool is fairly straightforward and makes it possible to interact with the API more completely, using all the available methods rather than limiting transactions to read operations as the browser does. `curl` is native on UNIX-based systems such as Linux and Macintosh, and you can install it easily for Windows from http://curl.haxx.se/download.html.

Let's take a quick tour through the API using `curl`. By default, `curl` uses `GET` (read), but you can specify other methods on the command line, as shown in the following examples. Remember that your responses may be different if other people have been changing things; go ahead and work with what you get. Don't be shy—this API is for this book, and you can't break anything important. The best way to understand this type of system is to work with it yourself.

First, let's use `curl` to look at a single topping. Lines beginning with a dollar sign indicate a command-line call. The other information is the information returned by the server itself.

Listing 2.3   `GET /api/v1.0/toppings/1`

```
$ curl http://irresistibleapis.com/api/v1.0/toppings/1
{
  "topping": {
    "id": 1,
    "title": "Pepperoni"
  }
}
```

That seems pretty reasonable. I'd eat a pizza with pepperoni on it. Let's list all the toppings and see what else is on the pizza. Remember that the list for the toppings is at the parent level, or `/api/v1.0/toppings`.

Listing 2.4   `GET /api/v1.0/toppings`

```
$ curl http://irresistibleapis.com/api/v1.0/toppings
{
  "toppings": [
    {
      "id": 1,
      "title": "Pepperoni"
    },
    {
      "id": 2,
      "title": "Pineapple"
    },
    {
      "id": 3,
      "title": "Pickles"
    }
  ]
}
```

Wait, what? Pickles? That's kind of gross. Let's delete that one. The id for it is 3, so the correct path to operate on is /api/v1.0/toppings/3.

Listing 2.5   **DELETE** /api/v1.0/toppings/3

```
curl -i -X DELETE http://irresistibleapis.com/api/v1.0/toppings/3
{
  "result": true
}
```

The response here says we succeeded. To be sure, let's pull a list of toppings again.

Listing 2.6   **GET** /api/v1.0/toppings

```
$ curl http://irresistibleapis.com/api/v1.0/toppings

{
  "toppings": [
    {
      "id": 1,
      "title": "Pepperoni"
    },
    {
      "id": 2,
      "title": "Pineapple"
    }
  ]
}
```

Okay, that's much better. But our pizza has pepperoni and pineapple, and I'd much prefer ham with my pineapple. Let's go ahead and change that first one to make the pizza how I want it. To update an existing item, the command needs to send a PUT to the resource with the new information required.

Listing 2.7   **PUT** /api/v1.0/toppings/1

```
$ curl -i -H "Content-Type: application/json" -X PUT -d '{"title":"Ham"}'
http://irresistibleapis.com/api/v1.0/toppings/1

{
  "topping": {
    "id": 1,
    "title": "Ham"
  }
}
```

Nice, now the pizza is looking pretty good. But as far as I'm concerned the pizza is merely a vehicle to get cheese in my mouth, so I'll add some extra cheese to go with the Hawaiian pizza I've built.

Listing 2.8   POST /api/v1.0/toppings/1

```
$ curl -H "Content-Type: application/json" -X POST -d '{"title":"Extra extra
 cheese"}' http://irresistibleapis.com/api/v1.0/toppings
{
  "topping": {
    "id": 3,
    "title": "Extra extra cheese"
  }
}
```

Let's do one final check to make sure that the pizza looks good.

Listing 2.9   GET /api/v1.0/toppings

```
$ curl http://irresistibleapis.com/api/v1.0/toppings

{
  "toppings": [
    {
      "id": 1,
      "title": "Ham"
    },
    {
      "id": 2,
      "title": "Pineapple"
    },
    {
      "id": 3,
      "title": "Extra extra cheese"
    }
  ]
}
```

Awesome! Now the pizza is just right.

Note that with `curl` you can also pass `-i` for slightly more chatty information, or `-v` for a much larger dose of verbose output. If you're having fun and you'd like to try those now, feel free. The extra details you'll see are HTTP transaction details, which are described in chapter 4.

2.4.3   *HTTP sniffers*

Browsers have become good at showing information about the calls they're making, but this is of limited use for a couple of reasons. As I mentioned earlier, a browser is only capable of sending a read request, which restricts the actions you're able to explore. When you submit a form, it creates a create (`POST`) request, but you can't arbitrarily call these operations in your browser.

HTTP sniffers are tools that allow you to explore all the HTTP traffic your system processes. HTTP sniffers watch and report on the network traffic your system is generating, whether it comes from a browser, an application, or a raw command-line call.

With these tools, you can see the entirety of the HTTP request and response, and this allows you to debug what's happening if you're running into issues.

If you're using a Mac, HTTPScoop (www.tuffcode.com) is a friendly choice. It's easy to set up and use, and the output is clear and complete. The downside to this tool is that it can't monitor secure transactions (HTTPS calls), and so it's not going to work with any API requiring secure calls. For the purposes of this book, though, you'll only be accessing a nonsecure API (the demo API), so HTTPScoop is a fine choice—it would be my first choice for any Mac users wanting a reasonably intuitive experience. The license cost is $15, but you can try it for two weeks for free.

Figure 2.6 shows an example of the windows in HTTPScoop. For this chapter, I'll focus on the main screen listing all calls and the Request/Response tab. Later in the book you'll learn about headers, status codes, and other HTTP details so you can understand how they all interact together. For now, though, consider the request to be a simple request and response, and don't worry about particular details if you're not already familiar with HTTP.

For Windows users, the best choice out there is Fiddler, which you can find at www.telerik.com/fiddler. For Windows, Mac, and Linux, there's a slightly more complicated choice in Charles (www.charlesproxy.com). If you're quite advanced in your network administration skills, you can try out Wireshark from www.wireshark.org. Wireshark is available and free for every major platform and sniffs all kinds of traffic, not only web/HTTP traffic, but the interface is complex, and it can be difficult to understand what you're seeing.

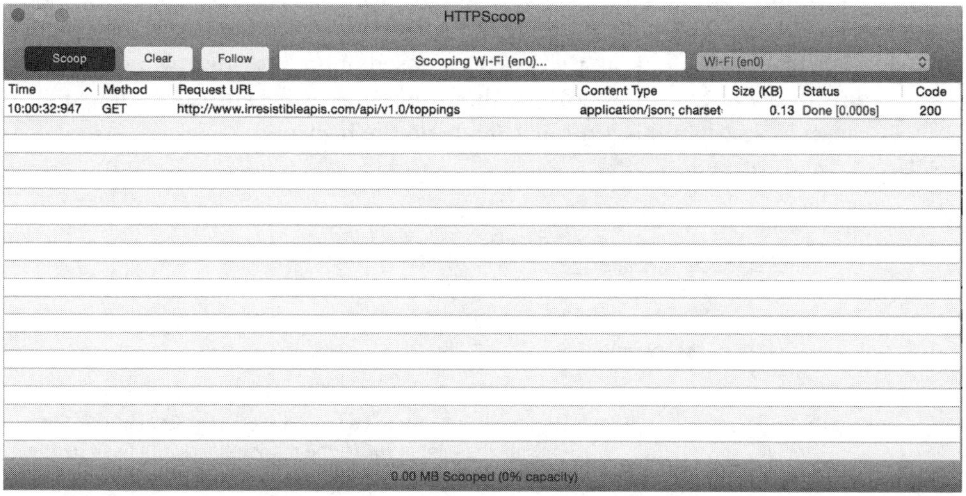

Figure 2.6   This is an example of a call being inspected by HTTPScoop. On this basic landing page, you can see the Request URL, representing the resource. The content type of the response, status code, and response size are also provided.

EXERCISE 1 Watch the traffic in an HTTP sniffer as you go through the exercises from this chapter. Use the `curl` calls to access the API directly and see what the calls look like. For more verbosity with `curl`, you can use `-v` in your command and see more information about the call from the client side. Compare the information in the sniffer to what `curl` sends and see if you can find patterns. Which debugging method gives the best information? Which one is easier for you to use?

EXERCISE 2 Make a deliberately incorrect call. Call `/api/v1.0/toppings /100`—there's not likely 100 toppings on the pizza, so this is a bad call. What kind of output did you get from `curl -v`? What did the HTTP sniffer show? The status code tells you how the system responded, which should give you the information you need to figure out what the issue is.

2.5   *Interaction between the API and client*

Seeing these GET calls to the API is somewhat interesting, but unfortunately you can't see the POST, PUT, or DELETE calls using a browser. `curl` isn't intuitive for exploring a system. Without some kind of application using the API, it's difficult to explore and visualize the elegance and simplicity of this kind of interface.

Keeping in line with the simple API, I've created a simple application to exercise the API, creating a list of toppings for your virtual pizza. Again, for a real application there would be a full pizza and a method to place the order, but this application is deliberately as simple as possible so it's easy to understand how it works.

I'll go through the same sequence I did in the last section. Here's our starting pizza, with pepperoni, pineapple, and pickles. Loading the initial page causes an API call to be generated, and we get the current list of toppings from the system.

First, take a look at the JSON representation returned when the API is called directly at `/api/v1.0/toppings`, shown in figure 2.7. Figure 2.8 shows how the application looks when this API call is made on the back end.

```
{
  "toppings": [
    {
      "title": "pepperoni",
      "id": 1
    },
    {
      "title": "peppers",
      "id": 2
    },
    {
      "title": "pickles",
      "id": 3
    }
  ]
}
```

Figure 2.7   Here you see a representation of the API toppings list in JSON, the markup language used by the platform. As described, the curly braces indicate an object, or dictionary, and the square brackets represent an array, or list of objects.

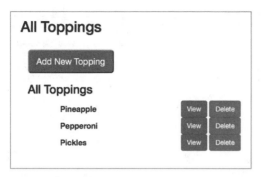

Figure 2.8 The application view for the toppings list shows the same information, as shown in figure 2.4. This screen is created by calling the toppings list and creating the HTML based on the returned information. If the list changes on the server, both figure 2.4 and figure 2.5 would change, with both showing the same information in different ways.

Now take a look at the main application at http://irresistibleapis.com/demo. With the JSON data, the simple application can build the front page. Some of the items are static—they don't change. The top half of the page, for instance, is always the same, with the title of the display and a button to add new toppings. The bottom half, though, is created based on the information retrieved from the API. Each topping is listed, and the ID of the topping is used to create an appropriate button to act on that specific item. The user has no need to understand the relationship between the ID and the name of the topping, but the IDs are used programmatically to set up the page to be functionally correct. Note how the information in the API in figure 2.4 directly maps to what's shown in the application in figure 2.5. The buttons on this page map directly to the other API calls, as shown in table 2.2.

Table 2.2 The mapping between the API calls and application functions

API call	Application function
GET /api/v1.0/toppings	Main application page
GET /api/v1.0/toppings/1	View button on main page
POST /api/v1.0/toppings	"Add new topping"
DELETE /api/v1.0/toppings/1	Delete button on either page

As we walk through the API actions, use the HTTP sniffer of your choice to watch the traffic as the interactions happen. Note that because this system is live, other people may have added, deleted, or edited the toppings, and they may not match. Feel free to use the buttons to adjust the toppings to match or follow along with your own favorite toppings (Jalapeños? Sun dried tomatoes? Legos?).

The first action in the previous example was removing the pickles from the pizza, and clicking Delete on this page for the Pickles entry will do that. This button knows which ID to operate on because it was embedded in the page when the listing was rendered.

Time	^	Method	Request URL	Content Type	Size (KB)	Status	Code
19:04:57:886		GET	http://irresistibleapis.com/demo/		0	Done [0.000s]	304
19:04:57:887		GET	http://irresistibleapis.com/api/v1.0/toppings		0	Done [0.000s]	304
19:05:04:896		DELETE	http://irresistibleapis.com/api/v1.0/toppings/2	application/json; charset	0.00	Done [0.000s]	200
19:05:04:897		GET	http://irresistibleapis.com/api/v1.0/toppings	application/json; charset	0.13	Done [0.000s]	200

Figure 2.9   This HTTPScoop screen shows a list of all the calls made by the system. In this case, you can see the DELETE method is called to remove the /toppings/2 resource from the system, and it was successful, as indicated by the 2XX response in the code column.

Clicking the Delete button will make the DELETE call and then make a call to the API to re-render the list of toppings with the deleted topping gone. If you're using an HTTP sniffer or have configured your browser to show you web traffic, you can see this call happening from your system. Figure 2.9 shows what it looks like in HTTPScoop.

As you can see, the application pulled a few different framework files and then got the full listing for the main page. When I clicked Delete, the application sent a DELETE request to the API server and then requested a new list of toppings. All the requests were successful, so the main page refreshed to show the new list. Figure 2.10 shows the list after I deleted the offending pickles from the toppings list.

To edit an existing topping, in this case to change Pepperoni to Ham, click the View button. Doing so makes the read call for the specific item and allows you to edit the title. Using this technique to edit the Pepperoni to Ham and then clicking Save causes a PUT to happen exactly as in the original example. Watch your HTTP sniffer or browser traffic to see how this progression works. Figure 2.11 shows what the Edit page looks like for a particular topping—in this case I changed the title from Pepperoni to Ham.

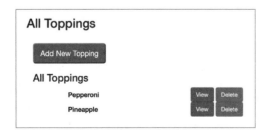

Figure 2.10   Once the topping has been deleted from the system, the HTML representation of the toppings list no longer shows the deleted topping. If the platform call is made (to /toppings) you'll see that the change is reflected in the JSON representation as well.

Edit a Topping

Title | Ham | Save

Figure 2.11   The Edit a Topping screen allows you to change the title of an existing resource.

When this change is PUT to the API, it will change the item's title from Pepperoni to Ham, updating the database to reflect the change permanently.

The PUT request, viewed in HTTPScoop, shows the request and response (see figure 2.12).

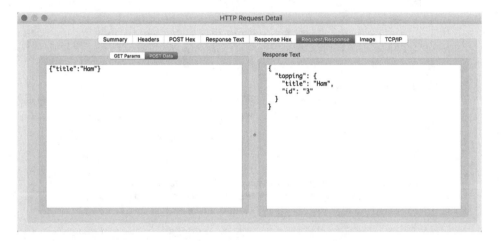

Figure 2.12   When you change the title of an existing resource, the information is sent to the server, and it sends back the new representation of that item. In this case, the object is quite simple; the title is the only field that can be changed. This is a simple demonstration of how an update works on an API platform.

As with the associated curl request earlier, the debugging demonstrates that the client sends a request including the new information for the requested item. A PUT request replaces information for an existing item in the system. In the response, the server returns a response showing the new values for the resource. This returned object matches the object that was PUT to the system. Without HTTPScoop, this seems a little magical, but you should be seeing a pattern by this point; these common operations are direct mappings to system calls on the back end of the application.

Figure 2.13   The list of toppings now includes Ham and Pineapple; the Pickles have been deleted (thank heavens), and the Pepperoni has been changed to Ham using an update. Again, if you made a call to the /toppings resource you'd see the changes shown in the JSON representation as well.

Again, once the topping is edited, the application redisplays the main page, now with Ham and Pineapple (figure 2.13).

What's left then? Now I need to add my extra cheese to the pizza, because it's my favorite sort of thing. Clicking the Add New Topping button on the main page gives me a page for adding a new topping, as shown in figure 2.14. Remember, adding a new item to the list is a POST action, and that's what will happen on the back end. Figure 2.15 shows what the API transaction looks like when this POST is sent.

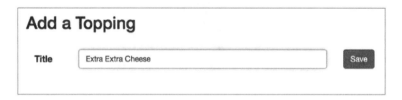

Figure 2.14   The Add a Topping screen is designed to add new toppings to the system. As mentioned earlier, a create action is generally represented by a POST operation, and that's what the system will do in this case.

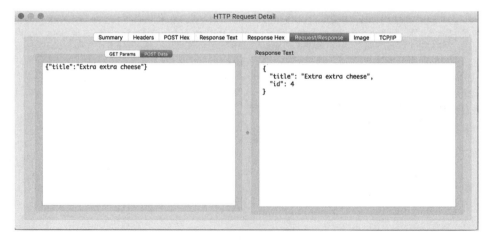

Figure 2.15   HTTPScoop POST request/response. The only field needed to create a new topping is the title, and it's set to Extra extra cheese (yum!). The response shows the ID and title— the entire representation—of the newly added item.

This example demonstrates again the difference between PUT, which updates a specific existing item, and POST, which creates a new item by adding it to the specified list. After adding this new topping to the system, the application again requests the list of toppings, which brings the web page back once again to the main page. This completes the circuit using an application to exercise the back-end API. The single page running this application is quite straightforward, because all the logic and actions are happening on the back end using the API.

Now that you've had the opportunity to view some specific traffic, take time to play with the example application with the various HTTP inspection methods. Because this sample application runs in your browser, you have the option of using developer tools in your browser to watch the traffic or an HTTP sniffer for this exploration. For the exercises in this book, you'll want to use an HTTP sniffer, so pick the one you're most comfortable with and start familiarizing yourself with its use.

Advanced Example Note

If you're a developer and want to install your own copy of this system, follow the instructions in section 2.6 to do so. Otherwise, skip to section 2.7 for a summary of this chapter.

2.6 *Install your own API and front end*

This optional section is designed specifically for developers who want to understand more completely the back-end functionality of the API and sample application. You can use a Docker container to run the system quickly on your own system or download the code from my GitHub repository. I'll walk through the steps to install and use the Docker container first and then give more general instructions for grabbing the code from GitHub to run on your own system.

2.6.1 *Installing the system via Docker*

Docker is extremely simple to install on Linux systems and quite easy on Mac OS X and Windows systems as well. Installing the Docker container is simple once you've got the Docker system set up. Using this container allows you to separate the code and processes from the main processes on your system while avoiding the memory and space-management issues of more heavyweight virtual machine systems. The Docker installers for installation on Windows and Macintosh are at www.docker.com/toolbox.

If you're an advanced user running Windows and already have virtualization working via VBox or another virtualization system, you need to be aware that Docker relies on VirtualBox, which may conflict with your existing setup. Additionally, boot2docker requires that virtualization be available on your system, which infrequently requires changes to the BIOS. Also, virtualization is only available on 64-bit systems. If your system is a 32-bit system, you'll need to install the code directly from GitHub.

Once you've installed Docker using the instructions at the Docker website, you're ready to pull and run the container.

On Linux, issue this command (on one line):

```
% sudo docker run -p 80:3000 synedra/irresistible
```

That binds your system's port 80 to the Docker container on port 3000.

On systems using boot2docker (Windows or Mac OS X), the command is as follows (root access isn't needed because of the nature of docker-machine):

```
% docker run -p 80:3000 synedra/irresistible
```

The application automatically runs in the Docker container. When using boot2docker, the Docker engine assigns a separate IP address for Docker containers. In order to determine the IP address of your Docker container, issue the command `docker-machine ip default`. Once you've done that, you can access the system at http://<docker-ip/. Because the server is running on port 80, the default web port, the browser will find the web server on that port.

If you'd like to start the container and explore the code, you can do so with the following command, which won't start the node server:

```
% docker run -i -t synedra/irresistible /bin/bash
```

You'll now be root in a shell within the container. Accessing the system in this way allows you to look at the code and figure out how all the pieces are working together. The application itself is composed of the toppings.js file, and the front-end web server is run from the static/index.html file. The previous command will allow you to access the application directly without cross-domain issues. You can read more about Docker port forwarding at https://docs.docker.com/userguide/dockerlinks/.

If you're running Docker directly on Linux, you can access the system directly at http://localhost. If you already have a web service running on the default port, you can assign a different port in the `docker run` command.

2.6.2   *Installing the system via Git*

If you prefer to run the applications on your own system rather than using the Docker container, you need to have Git and Node.js installed on your system. The commands needed to pull the repository to your system and install and run node are as follows:

```
% git clone https://github.com/synedra/irresistible
% cd irresistible/
% curl -sL https://deb.nodesource.com/setup | bash - && apt-get
  install -yq nodejs build-essential
% npm install -g npm
% npm config set registry http://registry.npmjs.org/
% npm install -g express@2.5.1
% npm install express
% npm install
% node toppings.js
```

From there you can access the system at http://localhost:3000 (or port 3000 on whichever server you're using). Node.js runs on port 3000 by default, so if you want to expose the system on the standard port (80), you'll want to run a separate server on the front end—something like Nginx or Apache—and then create a reverse proxy back to the node server. For security reasons it's best not to use root to run a bare web service, and you can't access the standard ports as a regular user. This is one of the advantages to using the Docker system—because it's isolated from the rest of your system at its own IP address, it's safe to run the front-end server on port 80.

2.6.3 Exploring the code

As you're running the system and exploring it, you'll see the logs for the system show up in the terminal window where you started up the web server. Using an HTTP sniffer, you can watch the API traffic your system is generating as described in section 2.3. Once you've started a web browser at http://docker_ip_address/, not only will you be able to see the traffic in an HTTP sniffer, but you'll start seeing server entries in the terminal window that you started.

The logs show you all the traffic—both front-end calls to / and the back-end requests to the API. This combined log data makes it easy to see how the systems are interacting.

If you used the Docker setup, you were placed directly into the /opt/webapp directory. The Git instructions will put you in the same directory: the webapp subdirectory of the repository. Table 2.3 shows a listing of the files in the program directory along with a description of what each one does.

Table 2.3   Files included in the program directory

Filename	Description
Procfile	Used if you want to deploy this to Heroku
Toppings.js	The main program for the system
static/index.html	A simple single-page application that exercises the API

The toppings.js file is used to run the node web server. When you type node toppings.js, the application looks for the index.html file in the static directory and serves it up.

The application uses Bootstrap, a single-page application framework that makes your simple applications look pretty. The formatting pieces are mostly contained within the Bootstrap framework, and overrides are made within the index.html file. This is all to explain what the id and style attributes are for each <div> on the page. In this case, it's using the main-single-template for the outside wrapper, and the inside is a main-single container. This function will present the table of items for the page to render.

The $.get function makes the call to /api/v1.0/toppings, at which point the back end returns a list of toppings, and this function is called to render the page.

EXERCISE 3   Play around with the page, see how each piece works, and try to see if you can make the application go directly to the Edit page from the toppings list instead of the View page.

2.7   *Summary*

At this point you've either played directly with my hosted service or set up your own. This chapter covered the following concepts:

- The structure of a simple web API system includes the required actions for a complete platform: create, read, update, and delete.
- A basic HTTP transaction includes a clearly defined request and response, creating a foundation for web APIs.
- From HTTP sniffers to Chrome Developer Tools, the ability to monitor the traffic makes it much easier to understand what's happening between the systems.
- RESTful API ideals define the endpoints as nouns, and not verbs. Between these ideas and the HTTP transactions they work with, the web API system is complete.

Now that you have an understanding of the various moving pieces in a simple API, you can begin thinking about your own API at a higher level: how to architect the entire system to use the simple pieces I discussed here to build a fantastic API system. This chapter was about the bottom up, and how the cogs and wheels work together to make things work. The next chapter will help you to learn how to think top down: what are the goals for your API system and how can you meet them most efficiently?

API First 3

> **This chapter covers**
> - Code consistency
> - Feature equality
> - Increased velocity
> - External/open versus internal
> - Examples of API First development

When you're setting up an API, the vision for the entire platform is quite important, from determining the business value through structure and design decisions. I'm going to step back for a moment from the practical description of APIs in order to talk about an overarching model that is generally superior to the old model of creating APIs in parallel with the main product.

Previous models for product lines with multiple different interfaces, such as mobile or integration, were created so that each of the integration points available for the different client use cases were built independently. This generally led to unfortunate consequences—APIs that were creating code already written for the main product, APIs that were perennially behind in features and functions, and a great deal of technical debt because each change to the system needed to be pulled into each type of client.

API First does what it says. Instead of *product first*, the API First model describes a model where the back end interfaces only with the API, and all products—the main front-end website, mobile integrations, and other integrations—interface with the API itself.

3.1   *Why choose API First?*

API First makes a lot of sense for any company. As soon as you have more than one product, you should have a layer to protect the clients from changes on the server. Your website and mobile application should both be able to get information from the system. A well-documented interface into the system, crafted with specific use cases in mind, allows you the freedom to change things around on the back end, as long as the interface doesn't change. You can switch out the database, add scaling, or refactor your back end entirely as long as you adhere to the documented interface. Integrated testing is easier, and the main products running on the API will, by their nature, test the integrity of the system on a regular basis through the daily use of that platform.

To understand why API First is a good idea, you first have to understand what the existing model looks like. Various architecture models are available that support web API platforms, but many existing APIs are created using a pattern where the API accesses the back end directly in parallel with the main product. This means that if you want to make new products, you have to either write more systems that access the back end or extend the API so that it supports both alternative products. Additionally, an API is frequently considered to be an "extra, nice to have" product rather than an important member of the product ecosystem. This attitude creates problems because companies are frequently focused on revenue-producing products; if there's no understood value for the API, it will likely suffer from a lack of needed resources.

3.1.1   *APIs as side products*

Figure 3.1 shows an example of the "usual" setup for APIs. As you can see, the API is separate from the main product, and even if all secondary products, such as mobile or partner integrations, run off of the API, a mismatch can exist between the features and functionality available in the main product and API-driven products. For instance, the main product may get a new activity feed, but because that coding is happening within the main product, it doesn't appear in the API (or as an extension in the mobile application or partner integrations). Keeping everything entirely consistent—from features and object structure—is theoretically doable, but it's a lot more work than restructuring the infrastructure to treat the API as a piece of core technology for the system. The back-end system is the critical component for both the APIs and the main product, and separating out the clients in this way makes it harder to triage and fix problems that might occur in the product or the API. Keeping everything in the same pipeline—from back end, through the API, to the product lines, including the main web product, the mobile clients, and APIs for partner integration—helps ensure consistency and reliability, and as your product grows, it makes scaling much easier.

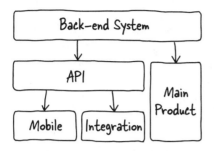

Figure 3.1 This is an API that was set up as many of the first platforms were created: the main product interacts directly with the back-end system, leaving the APIs as second-class citizens in the product hierarchy. Any new changes or features in the main product have to be duplicated in the API, resulting in feature inconsistency and incompatible resource representation.

Once you've established how you want your users to interact with your system, it's best to support that everywhere. Imagine that a company has a product for creating and updating contact information for users; we'll call it Addresser. Addresser's main product is a website where users can view their contacts and information, and there's also a mobile application to interact with the back end. The website makes a specific call to the back end and gets the result formatted exactly as it's requested. The mobile application, on the other hand, makes a call to the API, which provides the information in a different format. Figure 3.2 demonstrates this case, where the main product communicates directly with the back-end system and is likely to retrieve data in a different way as a result. When the back-end system team adds a new "Location" field feature, and the Addresser website starts using it, it doesn't show up in the API, nor in the mobile application, until an engineer has time to add it, doubling the amount of work necessary to keep the products consistent and increasing the likelihood of bugs in one product or the other one. This means that there will likely be a lag between the addition of this field to the main product and availability within the API. There's a lot of technical debt incurred when you have multiple systems trying to reproduce a single interface; this setup means that duplicate work is needed in order to maintain feature consistency. In this case, the mobile app wouldn't allow or see locations, resulting in developer dissatisfaction and customer confusion and irritation.

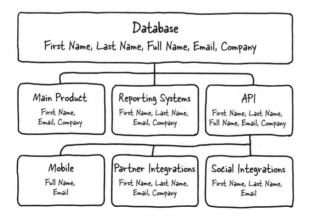

Figure 3.2 When an API is one of many different interfaces into the back end, the representation of a simple item (such as a user) can be different in many ways. Additionally, if the back end (in this case, the database) is changed to add more information, the interactions with each of the client systems will need to be changed, as will the clients of the API itself. This creates a large amount of technical debt because any change to the system has to be duplicated in several different places.

When you have multiple teams creating products without a shared vision, you also tend to have poor communication between those teams. The Addresser mobile team has no reason to interact with the main website team in order to help the back-end team create APIs that work for both products. This can lead to bug fixes in one code base but not in the other, or inconsistencies between the items available from the system, depending on which interface is being used.

3.1.2   *API First model*

What, then, would this system look like if it were designed API First? Figure 3.3 shows an API First model. The website and the mobile device get their information from the same API interface. This ensures that these resources will be consistent across the entire product line. Note that just because an API resource is available within the system, you don't have to expose it to the entire world—you can decide which of the API resources is internal, partner only, or open to anyone. It's still a great idea to have your API ready because when a major partner asks for access to some specific resources to support a use case, you have it ready to go. In the case of Addresser, the API may be designed to send users and contacts via the API to partners and client developers. At some point, there might be a location-based activity feed that a partner wants to create, but in order to create this feed they need to access the locations for the user's contacts. In the API First model, this API is available because it's being used by the website and the mobile application. You can make the decision to expose it to the partner wanting to create new and exciting functionality for your customers.

API First also encourages communication between your back-end team and each of the client engineering teams. Understanding use cases at a high level helps you create APIs that are easy to implement for the use cases you understand up front, and more likely to support future use cases that come up. Once you're creating the API as a larger team, you'll find many places where different teams offer complementary resources, adding to a more well-structured system.

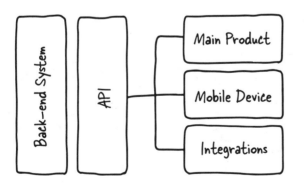

Figure 3.3   In an API First model, the back end only interacts with the API, which in turn drives the main product and all other implementations—the main product, mobile device, and other integrations. This reduces the need for duplicate code and allows each client to focus on exactly the pieces it needs.

3.2 Code consistency

When you have two separate systems doing the same thing, you create a world with duplicate code. In the case of Addresser, the user object would be needed for the main product, but this resource would also be required for interactions with the API. If the queries to the back-end system might use different fields or connected data, the end products will not be consistent with each other—a common reason for user dissatisfaction with the company as a whole.

When your code base diverges in this way, you start creating technical debt for your company, regardless of who is in charge of writing the APIs. Two testing systems are needed, and when a bug is found in the main product it's not necessarily fixed in the API—and vice versa. As you build more and more systems tied directly to the back end (for instance, you might have internal systems that access the databases for reporting), you create more dependency on that specific server implementation. If you share some code but not all of it between the different systems, changes to that implementation can break products unexpectedly. Additionally, when code is written in a highly coupled way (where dissimilar systems rely closely on other systems for convenience in coding), your system is highly interdependent and vulnerable to failure.

This issue has repercussions on the developer experience side as well. In a world where each project uses the back-end system individually, systems are likely to have different interfaces and represent resources differently, resulting in frustration for the developers and end users. Back-end systems are usually designed to meet specific needs, and unless the API is designed for a consistent developer experience across all interfaces, the developer may have to spend an inordinate amount of time trying to figure out what's available and how the application can retrieve it from the platform.

Where does API First not work?

Putting an API layer between your systems can hinder performance for highly scaled systems, such as a stock trading system, where the interfaces need to be completely secure, fast, and incredibly performant. There are going to be situations where it's necessary to couple the systems tightly to enhance performance. Many clients—whether they be main products, reporting, or administration applications—prioritize performance as secondary to consistency and reliability, and running all of your products' code through the same interface will speed development and reduce errors.

Figure 3.4 shows system interactions when each client (including the API) accesses the back end through its own interface.

As you can see, each of the clients grabs and uses a representation of a user, but each sends a slightly different request to the system. The API layer exposes the entire data structure, but the main product and the reporting systems grab only what they need. Because of this divergence, testing a change to the database requires working with each of the teams to ensure that nothing has broken, which requires the server

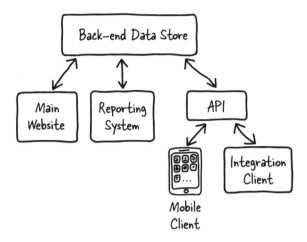

Figure 3.4   **When different implementations are maintained for different clients, the user experience is different—and if, for instance, the reporting system adds new functionality to include the company for a specific user, the API would need to add it. In this system, the mobile and integration clients would need to add it as well.**

team to track all the clients. In my years at major technical companies, this has been a serious issue; when one group owns a system and another group decides to leverage it directly, without an agreed-upon interface, client systems break when server systems change. For instance, if a developer discovers an undocumented method on the employee database to access employee data information in order to create an application for contact management, that application is vulnerable to changes because they didn't work with the originating group to make sure their use case was understood.

An API won't fix all the issues your production process may have, but it can make it easier to write code and architect changes with the right frame of mind. Once you've made the decision to attempt the API First approach, the focus moves from trying to maintain consistency across different product and code bases to designing, creating, and maintaining a strongly tested and well-designed shared interface. Decoupled code of this sort—code that doesn't rely directly on the bare interface of the other system—protects both sides from unexpected changes.

How can you create this kind of model? The API needs to have a well-documented and well-understood interface, and calls to the back end should be completely protected from client access through any other means. This process does take more mindful consideration up front but has huge advantages, as you'll learn in the following sections.

3.3   *Functional equality*

In the API First description, I mentioned a contacts application called Addresser. A common problem created by a model of this sort is where the main product gets a new feature in January but the API has to wait, sometimes for months, for the engineering resources needed to provide the same functionality. This issue can be avoided, but it's rarely the case that a company wants to delay the release of its main product for something that's considered "extra." Until the engineering organization determines that the API is a first-class product, this delay will exist, and in many cases the team who understands the new functionality is moved along to new projects before the API is created, resulting in an API created months later, if at all, by an engineer who isn't as familiar with the goals of the functionality change as the original team. The result is a poorly designed API.

If the API is integral to the main product, though, it's updated, tested, and deployed as part of the main change. It's ready to use and tested by the main product, and when you want to expose it to your other applications and developers, whether internal or external, it's ready to go. Having features available to release allows you to enable partner integrations quickly—trust me, your premium partners will want the functionality as soon as they see it—and open it up to your internal and external developer partners for use as you see fit.

Even if the API is ultimately used only by the engineering team for the main product, this approach still encourages consistency in the product's representation of resources and will help your product developers create integrations and applications easily. API First also allows the back-end engineering team to change the back-end database or server system without impacting the developers; the interface is documented and understood. Because the clients are going through this layer of abstraction, the engineering team knows exactly what they need to support with any changes to the back-end system. You've already documented the interface, so when your company decides to add new products, the available resources are ready and well documented. New clients wanting to use the API can work from the schema model to make sure that the use cases they want to implement are easy and efficient.

3.4 *Increased productivity*

It's somewhat counterintuitive that adding an extra layer to your system could reduce the amount of overall work that your engineers have to do—but remember that once you have the design for the interface defined and engineering teams start using it, they can share client libraries and other tools for interacting with your stable API interface. Although it's possible to write modular and decoupled code without this extra layer, it's much more difficult to do so well. Without a guiding vision, each development organization will determine exactly what they need to meet their goals, and so the clients will diverge rather than converge. API First means that you need resources assigned to make sure that your APIs will work to support your main product(s) easily and that your interfaces will be consistent. The goal is not to hamstring your developer partners by reducing their access to the data, but to make sure that they're getting what they need from a single source.

Once your developers are using the API to feed their products—whether internal reporting systems or third-party applications—they'll no longer need to write the duplicate code to access your back-end system. Each client will have access to new resources as they become available, and you can expose them to different classes of developers (internal, partner, external) as needed.

Running all your applications through the API may also reduce the need for multiple representations of the same object (for instance, First Name, Last Name, and Full Name). But having two different representations available is also of value; if the users of a client application prefer one representation over another, it's simple for the client to switch to using that representation.

The quality of your system will also be improved. When you have a single interface through which all of your data flows, you can test it more easily and consistently. Changes to the platform can be run through unit tests (as all code should be) as well as integration tests based on the use cases that you support. In fact, you can use the use cases for your system—including the main product, reporting systems, and integrations—as the guiding models for the API you create, and those use cases can also drive the testing you do against the system.

Although your back-end engineers may not appreciate the extra work up front, they'll start to realize that it's saving them time and effort. Your developer partners will thank you for the feature consistency they enjoy—where they are given access to everything that makes sense, rather than the features you've had a chance to implement in the API. If you make a decision to hold back features for only internal development, you can communicate it to your external development community so they understand that there's a business case preventing the access—and if they can provide you with a use case you want to support, you can revisit the decision. If the data is not available through the API, making that decision comes with much more overhead, and the inconsistency will stifle the enthusiasm and creativity of your developer users.

3.5 *Internal/external access*

On the flip side of open and transparent access to data is the gripping terror that enterprise companies experience when they consider opening all their data to the entire universe. The open API ecosystem started out this way, with open APIs making it possible for third-party developers to access the system and make changes or view people's information. This was a visible aspect of web APIs, and it caused some inaccurate assumptions about restricting access based on the application and/or user accessing the system. Large or heavily security-conscious companies were concerned that having an open API would expose their proprietary data without any control or restriction. The easiest way to dispel those assumptions is to understand how API management can allow companies to control access to specific functions. Figure 3.5 illustrates an OAuth request, one of the options for API authentication and authorization.

The authentication and authorization systems such as OAuth that have been developed for APIs make it relatively easy to define which pieces of an API are open to internal developers, as opposed to partner or external developers. Along with authentication and authorization, these mechanisms make it possible to know which developers, and which users, are accessing the API in which ways—a huge help when trying to debug problems.

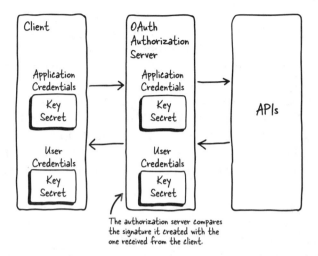

The authorization server compares the signature it created with the one received from the client.

Figure 3.5   In an OAuth request, the client and server both know the application and user keys, but they also have "shared secrets" at the application and user levels. The request is built using the non-secret data, and the encryption is done using the shared secrets. The client creates the request and signs it with the shared secret, sending it to the server. The server takes the request and also signs the request, and then compares the signature it created with the one sent by the client. If they match, then the client passes the authentication check and the request is allowed to proceed.

Authentication and authorization mechanisms give you total control over which people can access your system. Depending on how your data is structured and the types of information you want to keep back from the public APIs, you can decide to expose different fields for each type of data. In fact, this is one way in which an API abstraction layer makes it easier to provide system access to your partners without having to allow them direct access to your company's critical data systems. Adding an authentication system on a well-designed internal API to expose certain elements to customers and partners is much less work than creating a new interface from scratch for them.

That's not to say that it's a bad idea to expose information to the open developer ecosystem. Third-party developers can help by previewing new API resources, giving you feedback on what works, and validating those use cases for you to make sure they work as you expect. This is a type of "free" testing for your APIs, and if there's not a business case for holding back API functionality, you should definitely expose it. If writing to the system is something that the company is concerned about, allowing open developers read access to the resources can help you by exposing issues with your API that you hadn't previously considered. Take advantage of this potential; when you treat your developers as partners, they're usually willing to work with a beta or release-candidate version of your system in order to get a leg up on their competitors.

One other consideration when planning for your API is that even if your API is internal only, you want to create it with the same care as you would for an API that you might eventually expose to the world. There are a few reasons for this. First, you might eventually want to open up that API, and if it hasn't been crafted for a fantastic developer experience, you'll either have to suffer the consequences of a poorly designed API or start again to create a new API that duplicates the effort of the previous one. Second, and more important, it's a terrible idea to assume that because your customers are internal you don't have to create a great experience for them. When developers are forced to use an unusable system, it creates a huge support burden—when these developers can't walk away, they'll keep at you about the things that are causing them trouble. When designing your API, think about who will be using it (internal, external, partners). Authentication and authorization are less important when you're behind the firewall, but it's still much easier to triage issues when you can track down exactly who is doing what with the platform.

API First will provide your platform organization with the same advantages no matter who the customers of that API will be. Consistent and decoupled code will reduce bugs and regressions. Feature equality will make it easier to allow potential customers to integrate with your system—without scrambling to catch up after the need is clear. API First improves the quality and velocity of the code that's written, allowing your developers to focus on new functionality while spending less time chasing down issues.

3.6   *Case studies*

Although API First can seem like an excellent idea in theory, I've consistently heard engineers, managers, and executives say that they couldn't possibly implement this type of system for their company. It's true that adding an additional layer to your infrastructure creates more work up front, but the advantages can far outweigh the downside. For further context, this section talks about some case studies to demonstrate how companies have moved to this model, or started with it, and the results they've enjoyed as a result.

3.6.1   *API as the main product*

Twilio is a successful company that provides telephony services via API (see figure 3.6). For instance, if you want to add SMS or other phone capabilities to your application, you'd need to integrate Twilio using its APIs, and your development time would be reduced substantially. Telephony is something that's hard, and Twilio is a great example of a company that's making significant money by simplifying hard (but important) functionality.

Twilio's only real product is the API, and they charge for usage based on how much a developer uses. When the company started out, the APIs it had were restricted to the basic product, but as developer partners increasingly started using the platform in a more complex way, Twilio realized that it would do well to create APIs for the configuration, billing, and other website functionality that supported its main product. It still has some back-end systems that don't expose APIs, but anything that's available for developers to do with the system is available via API as well.

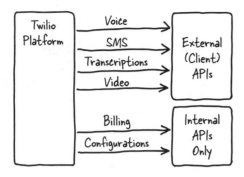

Figure 3.6 Twilio's system, with APIs for both internal and external functionality. Although Twilio uses its billing and configuration APIs only internally, the discipline it exercises in making sure that everything it does uses the same API system helps to ensure that the system is consistent and robust.

An important note here that we'll revisit in chapter 9: Twilio is widely considered the industry leader when it comes to developer support; it has a team of evangelists who attend hundreds of hackathons each year to help developers become familiar with its platform. Twilio has a strong commitment to developer support, even encouraging its evangelists to help developers work on code that isn't related directly to Twilio. It has a goal of providing documentation and resources so that new developers can make their first successful API call within five minutes. One of the major advantages to having a team of evangelists of this sort is that they're constantly getting feedback directly from developers that they can funnel back to the development team.

3.6.2 Mobile First

Instagram, a photo application, was initially created as a mobile application. The most efficient back end for the company to use was a web API, and Instagram created one for use only by its mobile applications. After several months, users started to request a website and integrations with other systems, but the Instagram team didn't have the resources or time to implement these things. Frustrated by the lack of access, some third-party developers reverse-engineered the system to create an API, which encouraged Instagram to open up its own API system to developers. But since it had started out API First, adding API management and authentication around the platform was relatively quick and easy, and the developers then had what they needed in order to create the products they were looking for.

3.6.3 Refactoring for API First

Etsy is a major online crafting marketplace, with over $1 billion in gross merchandise sales revenue in 2013 alone. In 2014 it decided to change to an API First model in one go. The previous API was a big success, allowing third-party developers to integrate with the system and meeting the needs of buyers and sellers. Unfortunately, the system was a mirror of the back-end database, not crafted toward specific use cases, and not efficient to use or maintain. Mobile application developers were frustrated that they had to make multiple calls to render a single screen—an antipattern that makes mobile applications fragile and nonperformant (users tend to walk into elevators or drive into tunnels, and it's important that the application can get the information it needs efficiently).

Etsy refactored its back end and APIs to support the new scheme and created strongly RESTful APIs on which it rebuilt its main products. To support its mobile clients and other clients who needed a slightly different setup, the company created a batching system called BeSpoke, where it could identify resources as bundles of other resources. Moving this complexity to the server meant that Etsy could better support all of its developers and keep track of how the resources were being used, and it could run concurrent requests for these bundled responses, which improved the efficiency even more. The business logic was maintained in the system at the API level, so authentication and visibility were consistent no matter where a user was interfacing with the system.

This ambitious undertaking had the outcomes Etsy was hoping for: increased velocity and consistency across resources and products. Its previous system had grown organically over time as the company grew, so taking this opportunity to refactor the system gave Etsy the ability to improve the responsiveness, scalability, and consistency of its system. There were unexpected benefits to this change as well. Etsy noticed that the communication between its development groups improved noticeably; the mobile team and website team were engaged with each other in defining customer experience and what was needed from the API. Etsy even had an unexpected bonus in that the activity artist feed—one of the products it hadn't targeted with the change—was able to go from an asynchronous call of several seconds to a subsecond call. This change meant that Etsy was able to move from regularly refreshing the resource offline to returning the information on demand when users requested it, reducing the resource need and providing a better, more accurate user experience.

As a second example, 3scale is an API management company, providing a platform with tools for companies to manage and administer its APIs (see figure 3.7). It should be no surprise to learn that all internal and external processes—indeed, all of the systems used by the company—run on web APIs. Anything customers can do with the product can be done through the API, because those products are running directly from the same platform.

When 3scale started, the company was looking to solve the problem of managing the traffic flow on APIs to ensure it was safe, scalable, and accessible. Steve Willmott, the CEO and cofounder of 3scale, has often said that his goal is for everyone to be able to have an API.

To start, the solution was to separate traffic delivery from management: deploy the management dashboards, analytics, and policy management in the cloud and provide code plug-ins in many languages (Java, Ruby, and Python, and more). Each of these clients hit a set of APIs on 3scale's cloud platform. Using the plug-ins, customers could deploy the functionality in their own applications. These plug-ins evolved quickly, and the API mediated all the calls, capturing stats and becoming the backbone of the service. Later 3scale added extensions for web proxies like Varnish and Nginx so these

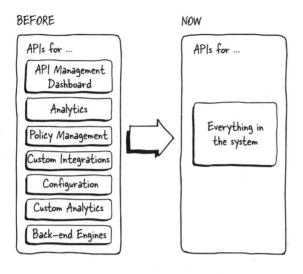

BEFORE
NOW

APIs for ...

API Management Dashboard

Analytics

Policy Management

Custom Integrations

Configuration

Custom Analytics

Back-end Engines

APIs for ...

Everything in the system

Figure 3.7 3scale's evolution from standard implementation to API First moved it from a system where most of the customer visible functions were available via the platform to a system where each function within their system worked via the same API platform. Again, this made 3scale's system more robust and made it easier to expose new functionality to users as requirements dictated.

could become fully fledged, high-performance traffic gateways, all communicating with the APIs.

The first versions of 3scale's dashboards didn't come with APIs. Given that it was capturing analytics data and had customers consistently asking for complex configurations, it became clear that the only way to meet these needs was to add APIs across all functionalities. In one of the major version changes in 2010, 3scale developed comprehensive APIs for every part of the platform alongside all of the user interfaces, switching those interfaces to run on top of the APIs—truly API First. Since then, the API and product have always been updated in parallel.

3scale is in a competitive market, and running its business on APIs in this way has allowed the company to enable many more customer use cases than would have otherwise been possible. Today, many customers use 3scale as a platform underneath other systems that add further functionality. The traffic management API architecture also means that today 3scale can apply management to APIs delivered across all sorts of systems—from content delivery networks to a customer's own homegrown web server layer.

3.6.4   *API First strategic direction*

Akamai is a company providing content delivery services for companies looking to add reliability and scalability to their web properties. Akamai's business model for APIs is slightly different than the other companies discussed here: rather than deal directly with the customers who are consuming the content, Akamai works with administrators who configure, maintain, and update their properties (websites) using Akamai's tools. The nature of this system is such that a great deal of the internet runs on Akamai servers, so any change to the access or configuration controls needs to be controlled carefully.

Historically, Akamai had many APIs for customers to use for reporting and configuration, but these APIs were inconsistent in authentication and interaction. Customers who wanted to integrate with these systems were required to learn a new model every time they integrated with a new API, and support, maintenance, and improvement were inconsistent and frustrating.

In 2012, the company made a decision to move all of the configuration and product behavior to an API First model using a single API system called EdgeGrid. Because of the need to protect stability and security, Akamai couldn't make a sudden refactor happen without potentially compromising its critical systems. Thirty percent of internet traffic comes off an Akamai server, so any errors or issues could cause serious repercussions for both the internet and the company itself.

Akamai was committed to making the change to API First in the best and most efficient way possible, so the decision was made to move to API First as a strategic direction: put the self-service portal and other products in front of the API and make those APIs available, where appropriate, to partners and customers. As new products were created or existing products updated, web APIs were created. An API architecture team assisted the product teams in creating APIs that were consistent with those of the other teams.

Akamai had an aggressive goal for bringing its system in line with this model: while keeping in mind the sensitivity of the existing system, the company aims to get most of the work done within the course of a couple of years. Given that most of the systems have been in place for many years, reimagining the components and rebuilding them based on the current and predicted usage takes time. An important thing to realize in this case is that when you're asking multiple business units or teams to come together and work as a larger team, you need guidance, vision, and support from both the high-level executives (the refactor won't generate new revenue on its own) and from an architecture team who can review the new APIs as they're created to make sure they're in line with the goals of the overall platform strategy.

3.7   *Summary*

In this chapter, you learned about the concept of API First, the advantages it can bring to your company, and how to choose the right level of privacy. We explored case studies of companies who have made the decision to implement their system in this way.

This chapter covered the following topics:

- The API First design methodology moves the web APIs in front of the back-end servers so that all products, APIs, and integrations are running off the same system.

- Without API First, API code that duplicates the main product code must be written and maintained, leading to reduced performance and inconsistent behavior in the system.

- When an API is a side addition to the product, new features given to the main product will lag behind on the API side until required. They should be created at the same time, with the same goals and vision—or, ideally, they should be the same thing.

- Removing the duplicate code and having strong communication between the teams, as well as strongly defined interaction points between systems, make it much easier for your platform developers to release new features or changes.

- Just because an API has some open aspects doesn't mean that you have to open everything up to the world. Creating a solid and consistent platform that meets your internal needs is a valid goal on its own—and if you do want to expose the information externally, you can do so with some additional security mechanisms to protect sensitive data.

- Etsy is the best example for companies who have gone API First from a more monolithic model. Moving to API First improved its velocity, increased cross-team communication, and improved sections of its product that it hadn't even targeted.

The next chapter gives you a solid introduction to web APIs—from the HTTP framework behind them to descriptions of how REST APIs work with that framework to create functionality.

Web services explained
4

Now that you're familiar with what APIs do and have some overall idea about the strategy, let's dive deeper into the technical aspects of HTTP and REST so that you understand how these systems work together. Knowing these details will also help you when you want to troubleshoot or understand how the interactions are working between a client and server.

Note that in order to grasp how HTTP matters in the API context, you need to know the protocol and practices from the point of view of the consumers—your developer partners. So while you're working to make a great API, understanding the interactions between client-server transactions from the point of view of a developer who is consuming the service is illuminating. This chapter is designed to give you a view of the user side of HTTP so that you can determine how the pieces fit together in an API. This chapter will provide an understanding of how APIs work, which is necessary to build APIs people love.

4.1 HTTP fundamentals

An API can be any kind of transaction between two computer systems, but this chapter focuses on REST APIs specifically. Although REST APIs don't have to use HTTP, this common protocol has all of the fundamental pieces needed to build a REST API, and so almost all REST APIs use HTTP as the *transaction* protocol (the layer underlying the REST API). First, we'll drill down on HTTP more deeply than we did in chapter 2, and then we'll explore the specifics of how the interactions work.

As mentioned in chapter 2, HTTP is the method browsers use to communicate with web servers. When you click a web link or type an address in a URL bar, your browser sends an HTTP request to the server, and the server sends back an HTTP response (see figure 4.1).

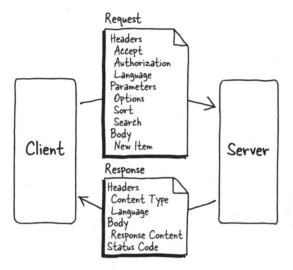

Figure 4.1 HTTP transaction between a client (application) and server (platform). The HTTP request will always be sent to a specific URL defining the resource; most requests will also have headers to add context to the request, along with parameters to refine the item itself. If the request is an update or create action, a body will be sent as well. The HTTP response always has a status code indicating the success or failure of the exchange, as well as headers describing the type and size of the content.

Several concepts are inherent in the HTTP protocol:

- Addressability
- Status codes
- Body
- HTTP verbs
- Headers
- Parameters

4.1.1 Addressability

One requirement for any system is a way to express exactly what you want to operate on. When you enter a web address into the URL bar of your browser, you're indicating the unique identifier for a specific item—in this case, a page on the internet. Every HTTP request must have an identifier; this address is called a *uniform resource indicator* (URI) in this case. Table 4.1 shows examples of addresses. In each address, there's a server component and a path component.

Table 4.1   URLs broken out by server and path

URL	Server	Path
http://www.google.com/	www.google.com	/ < This is the base of the website, the top page.
http://gmail.com/	gmail.com	/
http://irresistibleapis.com/demo/	irresistibleapis.com	/demo/

The unique identifier of a resource (or page) is the combination of the server name and the path. This format ensures that each request addresses a specific item on the internet.

4.1.2   *Status codes*

As every request must have an address, every response comes back from the server with a status code indicating the success or failure of the action requested. The HTTP status code system is fairly straightforward. The simplest explanations of the groups are shown in table 4.2.

Table 4.2   HTTP status code groups

Status code group	General description
5XX	We (the server) messed up
4XX	You (the client) messed up
3XX	Ask that guy over there
2XX	Cool!

Each status code group represented in table 4.3 expresses a broad meaning, and examples are given of what types of errors you might encounter in that group.

Table 4.3   HTTP status codes and specific examples

Status code	Meaning	Examples
5XX	Server error	500 Server Error
4XX	User error	401 Authentication failure 403 Authorization failure 404 Resource not found

Table 4.3 HTTP status codes and specific examples *(continued)*

Status code	Meaning	Examples
3XX	Redirect	301 Resource moved permanently 302 Resource moved temporarily
2XX	Success	200 OK 201 Created 203 Object marked for deletion

5XX errors (status codes between 500 and 599) mean that the server itself encountered an error. When writing your API, you must give good, strong error messages with the appropriate status codes. If developers encounter server errors intermittently on a particular resource when developing a client for an API, they may be able to retry the request, but you'll want to watch and log the number of errors and other status codes in your system. Otherwise, this is likely an error the API provider (in this case, you) will need to fix in the system. Table 4.4 describes the specific client error codes used in HTTP transactions.

Table 4.4 HTTP 4XX status codes

Status code	Meaning	Description
400	Malformed request	Frequently a problem with parameter formatting or missing headers.
401	Authentication error	The system doesn't know who the request is from. Authentication is like a driver's license, showing who you are. Authentication signature errors or invalid credentials can cause this.
403	Authorization error	The system knows who you are but you don't have permission for the action you're requesting.
404	Page not found	The resource doesn't exist.
405	Method not allowed	Frequently a PUT when it needs a POST, or vice versa. Check the documentation carefully for the correct HTTP method.

Authorization is the next step. Once the system knows who you are, it can determine what you're allowed to see and do in the system. As indicated in table 4.4, the 403 status code indicates that the system has determined that the user doesn't have permission to execute the specified request. Again, when returning a 403 status code, there should be an additional message describing the problem.

Almost everyone is familiar with the 404 status code, the code that's returned when a particular page doesn't exist. In addition to the well-known client error status codes listed in table 4.4, a huge number of 4XX errors are out there—for missing or unexpected parameters, headers, or incorrect data formatting. There's even a 418 status

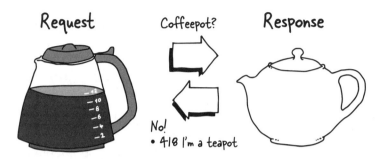

Figure 4.2   418 status code exchange demonstrating a somewhat silly interaction with the coffeepot protocol as defined by the W3C. Note, though, that it's similar to the other transactions we've seen; the client sends a request for a particular resource, and the platform responds with a status code indicating the answer—in this example, a response that the object isn't the expected coffeepot, but rather a teapot.

code put in by the W3C Standards Body for an April Fool's joke in 1998 (see figure 4.2); the W3C wrote a coffeepot protocol, and 418 was the error "I'm a teapot." It's a shame that people say that standards bodies have no sense of humor.

4.1.3   Body

When content is associated with a request or response, this data is sent as the body of the request or response. For requests, this is generally the case for create and update options (POST and PUT). The body gives the server the information it needs to create or update the resource specified by the client. Whether this is JSON text describing the new or updated object or an image file, the body is where the "meat" of the write operation will be placed.

In the case of a read operation (GET), the request doesn't need to have any data associated with it. In this case, the response will have a body with the content of the resource that was requested by the client.

4.1.4   HTTP verbs

Each individual request from the client to the server needs to indicate the action it wants the server to take. To create a fully functional system, it needs to be able to create, read, update, and delete (CRUD), as shown in figure 4.3.

The way this works can seem somewhat abstract, so I'll expand the example that was briefly given in the first chapter. I will order an iced tea from Starbucks, with the requisite additions and modifications I want in order to make it exactly how I want it (figure 4.4).

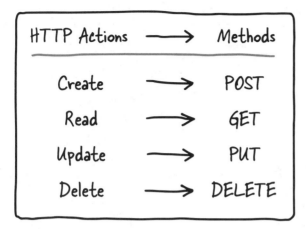

Figure 4.3 Actions and their associated HTTP methods. To perform all the needed actions for a complete platform, CRUD must be supported. HTTP contains methods for each of these actions, making it a great framework on which to build an API.

Figure 4.4 This is a human version of the programmatic transaction that follows. The interaction between the people demonstrates exactly how transactions work. As you can see, all the requests and responses between the client and the server map directly to an easy-to-understand interaction between people.

In the example in table 4.5, the list of orders is at the address /orders, and each individual order is at the address /orders/<number>.

Table 4.5 Iced tea transaction, translated into a set of HTTP transactions

Action	System call	HTTP verb address	Request body	Successful response code Response body
Order iced tea	Add order to system	POST /orders/	```{ "name" : "iced tea", "size" : "trenta" }```	201 Created Location: /orders/1

Table 4.5   Iced tea transaction, translated into a set of HTTP transactions *(continued)*

Action	System call	HTTP verb address	Request body	Successful response code Response body
Update order	Update existing order item	PUT /orders/1	```{ "name": "iced tea" , "size" : "trenta", "options": ["extra ice", "unsweetened"] }```	204 No Content or 200 Success
Check order	Read order from system	GET /orders/1		200 Success ```{ "name": "iced tea" , "size" : "trenta", "options": ["extra ice", "unsweetened"] }```
Cancel order	Delete order from system	DELETE /orders/1		202 Item Marked for Deletion or 204 No Content

Going through each of these steps in order will help you understand how the various resources work together to create a story. As I discuss each piece, I'll describe exactly what each is doing within the system.

First, I place the order with the cashier (table 4.6). "I want a Trenta iced tea." In HTTP parlance, this would be a create action, indicated with the verb POST. Now, if I were to request this multiple times, the system (in this case, the cashier at Starbucks, using the cash register) would create a new item each time I made the request. If I asked for this 15 times, 15 iced teas could be ordered (imagine that the cashier is as patient and accepting as a computer system might be). POST is the only HTTP verb that should reasonably be expected to create new items. All the other methods should work on already existing (and specifically identified by the URI) elements. The server response in the case of an HTTP POST usually includes the location of the newly created object.

Table 4.6   Place order

Action	System call	HTTP verb address	Request body	Successful response code Response body
Order iced tea	Add order to system	POST /orders/	```{ "name" : "iced tea", "size" : "trenta" }```	201 Created Location: /orders/1

The next thing I do is specify how I want the iced tea (table 4.7). "Extra ice, unsweetened." To do this with HTTP you'd use PUT, the verb that's used to update an existing object in the database. The address used for this action is the one that was retrieved from the POST operation before. The Location information indicates that further operations on this specific order need to use the address returned by the create action. As you can see in table 4.7, the body content for this request includes the entire ordered item, including the information in the originally created order as well as the information you want to add. Sending the update with the body, as shown in table 4.7, will update the system's version of your order to add the two new options. Note that sending an object that only had your changes (and not the original content) wouldn't update the object correctly. PUT is a full update on the item; you need to build the entire object and PUT it to the system rather than try to make changes piecemeal. Another HTTP method, PATCH, can be used in this way, but most API servers don't implement it, and using that kind of system requires a deep understanding of the data model.

Table 4.7 Update order

Action	System call	HTTP verb address	Request body	Successful response code Response body

Update order	Update existing order item	PUT /orders/1	{
			    "name": "iced tea" ,
			    "size" : "trenta",
			    "options": [
			            "extra ice",
			            "unsweetened"]
			}
				204 No Content
				or
				200 Success

The main difference between PUT and POST is *idempotency*. This rule says that a PUT transaction must be the same even if you send it to the server 10 times, or 100, or even a million times. Imagine that you're standing in that Starbucks repeating the phrase "Extra ice, unsweetened" 15 times. Unlike with the earlier POST, you'd be setting options for the same iced tea, and no matter how many times you made the request, the outcome would be the same (although the cashier might look at you somewhat crossly after the first few times). The system itself wouldn't change anything after the first request, and no extra changes would occur to your iced tea order beyond the first request you send.

That covers create and update. The next two verbs are more straightforward. Back to the Starbucks example, I want to check and make sure the cashier has heard me correctly. "Can you please read that back to me?" The cashier responds, "A Trenta iced tea, extra ice, unsweetened." In the HTTP world, this is a read operation, represented by the HTTP verb GET (table 4.8). This operation retrieves the server's current representation of the order in question. This representation matches the version sent by the update operation. No body content is sent with the request because the client isn't trying to change anything but is retrieving the current object from the server.

Table 4.8 Check order

Action	System call	HTTP verb address	Request body	Successful response code Response body

Check order	Read order from system	GET /orders/1		200 Success
				{
				    "name": "iced tea" ,
				    "size" : "trenta",
				    "options": [
				            "extra ice",
				
				"unsweetened"]
				}

Create, read, update . . . that leaves delete (see table 4.9). The HTTP verb for this is DELETE (note that all HTTP verbs are sent as all capitals in request transactions). To finish this transaction, imagine that I've left my wallet at home and must cancel the order. For an HTTP client-server transaction, this would be done by sending a DELETE to the item's unique identifying address. No body content is sent because there's no new information the server needs in order to perform the deletion. Sending the verb DELETE along with the specific address for the resource tells the server everything it needs to know to perform the requested action. Additionally, there will be no response body. Everything happens without content being passed around.

Table 4.9 Cancel order

Action	System call	HTTP verb address	Request body	Successful response code Response body
Cancel order	Delete order from system	DELETE /orders/1		202 Item Marked for Deletion or 204 No Content

With POST, GET, PUT, and DELETE, HTTP has verbs available to cover each piece of a full client-server transaction.

Figure 4.5 pulls the address, request information, and status together and demonstrates how the verbs, status codes, and addresses work for specific types of actions. For each of the verbs, an address is used to indicate where to look for the item, or resource, being accessed, whether it's an object or a list of objects. The verb along with this address combine to indicate what action should be taken with that item. Finally, the Status Code line shows the status code for a successful action.

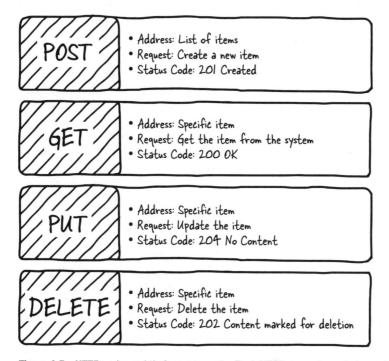

Figure 4.5 **HTTP verbs and their components. Each HTTP request must always have a method along with the resource: the address for the specific item as well as an action to be taken for that item. Note that the Success status code listed for each of the methods is slightly different but still follows the pattern of 2XX, indicating success.**

4.1.5 Headers

So far I've covered the address for an item, the verb for a request, and the status code in the response. For a simple transaction, this is enough to understand what's happening. HTTP contains *headers*, additional elements providing additional context for a request, and *parameters*, separate options for the request.

There are different ways to send options with a request (headers and parameters), and it's not obvious which kind of information should go where. Headers are used for context about the entire transaction, as opposed to a single request-response message. In some cases, headers or parameters can both be used for the same kind of information.

To make this clearer, let's go back to my iced tea example. When I walk into a Starbucks in Barcelona, Spain, the cashier may greet me in English or Spanish. Depending on how I respond, the rest of the conversation will be in the language I choose. In this case, I (representing the client) expressed my preference for English by speaking in English, and the cashier will respond in kind if possible. When you indicate to your browser what your preferred language is, it will send a header along with requests to indicate this preference to the server. If the server is able to provide the response in the requested language, that's what it should do.

Headers, then, are for context about the entire transaction. Common items passed in a request via headers include language preference, response format preference, authorization information, and compression preference. Table 4.10 shows common headers for requests, with a description of how each one is processed by the server to determine what response to send back.

Table 4.10   Common request headers

Header	Example value	Meaning
Accept	Text/html, application/json	The client's preferred format for the response body. Browsers tend to prefer text/html, which is a human-friendly format. Applications using an API are likely to request JSON, which is structured in a machine-parseable way. This can be a list, and if so, the list is parsed in priority order: the first entry is the most desired format, all the way down to the last one (which frequently uses */* to indicate "whatever might be left").
Accept-Language	en-US	The preferred written language for the response. This is most often used by browsers indicating the language the user has specified as a preference.
User-Agent	Mozilla/5.0	This header tells the server what kind of client is making the request. This is an important header because sometimes responses or JavaScript actions are performed differently for different browsers. This is used less frequently for this purpose by API clients, but it's a friendly practice to send a consistent user-agent for the server to use when determining how to send the information back.
Content-Length	<size of the content body>	When sending a PUT or POST, this can be sent so the server can verify that the request body wasn't truncated on the way to the server.
Content-Type	application/json	When a content body is sent, the client can indicate to the server what the format is for that content in order to help the server respond to the request correctly.

The response also includes headers, which generally specify the content type (the formatting used for the response), the language used, or the size of the request. Table 4.11 gives examples of common response headers along with what they indicate to the client.

Table 4.11 Common response headers

Header	Example value	Meaning
Content-Type	`application/json`	As with the request, when the content body is sent back to the client, the Content-Type is generally set to help the client know how best to process the request. Note that this is tied somewhat indirectly to the Accept header sent by the client. The server will generally do its best to send the first type of content from the list sent by the client but may not always provide the first choice.
Access-Control-Allow Headers	`Content-Type, Authorization, Accept`	This restricts the headers that a client can use for the request to a particular resource.
Access-Control-Allow-Methods	`GET, PUT, POST, DELETE, OPTIONS`	What HTTP methods are allowed for this resource?

Access-Control-Allow-Origin	`*`
	or
	`http://www.example.com`
		This restricts the locations that can refer requests to the resource.

4.1.6   Parameters

Parameters are frequently used in HTTP requests to filter responses or give additional information about the request. They're used most frequently with GET (read) operations to specify exactly what's wanted from the server. Parameters are added to the address. They're separated from the address with a question mark (?), and each key-value pair is separated by an equals sign (=); pairs are separated from each other using the ampersand (&).

Table 4.12 demonstrates different ways the request could have been made to get information about the order in question using filters and other specifiers.

Table 4.12 Using parameters to specify details of read requests

Action	System call	HTTP verb address	Successful response code Response body

Get order list, only Trenta iced teas	Retrieve list with a filter	`GET`
		`/orders?name=iced%20tea&size=trenta`
			`[`
			`  {`
			`    "id" : 1,`
			`    "name": "iced tea" ,`
			`    "size" : "trenta",`
			`    "options": [`
			`            "extra ice",`
			`            "unsweetened"]`
			`  }`
			`]`

Table 4.12   Using parameters to specify details of read requests *(continued)*

Action	System call	HTTP verb address	Successful response code Response body

Get options and size for the order	Retrieve order with a filter specifying which pieces to return	`GET`
		`/orders/1?fields=options,size`
			```{```
			``` "size" : "trenta",```
			``` "options": [```
			``` "extra ice",```
			``` "unsweetened"]```
			```}```

These two examples are somewhat different ways of understanding how parameters can be used in a request. The first example demonstrates the use of parameters to filter which items are retrieved from a list. As described earlier, the `/orders/` resource is a list of all of the orders in the system. So a `GET` call to `/orders/` would return all orders currently within the system. In this case, I'm only interested in iced tea orders, so I add a filter on the call to indicate that I only want items with "iced tea" as the name that are size `trenta`. Note that it's not necessary for the key names to match the variables within the object itself, but it can be handy for keeping track of what's being requested.

You probably noticed that this request has the question mark to separate out the parameters (sometimes called a *query string*) from the resource address, and that the two key-value pairs are separated from each other using the & character. You may have also noticed that `iced tea` became `iced%20tea`. Certain characters such as the space character need to be escaped in this way in order for a web server to process them correctly. In most cases your browser does this for you, but when a developer creates a client, it's important to remember to run the requests through an encoder to make sure that the server gets the right information.

The return value on this initial request also shows a difference with the original `GET` to the specific order. Instead of returning an object (indicated by key-value pairs encased in curly braces `{}`), this request returns an array (indicated by a list encased in brackets `[]`). That's because you're requesting a list, and the server is returning a list with one item in it. A list response should always be in the format of a list, even if there's only one item within that list. This consistency makes it easier for developers to work with the responses whether there are zero, one, or many elements in the response.

The second example shows how to ask for specific information about a single known item. The request is to the same single order used before, but in this case specific information about that order is being requested. Neither this nor the previous example will "magically" work, but it's a great way for an API/web service provider to provide developers with more ways to get exactly what they need from the system without getting extra, unneeded information. Trimming the response in this way is often useful for clients like mobile applications where the bandwidth is quite restricted and the application needs to get information as quickly as possible. In this case, the client is asking for the specific order numbered "1," but only the size and options for that order. The response is smaller than the full order in the original example and has exactly what the client wants for their purpose.

4.1.7 HTTP overview summary

This overview of HTTP isn't complete or exhaustive but should give you enough information to move forward with the rest of the concepts for web APIs. If you're interested in more detailed information about HTTP and how it works, you can find many resources on the web and in print.

4.2 REST web services explained

Now that you've got an idea how HTTP works, it should be much easier to understand the mechanics of the API you worked with in chapter 2. REST-style APIs (and many other similar web APIs) are effective when designed and built around HTTP. The HTTP verbs match exactly to the create, read, update, and delete (CRUD) actions needed. The existing error framework is more than sufficient for a strong framework.

There are some best practices for REST web services built on HTTP. For instance, the URI (web address) for a resource must be unique for each item. This is the item's unique identifier and is used for any action on that item. Because only POST transactions should add new items to the system, POST is generally used for create operations in REST by operating directly on a list resource rather than a single object. When you create a new object in the system, you send a POST to a list of items. If you look back at the pizza toppings example, you'll see that when new objects were created, that was done with a POST to the list of toppings, whereas update actions were done using PUT to the specific topping.

REST seems like a difficult and abstract way to describe a system, but if you take the HTTP fundamentals described and use them in a direct way, you're most of the way to creating a good REST API. As illustrated in the Starbucks example, the HTTP protocol supports all the needed methods for a complete transaction set. REST utilizes these methods to create interactions that are straightforward, consistent, and predictable.

As I discuss pitfalls and best practices, you'll learn to avoid the most common mistakes made when people are implementing REST-style APIs.

4.3 Exploring your API by inspecting HTTP traffic

In chapter 2, you were introduced to some ways to inspect HTTP traffic. Understanding how your developers will interact with your system is a critical component of API success, so you need to test your system as if you were one of the developers trying to use it. Inspecting API traffic is also helpful when creating support documentation or helping developers. Watching traffic using a sniffer is quite useful when trying to debug complex API calls, but for the purposes of understanding how HTTP traffic works in general, using a browser is a fine choice. For this discussion, you'll put together the information in section 3.1 with web calls. I suggest using Chrome or a similar browser with HTTP traffic inspection. To start, I discuss how to get Chrome set up correctly to give you the information you need, and then we'll explore how it applies more completely to the example application discussed in chapter 2.

4.3.1   *Setting up Chrome for HTTP inspection*

To set up Chrome for HTTP inspection, you first need to enable the Developer Tools. If you don't have one already, get a copy of Chrome to use on your system. One major advantage to Chrome in this case is that it's available for all major operating systems and works consistently across each of them. To download Chrome, go to www.google.com/chrome/ and get the appropriate version for your system.

After you've got Chrome up and running, the first thing to do is go to my website: www.irresistibleapis.com/demo. Figure 4.6 shows what it looks like in Chrome.

Figure 4.6   Go to irresistibleapis.com/demo to see the main HTML page. Remember that on the back end, this page is calling the /toppings endpoint in the API.

Now that you have the basic tool up and running, you need to configure it to give you the information needed in order to inspect the traffic it's processing. Find the Developer Tools in the menu, as shown in figure 4.7.

Once you've opened the Developer Tools, you need to tell Chrome that you want to be able to see network traffic (this parameter adds overhead to the requests, so it's disabled by default). To do that, click the Network button in the Developer Tools at the bottom of the page. Figure 4.8 shows what this will look like in your browser.

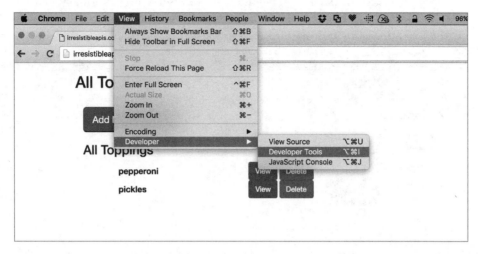

Figure 4.7 Once you've started the website in Chrome, you can activate the C Developer Tools using the path View > Developer > Developer Tools.

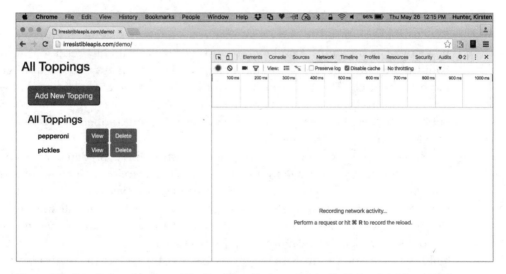

Figure 4.8 Now that you've opened the Developer Tools, switch to the Network tab to get to the information you want to see.

Once on the Network tab, you need to check Preserve Log. Normally, Chrome throws away old network traffic as it goes in order to keep the memory footprint low, but in this case, that's the information you want. Figure 4.9 shows where this checkbox is.

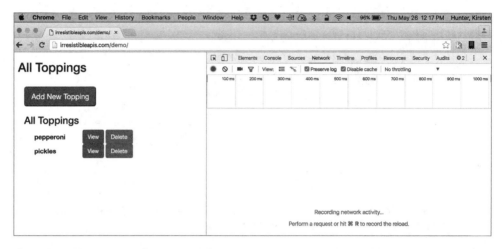

Figure 4.9   Change the settings to activate Preserve Log so that the HTTP traffic will stay in the queue for inspection.

Now Chrome is set up to show you what you want to see about the website you're browsing. The log in the Developer Tools is particularly useful, because you can see both the website page and the API interactions (because they're calls sent directly by the browser itself). Note that in most cases you won't be able to use a browser to debug or inspect traffic to an API because most APIs require complex authentication, but because this API doesn't have any authentication and is open to browsers, it's an excellent learning tool for this situation.

Reload the page you were on (www.irresistibleapis.com/demo or your local API/app server if you set one up in chapter 2). The Developer Tools section should now show you all the resources you're accessing and give you the opportunity to inspect them individually. Reload the page so that the elements will show up in the Developer Tools section. I'll start with the most basic piece—you've seen it before— and then I'll work up to the more complex pieces in the stack. All the elements used to build the page, such as the base page, the CSS, and any JavaScript, are displayed in the list. The first thing you want to view is the toppings call, the direct call to the back-end API. This will cause the network log to display both the front-end page and the back-end REST API calls. Figure 4.10 shows how to select this call from the Developer Tools.

Initially, the Network tab will likely show you the headers, as mentioned earlier. Check out the headers and compare them to the table of request and response headers so you can understand how the headers interact in this live call. This is the traffic that's flowing into and through the browser. Click the Response tab to see what the response content body looks like, as shown in figure 4.11.

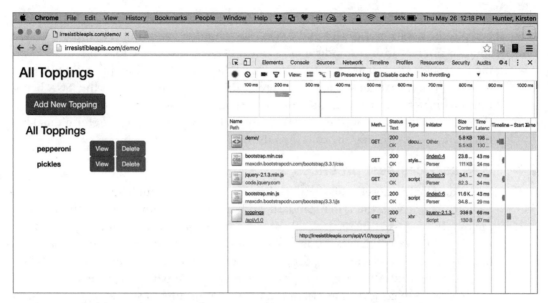

Figure 4.10 As calls are made through the browser, they each show up in a separate line in the Network Log section of the Chrome Developer Tools. To get to where you can understand the interactions, select the `toppings` resource in the network log.

What you see is that the main page at http://irresistibleapis.com/demo is making a back-end call to the API displayed in chapter 2. You can see here that as part of building this page, the HTML page is pulling information from the resource for the list of

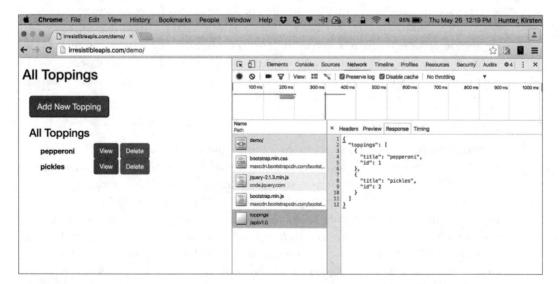

Figure 4.11 Once the `toppings` resource is selected, you'll be able to see information about the call in the right-hand column, including the response body, request, and response headers. Explore the various tabs on the right side to learn more about how the pieces work together.

toppings, in this case `/api/v1.0/toppings`, as you saw in chapter 2. So now, the JSON being returned from the back-end API is being used to build the HTML page so that you can interact with the individual actions: CREATE (Add new topping), GET (View topping), DELETE (Delete), UPDATE (View, and then change). This application directly interacts with the API described in chapter 2. It's no coincidence that the JSON being returned matches exactly what the web page shows. Try adding and deleting items in the system and watch how the JSON from the API changes; the page itself isn't making the changes—it's making the calls directly to the back-end system.

4.4   *Web services best practices*

When developing a web API, then, it's important to follow guidelines that keep your platform in line with the HTTP standard, and with the guidelines set forth in the REST philosophy discussed in section 4.2. Your resources should be nouns, not verbs (so `/orders/` instead of `/create_order`). REST best practices dictate that you should conform to the HTTP status and error codes and work hard to achieve and maintain consistency, making your API as usable as possible for the developers using your system.

Use cases are critically important even at the beginning of your design process, so think carefully about them. For instance, if you want to support mobile applications (ever) with your platform, you need to realize that mobile developers have different issues than standard web developers. The bandwidth is smaller, and mobile devices are unreliable in terms of keeping their connection up (the user can ride a train into a tunnel or enter an elevator, and the network connection can be dropped). You need to provide these people with a single call per page so that their applications can be performant and successful.

This may seem out of line with the idea of single nouns for resources as suggested by the REST philosophy, but realistically what you need is the system that will work best for the developers trying to use your system. Try to make your system as similar to the industry standards as you can, but when those standards clash with use cases critical to your developers, you need to flex in the right direction so the things you want them to do are easy and straightforward (and reliable, and scalable).

4.4.1   *Using the right status codes*

As discussed previously, HTTP status codes are quite flexible and able to handle most issues encountered during a client-server transaction: server errors (5XX), client errors (4XX), redirects (3XX), and successful transactions (2XX). Think quite carefully about how you plan to return information to the client indicating that an issue has happened. When returning 4XX and 5XX error codes, you can still return a body with a message indicating how the transaction failed. Was it a bad signature or a mismatched parameter, or was the request too large? Ideally you should make your system so talkative that anyone using it can tell immediately what's happened to make the request fail. Without this, there's an enormous support burden; any time client developers run into an error, they can't figure out what the underlying problem is, even though in most cases the problem is something they could fix if they understood the issue. Give your developers the chance to succeed without having to tap your support resources. They'll be happier, and you'll spend less time and money trying to hand-hold your customers through an awkward interface.

4.4.2   *Methods and idempotency*

Earlier I touched on the notion of *idempotency*, the idea that when sending a GET, DELETE, or PUT to the system, the effect should be the same whether the command is sent one or many times. When working with web developers, you should follow certain expectations about HTTP method behaviors. For instance, developers who are accustomed to working with well-designed web APIs may get confused if they find an API where a GET (read) command can be used to delete items in the database. This restriction was initially designed to avoid having web crawlers accidentally delete all the items in your system, but even now, with authentication in front of most systems, developers use the type of call into the system as an indication of whether the call itself can be destructive or change the state of the server. Follow the guidelines—a GET is for reading only and shouldn't be extended to perform other operations.

There are situations where the exact correct method can't be used consistently. For instance, Flash was originally unable to handle anything other than POST and GET, and as a result it was necessary to overload those two methods so that they could support faux DELETE and PUT operations. Many API vendors found ways to work around this, most of them settling on ways to extend POST to perform other write operations (using headers to indicate the desired action).

In any case, as much as possible you want to follow the existing patterns out in the API ecosystem. The less you can surprise your developers, and the fewer times they have to learn a new pattern for your API, the more likely they'll be to use the system the way you expect them to. This leads to happier developers, better street cred, and most important, a much smaller support load.

4.4.3   *Nouns vs. verbs*

As with the methods discussed earlier, it's critically important to use nouns for objects in a web service system. Although SOAP APIs used methods, we're focusing on REST-style APIs. In this case, we're not using a GET to /create_order; we're using a POST to /orders. The format of this call communicates to the developer that this is a system-changing call and that they're adding something new to the system. If a crawler did get out of hand with its GET calls, there's no way that it would accidentally change something within the system.

4.5   *Troubleshooting web API interactions*

One major advantage of a web API over one that's more tightly coupled is that the HTTP base of the API is easy to trace, making it much more efficient to determine what the transaction looks like—both request and response—and troubleshoot issues that might arise for clients of the platform. There are various ways of examining this traffic to triage issues or speed up development.

4.5.1 *Tools for API inspection*

Various tools are available for testing API and browser traffic. They'll show the headers, content, and values for requests and responses. HTTP sniffers like HTTPScoop and Fiddler can be used to determine how the traffic is faring in the journey between your client and server. These tools are covered in more detail in chapter 2, and you should definitely select one to use when working with web APIs, whether you're creating or consuming them.

4.5.2 *Error handling*

When you're developing an API, one of the best ways to make it irresistible is to make your error handling clear, consistent, and easy to follow. Choose the right status codes for the problems your server is encountering so that the client knows what to do, but even more important is to make sure the error messages that are coming back are clear. An authentication error can happen because the wrong keys are used, because the signature is generated incorrectly, or because it's passed to the server in the wrong way. The more information you can give to developers about how and why the command failed, the more likely they'll be able to figure out how to solve the problem. This is one case where having sample code that handles the errors can help demonstrate to the developers exactly how to handle specific problems that occur.

4.5.3 *Defensive coding*

Many developers are accustomed to a world where they own the entire stack of code. When this is the case, assumptions can be made about the stability of particular interfaces, with a strong reliance on unit tests to make sure each component works correctly and on integration tests to make sure that interfaces are in sync. But when the stack is fully owned by a development team, they can avoid strict coding standards where each item used in a system is carefully inspected to make sure it didn't change.

Although irresistible APIs are not likely to change unexpectedly, sometimes errors or changes do occur. Make sure that your sample code demonstrates how to handle specific status codes. Demonstrate checking that items exist in the object before using them. Write your documentation in a way that shows the best approach to interact with the resources. I've seen many cases where a developer using an API made the assumption that a resource would always be identical, and when it changed, their application broke. For web applications, that's annoying, but with mobile developers it can take weeks to push a new change through the application system for the mobile device, so it's critically important that they don't have incorrect expectations.

Encouraging and teaching your partner developers that they need to avoid assuming the system will always be up and running and identical to the day before will lead to a happier world. Web APIs usually have other systems behind them, and the larger the stack, the more possibilities there are for unexpected problems.

4.6 *Summary*

In this chapter, you've been exposed to some of the internals of HTTP, which should help you understand the underpinnings of REST APIs. I've shared some of the downsides to rushing through your development and given you some ideas to contemplate in terms of making items accessible and clear to your developers. Topics covered in this chapter include the following:

- HTTP fundamentals provide a closer look at the formats and sections of requests and responses. Understanding these fundamentals makes it much easier to follow the action in an HTTP sniffer and learn about the structure of the platform as a whole.

- A deeper explanation of REST fundamentals includes examples of REST APIs for context and demonstrates how you can leverage the HTTP protocol to easily create clean and functional web APIs.

- Inspecting HTTP traffic gives various ways to look at the traffic between the client and the server to understand the underlying transactions for a system.

- Web API best practices help you to avoid many of the common pitfalls encountered when creating an API without a well-thought-out plan. Taking the time to explore and understand other APIs will help you to guide and create a fantastic API product.

- Sometimes technical interactions don't work as expected, so a discussion of some common error causes and solutions gives you the tools you need to succeed, along with information on preventing these issues in your own web API.

The next chapter walks you through some guiding principles for creating APIs that are useful and successful in the real world. Topics include use cases, compact responses, consistency, social integration, and versioning.

Part 2

Designing web APIs

Diving more deeply into methods and choices for designing and implementing great APIs, the chapters in part 2 help the reader create an API with an excellent developer experience. After discussing some guiding principles to help keep your mind-set focused on the developer experience, these chapters cover the process of API creation. The chapters look at the process of determining business value and metrics and designing the API deliberately using schema modeling. Once you've completely designed your API, the remaining chapters guide you to the right path to drive your development. Finally, the chapters in part 2 discuss the process of empowering your developers.

Guiding principles
for API design

This chapter covers

- API design principles for successful APIs
- Cautionary notes on design antipatterns
- API examples highlighting these principles

The technical aspects of REST APIs are only part of the puzzle. This chapter and the next few focus on the process of creating an API that's not only functional but also delightful and usable.

Before I get to the meat of the process, I want to give you some advice to keep in mind during the process. This is definitely not a checklist; even when you've already done one of these things, you need to continue doing it. Think of it as learning to drive a car—even though you've checked your blind spot once, you need to continue doing so as you move forward. Similarly, this chapter is designed to help you create a mind-set while you go through the API design and development process that will help you make the right decisions to achieve success. I discuss the guiding principles of API creation and ideas to keep at the front of your mind while going through the steps to create your API.

The guiding principles in this chapter are as follows:

- Don't surprise your users.
- Focus on use cases.
- Copy successful APIs.
- REST is not always best.
- Focus on the developer experience, not the architecture:
  - Communication and consistency are critical.
  - Documentation should tell a story.

Following these principles will give you a great head start on building an API that's not only irresistible for your customer developers, but fun to develop and easy to support.

5.1 *Don't surprise your users*

First off, always remember that developers are people too. In fact, in the case of your API, developers are your customers, even if they're in the same company using internal APIs. In the case of an API, your customer and partner developers should be treated with the same respect and consideration given to users of your revenue-producing products, even when the API doesn't itself provide revenue for your organization. APIs that don't produce money directly can enhance the products that end users do pay for—your main website, the mobile applications, or integrations—and make those products more compelling.

When designing an API, you'll frequently encounter situations where it'd be easier to develop the API by cutting corners or moving away from standards. Using POST for all write actions, including updates and deletes, would be easier for the API development staff, but would also create more work and confusion for the developer customers of the API. Any decision of this type should be made to ease the burden on your customers even if it takes extra work on the development side. In short, put your customers ahead of your API development team, and make sure the experience is as smooth as possible. Whether you decide to use different verbs than usual for your methods, use nonstandard response and request formats, or organize your schema in a nonintuitive way, you should carefully consider the experience of the developers using the API. It's often tempting to try to focus on scalability and performance, but the basic truth of this is that if you don't focus on usability, you're not going to create a usable API, and nobody is going to use it—at which point scalability and performance aren't going to matter to anyone.

Any time you go off the beaten path, you create a "surprise" for your users, and they have to adapt their normal development style to suit the changes you've made. This design choice can result in a support burden in a couple of ways. First, users may be confused about how they're supposed to use your nonstandard system and need assistance in learning how to work with it. Second, and even more important, using a nonstandard approach creates a situation where developers are quite likely to use the API in a way you don't expect or support as they try to figure out the right way to interact with your system. Sticking with the standard interaction model wherever possible means that you and your users share the context of what that interaction should look like, whereas using a different approach means that the user is starting at square one and likely to make unexpected choices resulting in errors, or worse, code that works in one version and doesn't work in the next because they misunderstood the logic behind your API. In any case where you're considering extra work for your team versus ease of use for your developer customers, you should always perform the extra work on your side to reduce the support burden and increase developer engagement.

5.1.1 Flickr API example

An example of a company that didn't follow REST best practices is Flickr. When it created its web API, Flickr described it as RESTful (the company has since changed the description to *REST-like*). Rather than exposing data as objects, staying within the usual guidelines of REST, Flickr exposed methods (see table 5.1). Flickr's choice to make method-based calls limits the types of actions that can happen with the items in their system. The left column in table 5.1 shows what a method-based API looks like. Instead of operating on specific items within the system, each call is a command to do a specific thing. When compared to the RESTful calls on the right-hand side, the Flickr calls are much more difficult to understand as a complete system.

Table 5.1 Flickr calls and RESTful calls

Flickr call	RESTful call
`GET /services/rest/?method=flickr.activity.userPhotos`	`GET /services/rest/activity/userPhotos`
`POST /services/rest/?method=flickr.favorites.add`	`POST/services/rest/favorites`
`POST /services/rest/?method=flickr.favorites.remove`	`DELETE /services/rest/favorites/:id`
`POST /services/rest/?method=flickr.galleries.editPhoto`	`PUT/services/rest/galleries/photo/:id`

Flickr took a SOAP API—an API focused on actions, not resources—and tried to make it work in a more REST-like way, without the changes to the structure needed to make it work appropriately. That meant the API didn't have a contract to tell developers how they were supposed to interact with the system—and no objects.

The Flickr API accepts only two methods: `GET` and `POST`. This means that it supports clients who are using limited frameworks, but it also means that a developer with the full methods available has to think carefully about which method to use for a call. Additionally, the URL isn't used to describe the resource being accessed; rather, a method is called, and all calls are made to the same URL.

For instance, this is the easiest call in the Flickr API:

```
https://api.flickr.com/services/rest/?method=flickr.test.echo&name=value
```

This call is clearly not a REST call (even though it has `rest` right in the path). The "method" is the biggest clue that this system is working with verbs (methods) and not nouns (resources). But most developers can work with this, even though most libraries designed to work with REST expect a different URL for each specific resource.

Deleting a photo should be a `DELETE` to the photo resource, but instead Flickr uses the following call:

```
https://api.flickr.com/services/rest/?method=flickr.photos.delete&photo_id=
    value
```

To call this, a `POST` must be made (which in the usual case would create a new resource). Once again a method is specified for the deletion, and the `photo_id`, which should be part of the URL as a resource, is instead specified as a parameter.

The error codes used are also nonstandard and aren't passed back in the usual way. Figure 5.1 shows the list of error codes sent back for API calls that fail.

Error Codes

1: **User has not configured default viewing settings for location data.**
   Before users may assign location data to a photo they must define who, by default, may view that information. Users can edit this preference at
   http://www.flickr.com/account/geo/privacy/
2: **Missing place ID**
   No place ID was passed to the method
3: **Not a valid place ID**
   The place ID passed to the method could not be identified
4: **Server error correcting location.**
   There was an error trying to correct the location.
95: **SSL is required**
   SSL is required to access the Flickr API.
96: **Invalid signature**
   The passed signature was invalid.
97: **Missing signature**
   The call required signing but no signature was sent.
98: **Login failed / Invalid auth token**
   The login details or auth token passed were invalid.
99: **User not logged in / Insufficient permissions**
   The method requires user authentication but the user was not logged in, or the authenticated method call did not have the required permissions.
100: **Invalid API Key**
   The API key passed was not valid or has expired.
105: **Service currently unavailable**
   The requested service is temporarily unavailable.
106: **Write operation failed**
   The requested operation failed due to a temporary issue.
111: **Format "xxx" not found**
   The requested response format was not found.

Figure 5.1   As with the resources and methods described in this figure, using inconsistent error codes means developers have to hunt through documentation to learn what the errors mean. Using the standard HTTP status codes helps alleviate this problem and saves times for your client developers.

Instead of using HTTP status codes, as is the usual pattern, Flickr is using an antipattern where a failed call returns a 2XX status code (indicating success) and then includes the error as part of the response. Using the `photosets.delete` method within the API Explorer yields the response shown in figure 5.2.

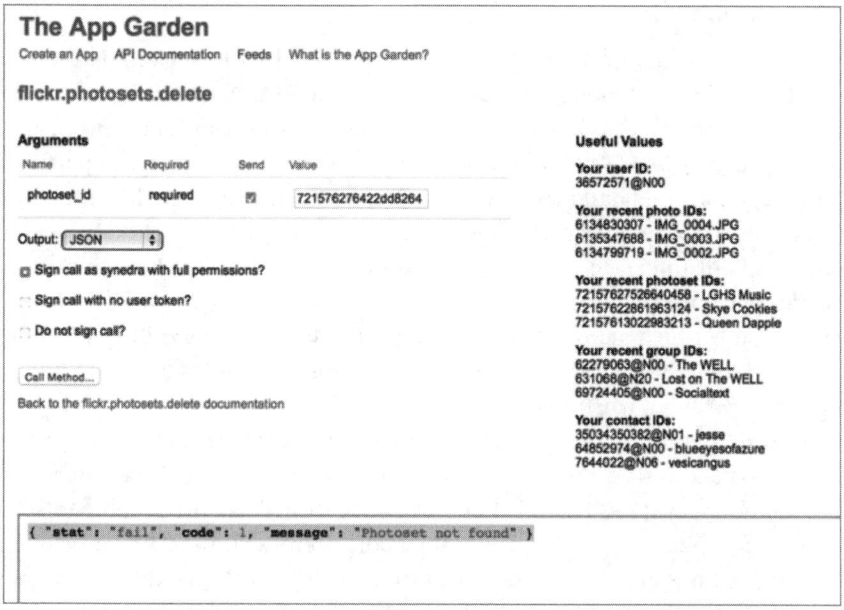

Figure 5.2 Even using the API Explorer for Flickr, you can see that there's no standard HTTP status code (although this API is using HTTP) and that the message format doesn't follow any standard industry pattern.

Again, when faced with this situation developers are unable to use the standard HTTP libraries, with their usual error handling, to write their code. The libraries designed to work with the Flickr API handle these methods, but when interacting with multiple APIs, the developer has to have special code targeted at the Flickr API.

All of Flickr's methods follow this pattern. It's a good thing that once you start working with its API you can get the hang of it and work through the issues caused by trying to get existing REST consumer libraries to work with a nonstandard setup. I know many developers who have decided not to use this API because of its poor design and implementation, who use other photo services because they trust an API more when it behaves as they expect. Flickr hasn't changed its API, probably at least in part because switching to a true REST system would require a complete overhaul of the API, which would break existing clients. This situation is a shame, because Flickr is one of the most popular photo-sharing applications out there, but the API it has makes it challenging to recommend Flickr as a good platform on which to build.

In learning from this example, when designing your API you want to stick to standards wherever possible, both the explicitly described standards and the best practices for API services. Don't stray from the path unless you must do so, and strive for consistency across your API endpoints in terms of organization, layout, behavior, and status codes.

5.1.2   *Don't make me think*

One of the mottoes for excellent web design is *Don't make me think*. This concept can be applied directly to API design as well. The flip side of not surprising your users is presenting your information in a clear and consumable way. Don't make your users think. Make sure that your API behaves as they expect wherever possible. In particular, don't expose your back-end database schema as the API, because it's highly unlikely to be the right structure for end-user developers. You need to create an API that's optimized to be an excellent interface to the front-end developer and avoid making decisions for back-end development that reduce this usability. Use cases are one great way to make sure you know which actions and workflows should be easy and fast. APIs that are created organically tend to end up being quite unusable, and developers attempting to integrate the API get frustrated or give up.

This is particularly true when you're developing external web APIs for your organization, but it's also true for internal systems. Remember that those internal APIs may well become external APIs, and they should be designed and developed so that they can easily be opened up to external users, consistent with the APIs you currently have externally. A huge part of the developer experience with an API is trust; developers have to trust that the system is reliable and that you've created an API mindfully and skillfully. It may not seem like a big deal if your server sends responses that are nonstandard or formatted incorrectly. It's easier to develop systems that use methods rather than objects even when you've defined your API as RESTful. But this type of mistake will make your users suspicious that you threw together the system; they won't know if you're going to "fix" it later, requiring them to change the code consuming the API, or if you're going to make other decisions that are nonstandard. They may even wonder if your poorly designed API will be deprecated because it doesn't have the focus to thrive.

Sometimes it's necessary to make exceptions, because your system needs to process information in a different way, or because some of your targeted users are working with platforms that can't interface in the usual way. For instance, in the past there were frameworks such as Flash that weren't able to send methods other than GET and POST, so in this case, an API designer who was targeting these users would need to make sure there was still a way to support these frameworks as clients. In such cases, most API developers chose to create headers to define exactly what the correct method was, and they documented it well. Because this was a common problem across APIs for this subset of users, a consistent method of working around it was extremely helpful for the client developers.

In a more general sense, when you need to move away from standards in order to support the needs of your system or users, how can you overcome the issues we're discussing? You can avoid many of these problems with the judicious use of documentation, communication, and sample code. You need to tell the users exactly what to expect and how to use the system, and provide them with as many examples of successful interaction as possible. It's important to create excellent documentation for any API, but when your API behaves differently than others, it's vital to provide extra documentation that helps the user understand the context correctly, above and beyond the normal documentation and example code required to get your users pointed in the right direction for using your system.

One temptation is to cover up these eccentricities by providing client libraries that mask the unusual interface. These libraries are frequently referred to as *software development kits* (SDKs). SDKs go only so far in "fixing" the problem, because you're requiring that users rely on these libraries in order to use your system, and if they step beyond the libraries, they'll discover those oddities you were trying to cover up. When you've built SDKs for various languages to work with your API, you've added a great deal of technical debt: every time the API changes, all SDKs need to change as well. Additionally, creating heavy SDKs adds an unnecessary layer of abstraction between your client developers and the API itself. This makes it more difficult to triage problems—there's one more point of potential failure. You've created a black box around something that shouldn't be opaque. In general, if your API requires an SDK more complicated than an authentication library, your API needs work.

> **EXERCISE 1**   Look for additional APIs that don't follow standard rules. If you needed to develop an API that required nonstandard practices, how could you make it easier for your customer developers to use and implement?

5.2   *Focus on use cases*

If you take nothing else away from this chapter, understanding the value of use cases is the key to creating an API that's successful and engaging. Without use cases to define the actions that should be easy in your API, it's far too easy to create an API that's technically sound but difficult to use. For instance, if you have a social application and you want users to be able to write to their activity stream, you should define the steps developers would need to follow and make sure that workflow flows smoothly for clients using the API. A use case is a set of steps describing the experience that an end user wants—a story-based workflow, if you will.

Use cases are vital throughout the process of creating an API. Once you've defined the business value you want to address with the API and how you're going to measure success, the resulting use cases drive the rest of the process. During the process of defining your API using a modeling language, make sure you can see how each piece works together to support each required use case. In the case of a social application, for instance, you'd need to make sure that the login/authentication system works seamlessly with the activity—and that reading back the activity stream is similarly easy. When developing your API, this focus gives you the opportunity to release sections of your API incrementally, guiding you to releases that enable specific use cases. Once the API has been released, you can create tutorials based on the use cases, and communicate clearly to developers what kinds of clients you want them to make.

Assuming you already have a product, that's a fantastic use case to consider. You already know what the user experience should be and how the pieces tie together.

Creating a use case supporting your product can sometimes be unnecessarily complex, so break down the functionality into smaller standalone pieces that make sense, which can be combined together to build the full functionality (or whatever functionality you want the API to support). Going through the exercise of breaking down your main product into individual use cases is a powerful way to discover what kinds of functionality your developers might need to leverage.

In the agile world, use cases are like user stories. "As an X, I want to Y, so that I can Z." A use case generally lists the steps a user should be able to follow to create a desired outcome.

5.2.1 Use case: mobile

One use case that's important to consider is mobile (see figure 5.3). Mobile developers have needs that will have a huge impact on the behavior of your API.

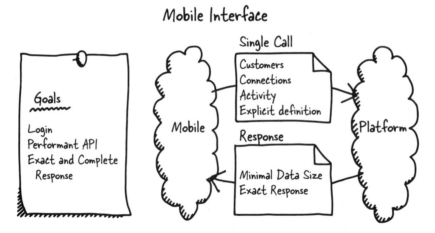

Figure 5.3 In a mobile interface, the main goals include logging in and user authentication, a performant and efficient platform, and an exact and complete response. The illustration on the right demonstrates what an ideal mobile/platform interaction looks like.

For a mobile application, the use case will almost certainly include:

- Logging in with the platform
- Avoiding unexpected application crashes
- Ensuring a quick response time

To support this kind of application, the platform must support the following developer needs:

- Single call per mobile screen
- Minimal data size
- Ability to explicitly specify which sections of data are needed

Creating a system that supports mobile developers adds a lot of extra work on the API development side, but it's likely unavoidable. Although it may be tempting to avoid this use case at the start, eventually your system will almost certainly need to support these users, and if your system hasn't been designed with this use case in mind, you may find yourself in a situation where you can't reasonably add this functionality. Here are the reasons for these requirements:

- Mobile devices have limited bandwidth.
- Mobile users frequently lose connectivity by walking into an elevator or driving into a tunnel (or hiking in the woods).
- Most mobile devices don't do parallel processing well, so a platform requiring several calls to obtain the information for a screen generates a poorly performing application.

If your API doesn't support this use case because it's hard to create, mobile developers will either work around the limitation or choose a different organization's API that supports their needs more completely and clearly. When they work around your system by, for instance, creating a caching server of their own, or scraping your website to avoid interacting with the API, there's a strong possibility that their system will get out of sync with your platform, creating a poor user experience. Although this seems like it's the mobile developer's problem, it'll come back to you because users tend to look to the main platform owner as the owner of this kind of problem.

5.2.2 Use case: application integration

Whatever kind of system you have, one of the most valuable use cases it can provide for you and your customers—or partners—is the ability to integrate your data into the developer's systems, and vice versa. Whether this is a shared login experience such as the ones provided by Twitter, GitHub, LinkedIn, and others, or a stream of activity that can be aggregated into a larger activity stream within their application, this kind of integration is an important use case to consider. If you don't plan for this up front, it may be difficult to present this information in a way that's easily used by your consumers. Remember, you should build all APIs as if they're likely to become external APIs at some point. Even if they don't, the consistency will improve the overall quality of your system, reducing your support burden at the same time.

TWITTER EXAMPLE

The first company we'll focus on is Twitter, because the functionality of this system is widely understood (see figure 5.4).

The most basic use cases for Twitter are adding to and reading from the activity stream, which could be done with a standalone application or as an integration with another product such as an online magazine or separate social system. For this, an agile user story might be, "As a Twitter user, I want to be able to post updates and view my message stream so that I can share information and keep up with updates from the

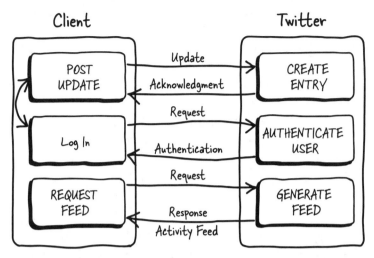

Figure 5.4   The interaction between a client and Twitter can include multiple types of interactions. The initial request and response is usually logging in, or client authentication. From that point, a client can either add new updates to the system or read the current feed of updates in the system. Each of these transactions works the same way: a request is sent from the client, and the server processes the request and sends a response back to the client.

people I follow." The use case could be expressed slightly differently. Viewing the action stream of the agile user story, a development-focused API use case could be the following:

- Log in with the platform.
- Post a message to the user's stream.
- Read the user's message stream to display the new content in context.

To support this use case, the platform must make it easy and fast to perform these actions. The documentation should include sample code showing how to make these calls in order so that it's easy and clear to developers. This sample code needs to be written by a developer or developer advocate and should include all potential client types: a native mobile application, a website application integrating with multiple facets of Twitter, or a website wanting to add the ability to share content on Twitter. Additionally, a narrative should be written by the technical team within the documentation describing the workflow for this interaction.

Twitter has also added new functionality based on use cases requested by its third-party developers. For instance, polling the API can be extremely expensive for a client and the server; making a request frequently is inefficient, and users don't understand why their updates don't appear immediately (see figure 5.5). To support this need, Twitter created streaming resources to which clients could "subscribe," letting them know when an update has happened.

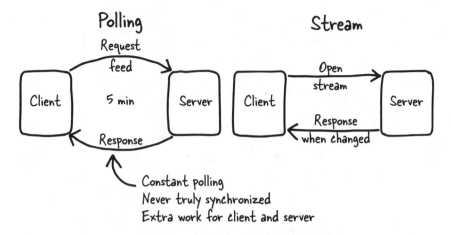

Figure 5.5 When waiting for changes from a platform, a client can continue asking the server whether there's been any change, but this is expensive in terms of time and resources on the client and server side both. A subscription model, where the client "subscribes" to receive updates from the system, is much more efficient.

Twitter is also an example of a platform where a particular use case was initially supported, but usage of the system indicated that it wasn't necessary. The API originally gave developers a choice between XML-formatted data and JSON-formatted data. Reviewing the usage of their API, the company discovered that fewer than 5% of clients were using the XML-formatted data, so it removed that option from the system and used its engineering resources for other, more popular features.

As a company, Twitter has generally been responsive to use cases requested by developers. Although it initially focused on one product without consideration for how it would be used to integrate with other systems, it quickly moved to a use case model to make it easy to target development and new features toward integration, as this became a large part of the reason for Twitter's success. The hundreds of millions of users are definitely a compelling reason to use the API, but many of those users are participating in the system because of the large number of places they can leverage a connection to Twitter. As a company, it focuses quite heavily on developer experience, which makes it possible for them to support the vast number of application and integration clients out in the ecosystem.

NETFLIX EXAMPLE

Netflix is an example of an API that follows use cases well. Although the Netflix API was originally designed for third-party developers, it has evolved to be targeted to devices such as consoles, television sets, and DVD players. These devices tend to have a large amount of bandwidth available in order to support streaming of movies or TV shows, but the end users are fairly impatient, and the device developers want to be able to grab all the information they need to display the information quickly (see figure 5.6).

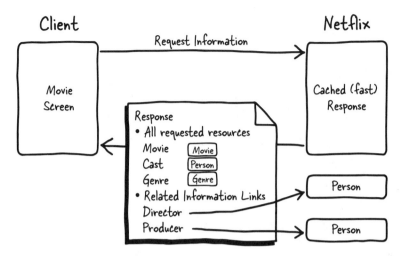

Figure 5.6   Common API interaction between Netflix and a client device or application

Here's what this use case looks like:

- Retrieve all information about a movie and related items in a single call
- Respond quickly to requests for this information (some devices, such as mobile devices, do have bandwidth limitations)
- Easily navigate to similar content

To support this, Netflix created a highly performant REST-based platform with the ability to expand similar information inline in a single call. A device can request information about a movie, including data about cast members, directors, genres, and similar movies. In addition, Netflix uses hypermedia within the calls to make it possible to programmatically find similar information dynamically within a call, so that subsequent calls can follow the chain to the related data a user wants to see. Adding information inline means that the payload is larger, but it's the client's decision as to whether to expand the information out to include more information or stick with the smaller, more basic default call.

Netflix has another specific challenge: many of the devices using the API are set in stone. Some TVs and DVD players, for instance, never update the firmware, so their use of the platform never changes. This has caused problems when Netflix wanted to add new functionality. In response, it encouraged devices to move to a system where the application itself was a shell into which the functionality could be injected. In this way, it became possible to add new functionality even when the system itself remained unchanged. Nevertheless, there are still old Blu-ray players out there that are chugging along using the old interface and will continue to do so on into the future.

When the API was designed, Netflix didn't know which way the usage was going to guide it. It targeted several use cases including these devices. When it turned out that their business model led them largely to devices as clients, it was relatively simple to continue tuning the platform to that use case, and the company didn't need to re-create the system from scratch.

5.3 Copy successful APIs

Once you understand how you want people using your APIs, copying from other exist-ing APIs is often a good idea. Chapter 1 briefly described the API Commons, a project designed to facilitate the sharing of API schemas between companies, where a new API can choose to implement some or part of existing APIs. This project is evolving slowly, as many existing API providers feel as if they'll be giving away their competitive advan-tage if they share the schema behind their API. This is an unfortunate choice by API producers, based on the unfounded fear of giving up a competitive advantage. The theory is that any information related to your company's intellectual property and plans must be held close to the chest, lest other people get the jump on you. Remem-ber that once your API is released, the schema can be determined by using the API itself. The advantage for your API should be in the quality of the data, the algorithms crafting the responses, and the integration with your presumably excellent product.

Using someone else's API as a starting point is relatively easy even without a *schema*—a blueprint or definition of the API in a more easily understandable format—but starting from an API definition can help you see which of the resources in the col-lection will work for you. For instance, if you're creating a new API based around fit-ness, you'll want your API to include resources for weight, steps, and calories burned. If a well-known API like Fitbit has placed its schema in the Commons, adding those items to your schema so that they're compatible for clients who want to implement both APIs would be simple. An API in the API Commons indicates that the organiza-tion owning that platform has explicitly invited others to use its API definition as a springboard for design. There's a huge upside to placing your schema in the Com-mons—and little downside. All schemas in this system have a Creative Commons license, so you can leverage them without fear of legal ramifications.

When you're creating a new API, you want to reduce the learning curve as much as possible for your users. Looking at schemas for existing APIs can help you create a sys-tem that can be integrated with other APIs quickly and painlessly. If your "User" model matches exactly with the schema of a complementary platform, a developer can tie those resources together with minimum effort. All fitness trackers keep track of the steps a user takes daily. If you're creating a platform for a system like this, with many existing models out there, pick one of the most successful platforms and model your system after it.

When organizations share design resources in this way, it speeds the process of arriving at the best practices for a specific industry or API type. Without a system like the API Commons, each platform is designed in an echo chamber, without learning from the experience of other existing systems. Because there are so many existing APIs in the ecosystem already, new APIs need to excel at creating APIs that make sense in the context of other platforms already being used by developers. Remember that hav-ing a schema isn't the end of the design phase—it's the beginning of the next stage in the process. If your development isn't guided by the schema you've created, the schema isn't doing its job.

API Commons, as of this writing, is relatively new. This means that organizations choosing to share their schema models in this way are creating a de facto standard describing the best practices for creating APIs using the resources they define. By sharing their model, they can help create a world where their API is easy to integrate with similar APIs, without changing their schema themselves.

How does the Commons work? An API is designed using a schema modeling system, or an existing API with no existing schema model can use a modeling language to describe the API. For this purpose, any of the existing schema modeling languages is fine to use—Swagger, RAML, Blueprint, or any other format that may be created. These modeling languages are covered in depth in chapter 7, but for now, know that there are several formats to describe what an API will do before it has been developed.

Once the schema has been modeled, an API Commons manifest is created, following the format shown in figure 5.7.

- apis
    - **name:** name of the APIs
    - **description:** short description of what API does
    - **image:** a png, jpg, or gif image icon to be used when displaying API listing
    - **keywords:** comma separated keywords or phrases to describe the API
    - **license:** reference to either CC BY-SA or CC0 licenses
    - **attribution:** a individual or company name to reference as behind the API
    - **url:** the URL of the raw, machine readable API commons manifest
    - **definitions:**
        - type: API definition format. either swagger, raml, api-blueprint,wadl,google,mashape,iodocs
        - url: the URL of the raw, machine readable API definition
- **tags:** must always be api-commons-manifest to be included in index
- **updated:** last date that API Commons manifest was updated

Figure 5.7   Manifest format for API Commons

This relatively simple format allows the API owner to describe the schema that they used for their platform. As you can see, this document describes the API, an icon to use for the definition, and the format used for the API definition (or schema model). The resulting information is used to add the schema to the API Commons index, which is shown on the API Commons website (see figure 5.8).

Although it's not necessary to use the same definition language as the platform(s) you're using as the basis for your API, doing so reduces the amount of work needed to create your own schema if you stick with the language used by the base platform. Chapter 7 discusses each of the schema modeling languages so that you can understand the pros and cons of each. For now, it's sufficient to know that they all have the functionality needed to model an API, even if it's quite complex.

The API Commons also supports versioning, so when your schema model is based on an API in the Commons, you can specify exactly which pieces you're using from several different APIs. The definitions are stored in GitHub so there's history available—which means versioning is possible.

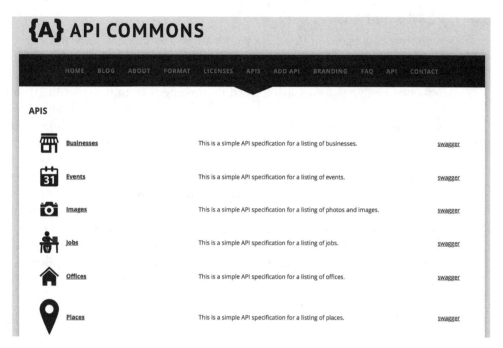

Figure 5.8 API Commons top-level definitions

Imagine you had a social event application and wanted to make an API so developers could create integrations with other systems and applications to improve your user experience. You could define this by choosing a People API from one API Commons definition (or schema), the Video API from YouTube, and the Events API from Google Calendar—each at the specific version you're using. By doing this, you make it possible for developers to explore your API even more quickly. Although no tools exist for building API consoles or data explorers out of the data in the Commons, these tools will no doubt become available as more APIs are included.

All that said, remember the Flickr example from earlier: you want to carefully evaluate the APIs you're considering using to make sure you feel they'll support the best developer experience possible. There's no reason you can't look at all the models out there, decide they're not going to work, and create your own—but the very exercise of looking through existing models should help quite a bit when creating your own API schema.

> **EXERCISE 2** Look through the API Commons at www.apicommons.org. Imagine that you are making a contact management system. Which of these APIs would you use to bootstrap your API model? Are they sufficient for your needs, or would you need to create a slightly different version—or another version entirely—for the system you're making? What APIs would you like to see represented in the Commons? Reach out to the API providers you'd like to see there and ask them to participate.

5.4   *REST is not always best*

You've probably noticed that rather than always describe the web APIs I'm discussing as REST APIs, I tend to soften the description. REST-based is an excellent way of describing most successful web APIs. For various reasons, such as the mobile case described earlier, you'll probably need to move away from the strict REST philosophy in order to best serve the needs of your users. Remember, the usability of your API is of paramount importance. Your users need an API that will meet their goals easily and efficiently, so follow the best practices listed here but remember the number one priority is usability.

The first guiding principle, *Don't surprise your users*, seems to indicate that you shouldn't move away from this philosophy, but you may remember that I've indicated, multiple times, that you shouldn't move away from existing best practices unless you have a good reason. Anytime there's a conflict between strict REST and making a use case easy, you should always err on the side of usability for all the use cases you're working with. Again, though, don't make the mistake of creating an API that's awesome for a single use case but useless for any others.

I discussed one use case you're likely to encounter that will make you move away from the model of a single resource per call: mobile. There are various ways to support the mobile use case, but none of them is particularly RESTful. That's because mobile applications need to be able to make a single call per screen, even if that screen demonstrates multiple types of resources. But if you don't implement something to enable your mobile developers to create a performant application, you're going to create heartache for them, and for yourself.

5.4.1   *Expand and include related resources*

One way to approach this problem is to do what Netflix did: allow developers to specify whether they want to expand related resources inline with the call. Figure 5.9 shows the difference in calls when requesting a movie plus related information in a strict REST API versus an expandable resource API.

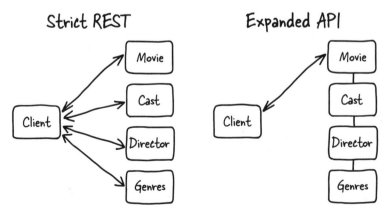

Figure 5.9   Strict REST versus API with expansion

In this case, the strict REST system requires that the client make four calls to show the movie with some related information. Because a mobile device isn't likely to have parallel processes, that means each call must complete before the next call can be made. If the mobile phone user walks into an elevator or tunnel, causing a call to fail, that call must be made again until it succeeds. This results in a nonperformant application in one of the places where people are least patient (mobile users expect quick responses from requests on their phones). Even if the calls all succeed, the time needed to wait for all the responses will result in a poorly performing application.

With the expanded API, though, the call is made to the movie, requesting expansion for the three other items desired for the page. It's a single call to the API instead of four separate calls, and though it might still fail, one retry on one call will still result in a more responsive experience for the mobile user than if all of the calls to the strict REST API had succeeded.

In addition to supporting expansion, Netflix uses hypermedia within results—which are covered in chapter 6 when we discuss business value and decisions, and in chapter 7 during the discussion about schema modeling—to help developers discover what related information can be expanded when making calls. Including this information makes it much easier for developers to understand the capabilities they have when using an API.

5.4.2 Create a query language

To solve the same problem, LinkedIn went with a slightly different approach. Its data structure is much more complicated than Netflix's, so a simple expansion wasn't likely to cover the needs of all its developers. Instead, LinkedIn created a query language to make it possible for developers to explicitly express what they wanted to see, what related information they wanted, and which fields they wanted within all the resources (figure 5.10).

The LinkedIn API was designed to encourage developers to explicitly specify exactly which fields they want in every single call, so the default representation of each resource was a minimal list with few fields included.

Here's an example of what you could request with a single request to the API:

- User's information
- User's contacts
  - School attended
    - ◆ Name of school
    - ◆ City of school
  - Organizations
  - Shared contacts
    - ◆ Name

This query language made it possible to say that you wanted all of a user's information, contacts, and the name and city of the last school each contact attended. The downside of this system was that the learning curve was somewhat steep. Because the

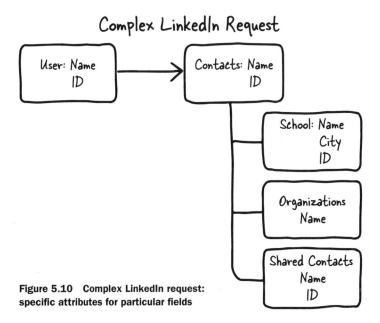

Figure 5.10   Complex LinkedIn request: specific attributes for particular fields

resources aren't RESTful—in order to get a reasonable representation of an object, the developer needs to specify more fields than the default—users of the API must learn how to determine which fields are available, how to access them, and what the restrictions are for use within the system. The LinkedIn API addressed this issue by spending time and resources creating example code and documentation describing how to make common requests. The consistency across the various endpoints made it easier to learn once a developer had made a single successful call to the system.

Unfortunately, due to business decisions, neither of these APIs is currently available for the public to use or test. But the general idea of creating query languages to allow client developers to express precisely what information they need, and in what format, is a good design model.

5.4.3   Create a comprehensive data transfer scheme

Freebase (recently deprecated) was a system not many people were familiar with. It was, in my opinion, the best web API out there. Freebase was a structured, user-editable, graph database. It included information from Wikipedia, MusicBrainz, and multiple other sources. It represented items as *nodes* (things) and *edges* (links). In this case, it wasn't a REST API at all. All queries hit the same endpoint, and users created an object expressing exactly what they wanted to know, receiving back exactly that object. Because Freebase was a graph database, extremely complex queries took only 50 milliseconds to return.

Here's an example of a Freebase Metabase Query Language (MGL) request. As you can see, it's in JSON format, which was the language used by Freebase.

Listing 5.1 Freebase MGL: searching for Tom Cruise and Katie Holmes

```
[{
  "type": "/film/actor",
  "ns0:type": "/film/producer",
  "/people/person/religion": "Scientology",
  "/people/person/height_meters<=": 2,
  "/people/person/spouse_s": [{
    "spouse": [{
      "name": null,
      "/people/person/religion": "Scientology",
      "type": "/film/actor"
    }]
  }]
}]
```

The request in listing 5.1 is asking for people who are film producers and film actors, and who are Scientologists less than 2 meters tall. Additionally, it wants to know about any Scientologists this person has married.

The response from the system (in the following listing) is a similar JSON object, containing the things that were requested.

Listing 5.2 Freebase response

```
{
  "result": [
    {
      "/people/person/religion": "Scientology",
      "ns0:type": "/film/producer",
      "/people/person/spouse_s": [
        {
          "spouse": [
            {
              "name": "Katie Holmes",
              "/people/person/religion": "Scientology",
              "type": "/film/actor"
            },
            {
              "name": "Tom Cruise",
              "/people/person/religion": "Scientology",
              "type": "/film/actor"
            }
          ]
        },
    ...
```

The response had other groupings, but this is the one I was looking for, and the response was almost immediate. For most systems, this kind of complex query would be time consuming, but even if I had asked for the films they had in common, or the name of their daughter, the response would still be almost immediate.

Although a graph database may not be the right back end for you, this example should show you that there are different extremes in requests to web APIs. The main constraint you should follow is that it's easy for your users to implement your use cases.

5.4.4 Create a separate batching system

When the developers at Etsy refactored their API, they wanted to stick with strict REST representations for their resources but understood that this wouldn't work for third-party developers creating mobile applications. For this reason, they created a system called BeSpoke, which batches commands and uses a separate address (figure 5.11).

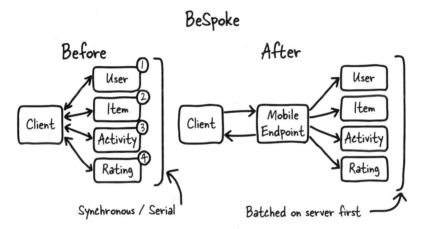

Figure 5.11   Etsy reworked its platform to be API First and strongly RESTful and decided to address the issue of mobile integration using the BeSpoke system, which batches calls together on the server end and sends back the aggregated information to the caller.

Etsy's goal was to create endpoints that were combinations of calls to its APIs. The company made the decision that it wanted to own the specific structure of each of these endpoints. If a client developer needs a new batched endpoint, they must request help from Etsy to get it implemented.

The batched-up calls are run in parallel wherever possible (sometimes the response for one changes the request for the next) and those calls are bundled up into a single response that heads back to the client. In this way, a mobile application can ask for information about sellers, their activity list, and the current things they have up for sale.

This system meets both of the company's requirements: it has a solid REST API, but it has built a separate system that allows its client developers to quickly request larger amounts of data as needed.

5.4.5   RESTful decisions

It should now be clear that although it's important for your system to behave as predictably as possible, you need to make sure that your system is usable. If that can't happen within the context of strict REST (or whatever other model you're using), then you need to step to the side and find something that does work.

It's vital in these cases that you communicate clearly to your customers exactly how your system does work so they can get up to speed as quickly as possible. If you use a separate system like BeSpoke, make sure that mobile developers can find their way to that information easily so they don't try to implement their application using the bare REST API.

5.5   Focus on the developer experience

I've said many times that you need to focus on the developer and use cases during design, development, and documentation, but your API still won't be successful if you don't pay close attention to the developer experience once you've released it. From the developer portal to the support you provide when people are struggling, everything you do for your users *after* you release the API is as important as the work you did to create it.

Developer experience for an existing API covers several different realms. Reference documentation should be solid and consistent across all of your API endpoints. It should be easy to get a list of endpoints for a particular API without searching through documentation. One of the advantages of using a modeling language is that these systems are designed to help you create automatic reference documentation for your API.

Developer experience, including documentation, is the heart and soul of a successful API. Chapter 9 explores this topic in depth.

5.5.1   Communication and consistency are critical

Throughout the process outlined in the following chapters, I want you to think critically about which pieces of information you want to share with your users. It's always best to assume you'll be sharing everything. Sharing your business value with your customers helps them to better understand what kind of clients they should build that will help your API to remain successful—and that will help them stay successful as well, because they're supporting your financial reason for having the API. Giving them the metrics you're using helps too; adding this to the context of the business value means the users have a great idea of what looks like success for your API, and they'll strive to help you with that, because it means they have a stronger position for their particular client or clients.

The use cases you create should be turned directly into tutorials for your client developers, to give them working code with an understandable story to follow. Sharing your schema model (even when the API is under construction) opens up the ability to have conversations with your customers about how the design meets their use cases. And they can use the blueprint to identify potential error cases they should handle and understand better how to implement their code most efficiently. Too often the client developers are seen as intruders into the system, and API providers try to hide away their business choices from those developers—but treating these developers as partners means telling them everything you can.

Whenever you make a decision, whether it's in line with everyone else or a new path you're blazing, it's vital to communicate with your users. Too often developers are kept in the dark about important decisions being made by the platform organization, which leads to frustration and mistrust. When you treat your developer clients as partners, keeping them in the loop wherever possible, you'll find that they're forgiving, helpful, and as interested in your success as you're interested in theirs.

It's tempting to treat these people as competitors because they're implementing functionality that may compete directly with your main product. But providing a different user experience for a subset of users is sometimes exactly what your user base needs to feel more excitement about the whole organization. If you're willing to let developers use your system, then you should be willing to be transparent with them wherever possible.

Sometimes you can't share the business reason for decisions you need to make. In those cases, it's still important to tell your client developers that there has been a change and that it was made because of an underlying business decision. If you don't tell them this, they're likely to think the decision was arbitrary and can be changed, or will feel slighted by the decision. As a company, Google has always been transparent with the developers utilizing its APIs. It does get a lot of flak for the choices it makes, but developers using its system can be assured that it will give notice before the API is changed drastically or deprecated.

Relying on a platform for functionality within your application or website is a frightening prospect for anyone. Reaching out to your customers to keep them in the loop when changes are made is one of the best ways to build trust within the developer community. Remember, these developers are giving you their time and skills to integrate your system into theirs, and you need to treat them with respect.

These guiding principles are important to keep in mind while building your API, but the most critical thing in implementing your API is consistency. Your API needs to be consistent in terms of resource formatting, status codes, formats, and any other design choices you make. If a developer gets a user by drilling down through an organizational group, that user should be identical to the user when found via a search. Status codes for users should behave the same way as status codes for locations. If you choose to use an expansion or query method to allow for more complex queries, it needs to be implemented consistently throughout the API. Your documentation should also be consistent across the system. It's likely that different teams will be building different parts of your API, so you may need a guiding team to help each group create resources and documentation that speak directly to the use cases and flow naturally from one section to another. Consistency can be a challenge, but as with everything else, when you have a choice between extra effort for the developers of the API and the consumers of the API, you should always make the experience as easy as possible for the users of the API.

5.5.2 Documentation should tell a story

When developers are initially exploring your platform, the questions they're likely to ask are "What can I do with this?" and "How do I do something?" Unfortunately, most documentation for APIs focuses on "How does this work?" That's a question that generally doesn't come until after the developer is already engaged with the platform. The pretty example in figure 5.12 demonstrates what most API resource documentation looks like.

The problem with this type of documentation is that there's no story or context for developers to use to understand why they should care about this API. Sometimes the thought is that if a developer finds her way to the API, she already knows what she wants to do with it, but it's not a good idea to make that assumption for several reasons.

First, developers who are new to your system and find it through spelunking on the web may well not know what they want to do with the API. Making the assumption that they do know means that developers who aren't already familiar with the data space and why they want to use it will likely give up and leave. This seems like it would pertain only to external or open APIs, but for developers starting out with your API, you

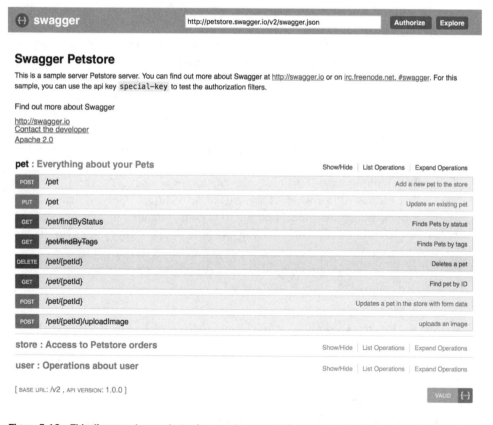

Figure 5.12 This diagram shows what reference documentation can look like in a system that has been designed by modeling a schema. The documentation you see here, which is dynamic and allows for exploration, is created entirely from an OpenAPI specification.

need at least a "Getting Started" story, or they're more likely to fumble around trying to figure out what to do.

Second, tutorials that read like stories tell your users a tale about how you expect them to use the platform. When developers can get started with an existing example of a flow through the system, they can more easily create applications that use the API in a way that's supported. If you leave developers to try to find something that works without guiding them, they're more likely to work around the functionality that you want them to use. It may seem like all you're doing with use cases and story-based tutorials is teaching people how to do specific things with your platform, but that's not true. Particularly when you provide some structure to the stories you're providing, as the client developers work through them they gain a greater understanding of how your system works and are more likely to have their creativity sparked by the examples you've given.

Third, stories help users to better understand how the different parts of your system interact together so they can be successful more quickly. I've seen many cases of developers who cobble together a mashup between different resources to create a particular function, when that data is available directly from another resource. It may seem obvious to you how your data is structured, but without that context developers will do the best they can.

Fourth, and most important, developers love to get up and running quickly. Taking the time to provide them with documentation that helps them solve their problem effectively communicates to them that you value their time. It shouldn't be an arduous chore to figure out how to combine your resources to create a meaningful application or integration. Don't make them reinvent the wheel. Give them examples of successful stories they can use to inspire their own ideas. These developers are your partners, so treat them with the consideration they deserve, and they'll reward you by creating awesome applications with your API.

It's challenging to find examples of story-type documentation in the wild, but at the least many API providers have started providing a "Getting Started" story to help developers make the critical first call to become engaged in your API. As the creator of an API, challenge yourself and your documentation writers to create documentation that helps users make the first call in the minimum amount of time.

Here are some questions that your documentation should answer in a "Getting Started" guide:

- Do you require authentication?
- How does a developer quickly get the pieces he needs to make the authentication work?
- What does an example call look like?
- How can a developer make a call to the system using a common library or on her own?

Don't assume that your developers already know *anything* about using your API. If you're worried about scaring developers away by seeming condescending, don't.

They're more likely to be grateful that you took the time to guide them to a successful call, and trust me, many of your users won't be familiar with systems like yours and will be happy to see documentation that guides them through the process of making a call and teaches them what they can do with the API. There are many, many skilled developers out there who haven't ever interacted with a web API before; this has been clearly demonstrated to me by the enormous number of people who attend my "REST Demystified" talk at conferences. Great developers are not all client developers . . . yet. Help them get there.

Once you've started making documentation that's story-based, don't stop there. Give some use cases to your developers to show what kinds of things are possible given the way your system works. Spark their creativity with ideas.

Remember that new users want to know what they can do with the system and how they'd do that. It should be as straightforward as possible to find this information in the front of your documentation. A new user doesn't know where to look, so the most obvious call to action needs to be a button leading developers to the documentation they need to figure out the answers to these questions.

5.6 Summary

Even before you start creating an API, you need to get into the mind-set of the people who will be using your system. All of these guiding principles will help you to put yourself in the shoes of the people you want to succeed. Keep these principles in mind as you work through the process of creating your API, and the system you build will be more compelling, successful, and easy to use.

This chapter covered several guiding principles for creating a successful API:

- *Don't surprise your users.* Be mindful of the decisions you make and make sure to communicate your intent clearly and consistently. Arbitrary decisions made in a rush frequently come back to bite you when those decisions lead to developer confusion.
- *Focus on use cases.* If you can't describe what you want developers to do with your API, they won't know what you're expecting, and you won't have any guiding vision to drive the development of the API.
- *Copy successful APIs.* Stand on the shoulders of giants. There's no shame in cribbing from a successful API to make the experience of the application developers that much more consistent and easy.
- *REST is not always best.* Although the focus of this book is on REST APIs, it's important to keep a critical eye on the development to make sure that idealism isn't trumping usability.
- *Focus on the developer experience.* Again, this is the focus of chapter 9, but it's worth reiterating here that a great developer experience is the number one way to ensure success for your API.

The next chapter covers the process of determining business value, establishing metrics, and designing use cases for your API.

Defining the value for your API

This chapter covers

- Business goals
- Metrics
- Use cases

Designing an API should always start with the process of determining business value and how you'll measure it, followed by determining use cases to make sure you can build your design and strategy with confidence. Doing this for a web API brings it into line with other company products and helps you to both communicate your goals and success to your executive team and make sure your API is staying on track to success. Having these goals and metrics in place will also help you verify that the API is moving in the right direction, so you can determine whether you need to "pivot" your goals, metrics, or use cases to more directly match how client developers are using the API product.

6.1 *Business goals*

Understanding and communicating the API's business value to your company, including goals to measure success, is critical. This is the information you're going to communicate to the executives and other teams at your company, helping them understand why you have an API for your company. A product that can't demonstrate success to the executive team is at serious risk of losing the resources needed to drive it. The ability to track and communicate the goals and strategy for the API and how it will contribute to the company's bottom line will keep your product on track. A solid grasp of the business value will additionally help guide your design and development and make sure you end up with an API that meets the need you're trying to address. Without a clear vision for the API, you'll end up with a process that feels like herding cats, where you try to create a cohesive strategy on the fly. Take the time to figure out exactly what you want to get out of the API before you start working on the next steps. The easiest way to do this is to determine what your company is striving to accomplish in general and decide what web API business value would best support these goals.

Common goals for successful APIs vary widely. This chapter discusses several existing models, but asking, "What's the API going to add to my company's success?" will help guide you to the correct type of goal for your product. The values I discuss in this chapter cover monetization, usage, partner retention, and market dominance.

6.1.1 *Monetization*

Monetization is the most common business value that people attempt to accomplish. When the API is the main or only product for the company, this is an obvious necessity. In other cases, this is not an appropriate goal for the API. The reason is that it's quite challenging to drive usage of your API when it is competing with the goals of the main product. When an API is supporting the main product, it's important to make sure that the goals for the API are complementary to that product. In that case, your API will suffer from a lack of uptake if developers need to contend with money issues with the API. Ensure that the API encourages those client developers to create applications that strengthen the core value of your company's main product or add new ways for users to interact with the system. When your API is not your main income stream, find ways to add to the company's success without adding friction to the adoption of your API with a monetary cost.

Twilio is a company where the API is its main product, and a great example of a company where monetization is the main goal of the platform. It's made difficult telephony interactions simple for developers, and in return its customers (client developers) pay Twilio for usage. The whole company is designed to support the web API platform, and it's been successful as a result.

Marketing at Twilio is based on driving usage to the API. An army of developer evangelists works in the marketing organization and is constantly attending hackathons, helping developers integrate phone or SMS services into their applications. By providing the ability to integrate easily with telephony services, yielding a huge value for many application users, developers are motivated to pay money for the services they receive from Twilio.

Monetization for Twilio is directly tied to the developer usage of their API. Each call to the API costs a small amount, so an application using Twilio as part of its stack will provide Twilio with income relative to the success of the application. In this way, Twilio gets a small part of the income generated by each developer for a part of the functionality of the developer's application itself.

Its developer portal is one of the best in the industry (see figure 6.1), because developers *are* their direct customers, and in order to thrive they must support those customers well.

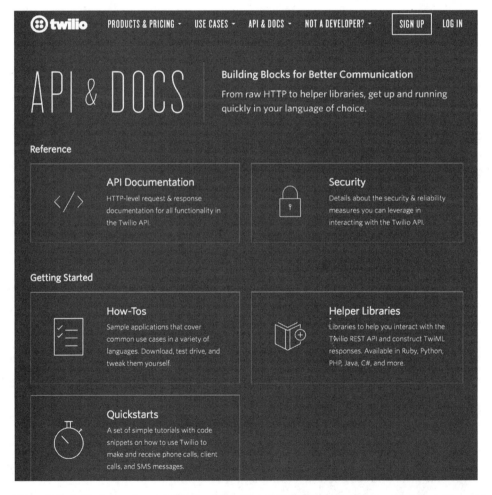

Figure 6.1 Twilio has a strong developer portal. All portals should have API documentation as a quick link, but many other items are required to make a great portal. Articles about the system can help developers understand the underlying technology, such as the Security section here. Most important, the Getting Started section includes guides and libraries to help developers get going quickly, keeping the Twilio five-minutes-to-first-call goal in mind.

Twilio has a strong focus on making the developer experience easy, striving to make sure that a developer who visits its site can make a successful call to the API within five minutes—an aggressive goal that helps ensure that developers don't get frustrated and give up on the API quickly. Twilio is also quite determined to retain its place as the dominant player in the SMS API industry. When your business case is tied so closely to revenue for the company, it's not that difficult to generate support from the executive team. But don't despair if this isn't your business value—I talk through various other models throughout the chapter.

Twilio's model for its API is currently represented by figure 6.2. As time goes forward, it's added new features into the system. But the interaction for the client developers remains the same. That makes the platform increasingly valuable for those application creators.

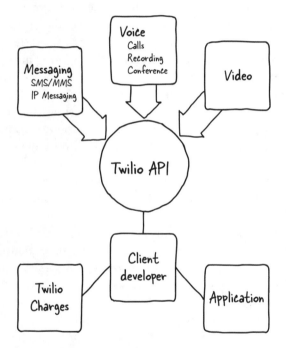

Figure 6.2 Twilio's API interacts with services in the messaging, voice, and video space. Each of these functions works directly with the same API, making it easy for developers to integrate multiple segments into applications. The API is like a central routing station, moving requests from the client developer's application into the correct part of the Twilio API portal.

In figure 6.2, it becomes clear that Twilio has set up the system to be a single interface to each of the telephony systems. In this way, developers never need to interact directly with the systems themselves and can leave all that heavy lifting to Twilio. Because the functionality provided is time-consuming to implement for a single application, Twilio's offering is generally considered by developers to be well worth the cost.

Monetization, then, is a valid business goal. In this case, it's not hard to explain to your executives or other teams why you have an API. But if your API is an enhancement to your main product, it's easy to fall into the trap of expecting your API to directly generate revenue. Without a strong business case around the API, you're not likely to generate enough revenue to justify the resources needed to create and maintain the API—

and these are the APIs most likely to be deprecated in favor of other, more profitable products. When your API is an add-on product, strongly consider one of the other business value choices, and see if one of them is more appropriate to your overall business strategy.

6.1.2   *Usage*

Sometimes the goal of the API is to drive usage, or how many times the end user interacts with your system. These users probably won't spend all their time in your application, but if you have a product with an activity feed or other stream of information—if you have any type of social-based application—encouraging users to write to your system will drive interest and increase platform functionality for all your users, including the ones who don't actively share information within your system. Providing a means for other applications to write activity into this stream will increase the perceived value of your system for your end users. Most social systems rely on advertisements to generate revenue, so the more compelling and engaging the activity stream is, the more eyes they'll be able to sell to advertisers, and the more money they'll bring in.

Twitter, LinkedIn, and Facebook are excellent examples of this type of product. Each of these systems relies heavily on content generated by users in order to create interest and engagement. Making it easy for a user to share interesting content with their network—and extended network—encourages people to contribute meaningful content to your ecosystem. If users are reading articles they enjoy on a news site or blog, it should be simple for them to share that information with everyone in their network and add that content to the ecosystem for your product. Figure 6.3 shows a blog post from my blog with sharing buttons for major networks, allowing people to share my page among their social networks.

As you have probably noticed, these sharing icons are everywhere throughout the web. Social systems want to drive the addition of fresh content into their platform to add value for their users, and content owners want to encourage people to read the information they've posted. The use of these buttons drives new and relevant information to users' information streams, increasing the value of a social platform. This interaction is generally a widget that uses the web API to provide the functionality. In this case, the ability to add the ability to share content back to Twitter (or other social systems) is extended to content owners, such as bloggers (as demonstrated earlier) and news websites. When you're designing an API for usage in this way, it's important to make it easy for end users to add content into your system to keep it lively and engaging.

Twitter makes money largely from advertising and selling data about the information in their system. In order for the advertising to be compelling to users, Twitter can use the activity stream to better understand each customer's interests. Additionally, constant generation of new content ensures that the data remains germane to the partners who consume it. Its APIs are focused on engaging new users and keeping its existing users active and involved in the ecosystem.

Designing Irresistible APIs

I spend a lot of time traveling around and teaching people how to make better APIs. The current focus of my talks is Designing Irresistible APIs – I'll be giving this talk (or a version of it) at OSCON, and just presented it at Future Insights Live, as well as doing a webcast to get people excited about OSCON. I've uploaded my slide deck on slideshare but I thought I should make a brief post summarizing the ideas in there. There's a newer one here, and a copy of my API 101 slide deck from APIStrat Chicago.

API Design Process

1. Understand the business value of your API. Are you trying to drive usage, integrate with partners, attract new users, excite existing users? Your API is unlikely to directly drive revenue unless it's your main product, so understand what you want to get out of your API before you even start creating it. Note that partner integration is a very strong business value, but what you want to know here is what would you tell your CEO if you were trapped in an elevator with him and he asked why you have an API.
2. How are you going to measure success? API usage? How many people use the API vs. the website (APIs are not as resource intensive and can be automated, helping you to create more solid integrations)? How many partners are integrated? Again, this

Figure 6.3 Blog using a widget that creates and drives sharing icons for the main social platforms. Because each platform has a well-understood, well-described, and consistent API, developers can easily create integrations into these social platforms, and blog owners can plug in widgets with this functionality in a few minutes.

LinkedIn had a complicated API, but it has since been throttled back, largely due to the determination of business value and the excessive cost of providing the majority of its APIs to third-party developers as well as partners. LinkedIn's success is largely driven by revenue from advertising and recruiting. This revenue is increased by the number of users in the system and how often they interact with the system. LinkedIn wanted to bring new users into the system, engage existing users as frequently as possible, and make it easy for recruiters to find qualified candidates. Because of this they've recently focused on a few API-related offerings for developers and content providers. For instance, allowing developers to enable their users to sign in with LinkedIn gives them the opportunity to manage the user identity for those applications, staying at the front of the users' minds. The sharing widgets, built on a back-end web API, provide content providers with the ability to allow readers to share interesting content within the LinkedIn ecosystem.

Facebook continues to offer several different API products (see figure 6.4). It has always wanted to drive usage of applications to its system, encourage the development of third-party games and applications that use the Facebook system, and generally drive up the percentage of time users spend connected to its system.

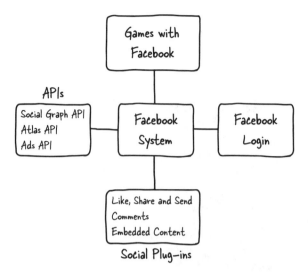

Figure 6.4 Facebook's multitude of API offerings show the vast number of integration points it has created into its system. The most basic social platform integration—sharing widgets—is quite easy to use, but the Facebook platform includes complex integrations into the social graph (how people are related), monetization for games, and a game platform that provides much of the needed functionality for creating Facebook games.

Facebook has an SDK system for developers to use to integrate their games or other applications into the system, encouraging users to interact with Facebook more frequently as they play with these applications. Facebook additionally provides an API to add monetization to games, allowing users to purchase items for use within the game by interacting with Facebook directly. The combination of these two interfaces has helped Facebook become the most successful game platform among the social networks.

The Facebook graph web API allows application developers to integrate Facebook's social data, including friend and demographic information, into their applications once the user has approved this access for the application. Any time you're asked to check with Facebook and give permission for an application to access your own data, this developer is using the Facebook graph API to bring your information into an external website or application.

In short, usage is a strong driving force for social media. These three companies aren't the only ones that derive value from a strong, relevant stream of new information. Any company wanting to increase the amount of information created for its system can consider whether this type of business value makes sense for its platform. Note that in many cases this functionality is extended via a plug-in or widget, but these features are driven by web APIs and are consistent with the general purposes of other REST-style APIs, even though they're wrapped in handy packages for website creators to use. In these cases, the widgets and plug-ins are the customers of the API itself, but their existence is reliant on the existence of a strong, healthy platform.

6.1.3 *Partner retention*

One of the strongest business values for an API is partner retention. When your company has a solid relationship with another company, it helps create a strong revenue stream on which to build your other income. Losing these partnerships can create unstable revenue streams, causing problems for your company. To help avoid this problem, create an API that focuses on usability targeted at the use cases your partners may want. This could include automation within your system or integration of your reporting with their own dashboards. Partners who have already spent the time to integrate your systems into their own products or applications are less likely to move to a competitor, particularly if your API is in fact a first-class product and you keep new features in parity with your main product.

FEDEX

FedEx is in a highly competitive market, but it was the first to create a strong API system for logistics, shipping, and tracking. It has enabled many small companies to become competitive by reducing the need to create extensive infrastructure to market and deliver their product.

For example, the flower delivery company FTD has historically been a major dominating force in flower delivery. It provided nationwide flower delivery to customers by partnering with local small delivery shops, which could bring flowers to people in their area. This allowed them to hold a virtual monopoly in the industry, as local flower shops didn't have any way to attract customers in their area as easily as FTD could, and had no way to deliver flowers in other areas without arranging for shipping manually (see figure 6.5).

By integrating with FedEx, though, smaller companies have been able to enter this previously closed market (see figure 6.6). Customers of these client developers have a

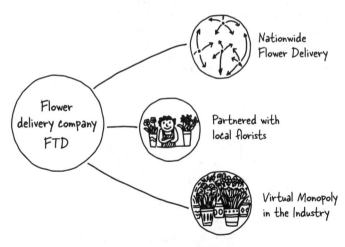

Figure 6.5   Before the FedEx platform became readily available, FTD enjoyed a virtual monopoly in the flower-sending industry for nonlocal deliveries. It worked with local florists (and was able to impose strict guidelines and pricing) and made it easy for consumers to send flowers anywhere in the country. But the system wasn't set up so that the best florists were successful; FTD made it so that partnering with FTD was an important business decision for florists.

better way to track their packages without reaching out to either the application owner or FedEx, and the partners can focus on the core business case without becoming experts in the shipping industry. Once this integration is done, it's a lot of work for a company to switch entirely to a competitor, which cements FedEx's place in the industry. In this way, FedEx has created a situation where it's likely to retain partners who are integrated deeply with their reliable API and who have improved their own processes as a result. It would be quite difficult for another shipping company to entice one of their partners to switch to its service, because that would require proving that the new service was good enough to cause a shift in experience for their customers and a significant amount of development time to change the integration.

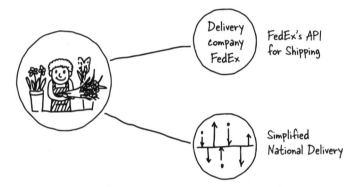

Figure 6.6 Once FedEx provided a platform for local florists to use, it was no longer necessary to partner with a large company such as FTD in order to receive and process floral deliveries remotely. Now that there are ways for local companies to deliver their specific products with a minimum of effort, the competition is focused around the value of the products and not partnerships with specific companies.

6.1.4 *Market dominance*

Market dominance is different from partner integration in that the goal is for the company with the API to become the leader in its industry, rather than enabling its customers and partners to succeed in theirs. Having a focused, agile API makes it easier to establish your dominance in your market and maintain this status into the future.

NETFLIX

Netflix is an example of a company that has established market dominance in the video-streaming industry based on the use of its API by different consumer video devices. It has innovated and changed its API to remain the most dominant system in the movie-watching industry—from integrations with partners that make DVD players, to online movie rating and ticketing services. Netflix's main business value is dominating its industry by enabling integration with devices within this space to increase its user base and provide value to its existing users.

Netflix tuned its API to make it highly usable for devices such as consoles, DVD players, televisions, tablets, and smartphones. It removed the parts of the API that weren't important for these partners or germane to their current system—such as the DVD queue and search APIs—leaving a tightly tuned set of APIs that it offers to these device companies. Netflix restricts its partners to platforms that will reach tens of thousands of its own subscription users. In addition, the products provided by Netflix itself, including its phone, tablet, and desktop computer applications, use the same APIs they provide to these device manufacturers. Everything is highly optimized to allow users to have a high-quality browsing and viewing experience, whatever platform they're using (see figure 6.7).

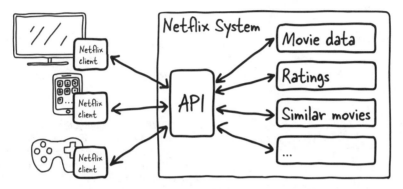

Figure 6.7   Netflix is an excellent example of how an API can streamline a user's experience. The API itself provides basic search and information about movies, including people and genres associated with them. The company additionally provides a movie player on most major platforms, which is integrated with the Netflix platform via the API, so a user can always find and learn about movies before watching them. The API makes it possible for other devices and applications to do the same thing so that users' experience is consistent across all the applications they use.

Netflix has been so successful in this space that creating a movie site or new video-enabled device *without* direct Netflix integration places a potential video-viewing product at a disadvantage. The reach and established base of the Netflix API is so strong that all new entrants to the space are compelled to integrate with Netflix, and existing vendors are highly unlikely to remove or replace Netflix in existing products. This is not to say that these device companies won't add other video-streaming services, but excluding Netflix reduces the value of a product in a significant way. Device manufacturers and movie sites are motivated to partner with Netflix and to continue doing so to maintain their own place in their specific industries. The synergy between Netflix and device manufacturers enhances both of their places in their relative industries.

6.2   Metrics

Once you've determined what your business value is and what you're trying to achieve with the product, it should be relatively easy to determine how to measure the success of your platform in this area. Frequently, companies are tempted to create metrics demonstrating the reach of the API without demonstrating how it's adding to the bottom line. Metrics such as "number of developers who have signed up for the API program" and even "number of calls to the API" aren't going to be compelling to the executive team. Although API usage statistics, including applications and users, can show that the system is growing to be able to provide the value desired by the company, the most meaningful metrics are those that demonstrate how the platform is contributing directly to the established business value.

6.2.1   Poor metrics

For any API, the most common initial choice made in creating and tracking metrics is to track the number of developers who have signed up for an account within the system (see figure 6.8).

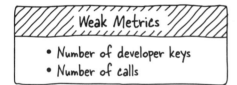

Figure 6.8   When determining the success of your API, the simplest things to measure are the number of developer keys and/or number of calls. Without measuring the types of calls or number of end users, these pieces of data aren't at all indicative that the API is creating value for your company.

In the case of these metrics, the analysis will not help you translate the activity into the business value you've already determined. It would seem that the number of calls is a good thing to track, and it's a fine internal metric for the API team. But when communicating with other groups outside of the development team for the API, your business goals need to be broken down into metrics that are more meaningful in the context of your value proposition.

A member of your executive team may initially be interested in the general usage of your API, but in the medium and long term they'll want to see how the API is contributing to the bottom line of the company. An API that's not showing success in other areas is costing money for the company with no obvious path to creating success, so you need to share metrics that demonstrate how the API is improving success for the entire organization or face the chance that your API will be deprioritized by the company.

6.2.2   Monetization

When the API is your main platform, you can easily measure success by looking at the revenue generated by that product. In many cases, though, you can target growth for your product by watching related analytics to determine how well your system is scaling and helping you fill the pipeline for future success. In the case of a company like

Figure 6.9 As a system with an API as its main product, Twilio can easily measure things that demonstrate API success. It can measure standard company metrics like revenue per employee, because all of its revenue comes through the API. Additionally, it can measure things about the accounts such as the number of conversions to paying accounts and the number of accounts with a high and consistent volume of calls.

Twilio, for instance, it probably wants to figure out which metrics speak most clearly to its platform's ability to continue growing. Figure 6.9 demonstrates how a company like Twilio can effectively measure performance and progress.

Even for a company where the main product is the platform, the easiest things to measure are of limited use to the company in terms of projecting growth and revenue. Measuring the number of people who have signed up or the number of calls per month (which includes a significant number of "free trial" calls) won't help the company become more successful over time. Focusing on the exact items that can improve the business value you identified is tricky, but worthwhile.

The easiest data to measure in Twilio's case would be revenue-per-employee, as there's only one product to consider. Yet this doesn't help plan for the future or use metrics to measure not only past and present success but future revenue. Revenue-per-customer would be better (because it would include newer customers), but is still too indirect to help identify what needs to happen to drive future improvements.

Because Twilio is striving to be the market leader, introducing new developers to the system is important. But many times developers may not use Twilio beyond their initial introduction to the system, usually at a hackathon or conference. These developers don't contribute to the bottom line of the company. How, then, could Twilio measure success?

Twilio provides all new developers with a decent-sized allotment of money for their initial calls. So, are developers who recharge their accounts from their own money more likely to go on to continue using the API into the future? If so, the number of developers who convert to paying customers could be a good thing to track.

The company is also interested in increasing the volume for existing applications. The army of developer evangelists is an awesome way to drum up awareness and interest in the platform, but real money is made with customers who create a steady stream of revenue over the long term. This being the case, the number of *high-revenue* customers—customers over a certain volume of calls per month—is something that's important to keep track of.

6.2.3   Usage

When determining metrics for usage, a company needs to dig a little deeper to determine the measures and statistics that will be meaningful for the company itself. If the goal is to increase usage, that's a relatively easy measure. But you might extend this a little to capture your goals.

Do you want to measure writes to the API as a percentage of overall updates to your system? Is signing in with the social system valuable to your company? This gives you identity management for your users, keeping them connected to your system even when they're not directly interacting with it. Figure 6.10 lists a few ways you could measure the performance of a platform that's heavily directed at increasing usage within the system.

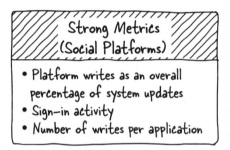

Figure 6.10   Social platforms have a specific set of goals; increasing the amount of activity in the system and the frequency of interactions by users both indicate a healthy ecosystem. When determining strong metrics for your social application, think carefully about what kind of metrics will indicate that users are more closely tied to your system (frequency of interaction) or providing new interesting content (frequency of writes).

6.2.4   Partner retention

This business value is more difficult to measure than the previous two choices. How do you measure the success of a platform that's aimed at maintaining partnerships with your customers? The overall effect on your bottom line will be adding stability and growth to the number of customers using your main product. The value here could be derived from the number of customers using the system who continue to use it for a set amount of time into the future. You could measure the percentage of applications that are still active 3, 6, or 12 months into the future and determine how successfully you're retaining those valuable partnerships.

Using FedEx as an example, the company is in a highly competitive industry. UPS and the USPS, as well as countless smaller shipping and logistics organizations, compete directly with FedEx to achieve and retain the status of primary shipment company for their customers. The ability to integrate the shipping, tracking, and logistics information into customers' applications with a minimum of fuss is quite important.

6.2.5   Market dominance

When working toward market dominance, you want to measure the reach of your platform and your position in the marketplace relative to your competitors. This type of metric is much more in line with the metrics frequently considered important by businesses.

Netflix is a great example of this type of measurement. As the DVD business waned, it became critically important to establish a position of dominance in the market, and several other competitors were entering the space at the same time. Netflix started early on this strategy, partnering with video device and game console manufacturers to make sure their users could watch Netflix on whatever screen they were near.

To measure the success of this strategy, Netflix might track the number of devices it appears on compared to the devices' relative position in electronics sales. Netflix is selling a service, so the amount of time a user spends watching movies increases the value proposition for that user. It could also measure the number of hours users are watching movies on its devices.

6.3 Use cases

In chapter 5, I mentioned use cases as something critical to the success of an API. In this section, I describe how you can map your business goals to your design and development phases. Once you've determined your business metrics and how you'll measure them, it's time to think of use cases that will help guide you to increase those metrics in the way that's meaningful for your platform and that will support your business goal. Don't be shy during this part of the process; think about exactly the kind of use cases you want to support and make those workflows as easy as possible.

6.3.1 Mobile

Although this isn't one of the business goals I mentioned, mobile is a use case that almost every API designer should consider. It's one feature that's hard to add after the fact, so you need to design with the mobile developer in mind so you don't end up having to refactor your code even before the platform is released.

Mobile is a tricky case (see figure 6.11). As I've said, developers who are creating mobile applications need to be able to make minimal calls for the system. Back-end calls to your platform must be quick and efficient. The more calls the end users can make, the more revenue your system will generate.

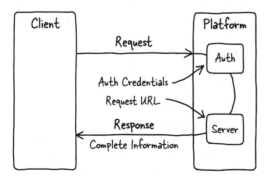

Figure 6.11 Basic mobile interaction. Without focusing on the specific information in the call, an initial call from the client to the platform will include authentication information and specifics about the resource being requested. On the platform side, the authentication data will be processed by the auth segment of the platform, and if the credentials are authenticated (who is it?) and authorized (can they do the action?), the request is passed through to the platform, and a response is sent back to the client.

For each of the actions in your system, it should be extremely simple, in a single call, to do the following:

- Authenticate or verify credentials for the user
- Make a complete call to your system, returning exactly the data needed by the application
- Provide the ability to gather all information for a screen, or accept all the information needed for an action, in a single call

Mobile, more than most other use cases, requires mindful development and sometimes requires additional work to make it successful. But mobile usage is one of the main uses for an API, so it's worth your while to make these calls as easy as possible. Remember, any time you're faced with a decision to improve usability or reduce development use on your side, the right call is almost always to make your system easier to use.

6.3.2   *Monetization*

When your API is your main product, monetization must be the business goal for your platform. You can achieve this in various ways: usage-based, subscriptions, or other mechanisms. The trick is to make sure that the client developers get enough perceived value out of your platform to justify the expense.

TWILIO

In the case of monetization, it's critical to make it extremely easy for people to interact with the platform in whatever way makes sense. You want people making as many calls as possible, so you want to make it easy for your customers to make calls from mobile, desktop, or sharing applications. Ideally you'd support all these use cases, with easy-to-use interfaces that support all user models for your direct customers, the developers.

As an example, Twilio supports (among other things) sharing out to multiple friends using SMS, sending voice messages, creating conference calls, and handling video. Twilio's main value to customers is that it makes telephony easy. If you have ever tried to create a system for interacting with a telephone network, you know how difficult and time-consuming it can be, and when application developers are working on their own, it's nearly impossible to get a contract with those systems for top-tier service and support.

Here are some example use cases for a telephony application of this type: using easy authentication, performing quick single-call interaction, sending SMS messages to multiple friends or a group, sending a voice message to users, or creating a group conference call. Although it's clear that sending information to users could use push notifications, SMS and voice are two modes that are much more immediate than push notifications to grab their attention. It becomes easy to use SMS as an immediate chat channel for a group of people, to grab people's attention when they're near someone they know, or to seamlessly alert users that someone who shares their interests is nearby. These would be great supplements for a social/dating system. Twilio also makes it easy for people to opt out of these interactions easily, so the client developers don't have to worry about that aspect of this interaction.

SENDGRID

SendGrid is another company that makes hard things easy (see figure 6.12). Most companies need to use email to interact with their users—sending out alerts when important events have happened, initiating a user verification or password reset, or sending announcements about activity within the system. SendGrid is designed to manage all aspects of sending mail. It has white-listing and prescreens all customers to make sure the system is clean and not sent to junk mailboxes. The scalability is baked into the system, freeing customers from needing to be concerned with email growth. All transactions are as secure as possible. Metrics are strong and targeted at transactional email and marketing campaigns. SendGrid has demonstrated its value for companies like Foursquare and Ladders, both successful companies that started out having their engineering team attempt to manage the high volume of email required by their business model. SendGrid has made it extremely simple to manage the email that your company needs to send and track. In this case, the use case is making mail simple and quick for their users.

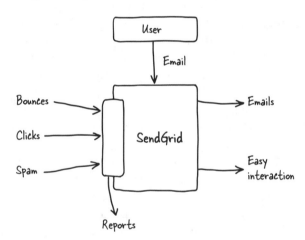

Figure 6.12 The SendGrid platform is like a central routing station for email interaction. It can schedule and structure outgoing emails to provide for tracking clicks, bounces, and spam filtering. The user interaction with the system is simple and straightforward.

The APIs provide the ability to get real-time event data such as bounces, clicks, and spam reports. SendGrid provides several different interaction models for its customers so that they can use whichever protocol works for them, whether it be SMTP (Simple Mail Transaction Protocol, a standard email protocol for the web) or the web API. Several different functions exist within the APIs designed to support marketing or transactional use cases, or to integrate more deeply with the system.

SendGrid realized that email is frequently something that needs to be triggered by an application action or system event, so it made automating transactions with webhooks (a relatively simple system) possible, as well as providing the ability for developers to integrate deeply into their own system to support their own needs.

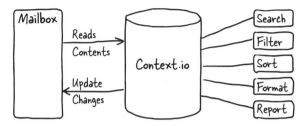

Figure 6.13   Context.io creates a database out of an email box. The contents of the email box are read, and functions are exposed for searching, filtering, sorting, and formatting that data. Additionally, when changes are made in the data by Context.io to add tagging or other additional information, Context.io writes these changes back to the originating email box.

CONTEXT.IO

Context.io also works with email, but instead of focusing on sending emails, enables access to information in your users' inboxes as if they were databases (see figure 6.13).

It supports queries on the mailbox and allows you to query by keyword, user, or thread. Additionally, it will POST back to your server information about actions in the inbox, allowing you to configure actions that can trigger webhooks to do whatever you want. Again, in this use case, the company is working to make something that's challenging easy for anyone wanting to analyze the data in a user's mailbox to create valuable metrics, track and report specific actions, and work with email the way users tend to do: by thread.

Monetization is a great business case when a company is striving to make difficult things easy for developers. Any time someone can offload a needed functionality to another company that provides useful actions for the money, it's going to be a great value for companies wanting to focus on their core competencies rather than expand their engineering team to re-implement functionality that can be purchased elsewhere. In all of these cases, the monetization metrics of "calls per user" or "growth over time" are easy to understand when the success of the company is tied to making critical functionality easier and more reliable.

6.3.3   *Usage*

Usage tends to be a business value well suited to social applications. There are many such systems; Twitter is the most obvious, with Facebook and Tumblr also providing interactive functionality for millions of users. Whichever system you're working with, there are two critical actions you want to be able to support with simple interfaces: writing to and reading from the stream. Each system features other interactive actions that are tied to the specific goals of the company. In this section, as I discuss each of the companies that are focused on social interaction, I'll discuss their main use cases as examples.

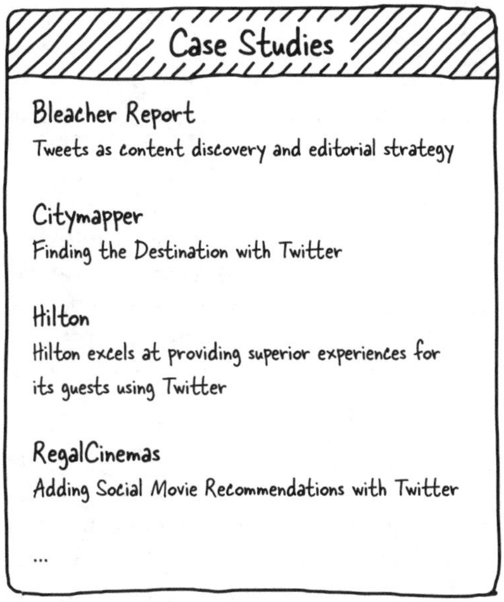

Case Studies

Bleacher Report
Tweets as content discovery and editorial strategy

Citymapper
Finding the Destination with Twitter

Hilton
Hilton excels at providing superior experiences for its guests using Twitter

RegalCinemas
Adding Social Movie Recommendations with Twitter

...

Figure 6.14 Twitter has examples to help understand how use cases are mapped to API functions. For each of the examples listed here, the interaction point provides benefits for both Twitter and the end user. Great APIs will always create this kind of mapping—if an API improves the end-user experience as well as improving the system itself, it's most likely to become successful and well used.

TWITTER

Twitter, for instance, doesn't provide complex profile data, games, or other interactive applications. Writing to the activity stream is the most valuable interaction a user can provide for the system's business. To encourage application developers to write status updates to the system, Twitter implemented the items shown in figure 6.14.

Twitter doesn't charge for this service, which encourages application developers to help Twitter users to add new content to the data stream, keeping it fresh and interesting.

In addition to writing to the system, Twitter wants to add even more value by making it easy for client developers to enable Twitter's users to read from the system and track things of interest to them. Users can retrieve information in a few different ways, all easy to do via the API so application developers can match the ideal activity stream with the use case they have for their own application.

The main type of read access client developers can offer to their users is status, or timelines. Users can see their home timeline, which is what they see first when logging into the Twitter application itself. In addition, they can see another user's status, mentions, or retweets. All of these are individual resources within the application, and quite easy to access. Application developers can also provide their users with the ability to read and write direct messages.

There are some more complicated interfaces in the Twitter system. Search is necessarily somewhat more complex. The application needs to create a query to communicate exactly what type of search is being made, and building this query is more complex than the retrieval of a single, well-defined piece of data from the system.

Similarly, an application can access the streaming API to watch for new posts that match a particular query.

In fact, because Twitter runs completely on its own API system, client developers can provide virtually all of the Twitter functionality to offer users within their own application.

FACEBOOK

Facebook has a much more complicated system to offer to users, but the first and most popular is the Wall, which provides the activity stream for client developers to integrate into their application. Writes and reads work much as they do for Twitter, and searches are available as well. There are widgets for reading from and writing to the activity stream.

But Facebook's system is much more complex than Twitter's. Although Twitter encourages application developers to create applications outside of the system and post updates inside Twitter, the sharing of game or application activities is discouraged. Facebook encourages application developers to create games or other applications designed to run within the Facebook ecosystem and write to users' walls so that other users are encouraged to play. Facebook even provides a system allowing application developers to charge users for game enhancements.

The widgets offered by Facebook allow for much easier implementation of certain types of functionality, particularly social interaction. Facebook even makes it easy to add Comments, Likes, and Shares to your own web pages with the installation of a simple plug-in on your site. By simplifying its API even further for these types of actions, Facebook makes it extremely simple for content providers to leverage the Facebook system to enhance their websites without writing any code.

Although I don't tend to like SDKs for simple REST APIs, I do appreciate the SDKs provided by Facebook. These tools are designed for a few things:

- Assist developers in creating applications that can be accessed and played outside of Facebook
- Allow developers to use Facebook to make the games or other applications more social
- Allow developers to leverage the money-making functionality Facebook offers to developers

In short, Facebook provides several types of APIs for integration. Simple widgets allow content providers to integrate social sharing and conversation around their content without writing any code. The REST APIs, including the Graph API, allow developers to leverage the complex Facebook social graph for use within their applications. SDKs assist developers in creating applications that can utilize the monetization and social interaction from Facebook in applications residing on other platforms.

TUMBLR

Tumblr is a super simple blogging platform, allowing users to post media, such as video or photos, thoughts, or replies to other posts. Many application developers have found new and interesting ways to utilize the functionality provided by the Tumblr system. The simple API makes the system quite interesting; several applications use the system to create their own blogging or photo-sharing application on top of the Tumblr platform. Tumblr can be considered, at its heart, a sharing platform for users.

Tumblr has gone even further than other social applications in simplifying authentication. Just as much of the content is available without logging in on Tumblr, certain items can be accessed without any authentication in the API. For instance, getting the avatar for a user can be accomplished by a bare call to the avatar endpoint for that user, without any credentials at all. Many of the calls can be made with a simple call, identifying only the application making the call, but not the specific user retrieving the information. Making these calls simple means that an application could be created that never requires a login by the end user. This system is designed not only to be easy for users to interact with directly, but to encourage applications to provide simple access as well.

The simplicity of this system, both via the web interface and the API for developers to integrate with their application, reduces the friction in adding content or including it alongside other activity streams.

6.3.4 *Customer/partner retention*

Partner retention can be one of the most valuable goals of a company's platform. If you can make it valuable for partners to continue using your system once they've integrated—and difficult to replicate that information with other systems—you're adding friction to the process of integrating with your system. This retention can be created in multiple ways; I'll mention a couple of different examples so you can have an idea of what kinds of things will make partners think twice about jumping to a different platform.

UNIQUE CONTENT

When you have a specific type of functionality that's unique to your platform, it becomes a compelling reason for partners to integrate with you and also creates some reluctance for them to remove that functionality. An example of this is LinkedIn. This business-focused social platform provides several pieces of valuable functionality available only to partners.

Flipboard largely uses the LinkedIn functionality to get users' activity and their news stream from LinkedIn, which has one of the best user-targeted article ecosystems out there. Removing LinkedIn from the application would lower users' satisfaction with the system, so Flipboard is unlikely to want to leave the system. Additionally, though multiple news-focused systems are out there, few of them provide the user-centric newsfeeds available via LinkedIn.

Hootsuite is a social system that schedules and batches updates to various social systems, including LinkedIn, Twitter, and Facebook. The main use case for Hootsuite is business, and its pricing structure is designed to help companies manage their social media strategies. If Hootsuite were to remove this dominant business-focused social platform from its application, a great deal of its value to users would be eliminated.

AUTOMATION/INTEGRATION

Many companies provide services for their partners and customers. As time has gone on, more and more companies are providing Software as a Service, Platform as a Service, and Hosting as a Service. No matter what service is being provided, the configuration, metrics, and automation for the system is critical to a healthy relationship between the provider and the customer.

Amazon and Rackspace provide various hosting platforms. Akamai provides content-delivery services for companies wanting to improve their web performance. All of these, as well as many other hosting platforms, have APIs for their customers to use to integrate configuration and reporting with their own systems. This provides customers with the ability to track data from the service into dashboards they have for their own functionality, automation for alerts and events, and the ability to integrate frequent actions into their own systems. For instance, Akamai allows customers to add cache purge functionality to their content management systems.

When you're providing a service for your customers, frequently you can encourage them to integrate your administrative functions into their own systems. This integration generally requires development resources from the customer, and as a result the customer won't be inclined to redo this work to move to a new provider. Those APIs must be reliable, scalable, and usable. This is a case where moving to an API First system works in your favor, because those administrative functions will be available to your customers, to integrate at whatever level works best for them.

6.4   *Summary*

To wrap up this chapter, I want to point out that these items are critical to creating a healthy, successful API. Without knowing what your business goals are, without knowing what metrics you're going to track, and without setting up strong use cases to drive those metrics and value, your API is not likely to make it. These items are required when creating any other product for your company, and your API is no different. The process for working through these steps is as follows:

- *Determining your business goals*—This is critical for any product, and an API is no exception. Determine how your API product will contribute to the success of your company.
- *Defining your metrics*—Once you've determined the business value, spend some time considering how you could measure the activity of the API to provide meaningful insight into the progress toward the business goal.
- *Creating meaningful use cases*—Now that you know how to measure the success of your API, it's time to create use cases that support those values and metrics.

The next chapter covers the process of modeling the schema for your application. We'll explore two of the main schema modeling languages, OpenAPI and RAML, and talk about ways to approach the modeling based on the use cases you've created. We'll also discuss the value of schema modeling for improving the clarity of your conversations with customers and other teams, and I'll use these schemas as a basis for guiding your development strategy in future parts of the process.

7

Creating your schema model

This chapter covers

- Understanding schema modeling basics
- Creating a RAML schema model
- Creating an OpenAPI schema model

At this point, you should have a good idea why you have an API and what it needs to accomplish to be successful. You have a business value as your foundation, metrics to support them, and use cases to make sure you can meet your customers' needs and understand what you want your client developers to be able to do.

This chapter moves to the next stage—modeling the schema for your API and creating a design document that can be shared with other teams, customers, or executives. This document should help you find a development path that gives you the best chance to succeed with your API. This schema model is a contract between your organization and the clients who will be using it.

With a schema model, you can utilize design-driven development to ensure that the developed API matches the schema—and so meets your use cases. You can create a mock service that will allow customers or testers to create test clients against

135

your eventual API before any code is written. You can use this schema model to run tests or create code for your API developers to use. The schema model is a powerful tool when creating successful, engaging, and irresistible APIs.

I'll show you two different modeling systems for creating schemas, using two different markup languages. Some people choose their framework for schema modeling based on the markup language, because they prefer the readability of one over the other. All the frameworks I discuss in this chapter are excellent, usable, and well defined. The choice of framework can be based on anything, as long as it supports your desired workflow.

We'll go through the top two schema modeling systems, and you'll learn how to model a basic API that's an extension of the demo API you saw earlier. We'll discuss some of the tools each system provides to ease into the development, make sure it follows the right path, and leverage the model to test your API and make sure it's meeting your needs. Here are the two most popular schema modeling systems and the markup languages they use:

- RESTful API Modeling Language (RAML), which supports Markdown
- OpenAPI format (previously Swagger), which supports JSON and YAML

7.1 What is a schema model?

A *schema model* is a contract describing what the API is, how it works, and what the endpoints are going to be. Think of it as a map of the API, a user-readable description of each endpoint, which can be used to discuss the API before any code is written. Like a functional specification, this document describes how the API will behave. Creating this model before starting development helps you ensure that the API you create will meet the needs described by the use cases you've identified.

With a schema model, you can ensure that everyone has a shared understanding of what the API will do and how each resource will be represented when the API is complete. Each of the schema modeling languages has tools available to automate testing or code creation based on the schema model you've created. But even without this functionality, the schema model helps you have a solid understanding of the API before a single line of code is written.

7.2 What does the API need to do?

Before starting with the schema modeling sections for each of the modeling languages, let's go over the needs we have for the resulting API. It will be the same as the example API in chapter 2, with some extensions to finish off the functionality. Remember that a *resource* is a single object or list within the system. It's the "noun" you'll be working with.

7.2.1 Top-level resources

First, let's start defining the resources within your specification. This is where you'll use the use cases defined in chapter 6 (see figure 7.1).

```
Toppings and Pizzas (lists)

List Toppings:      GET /api/toppings
List Pizzas:        GET /api/pizzas

Add Topping:        POST /api/toppings
Add Pizza:          POST /api/pizzas




Individual Toppings and Pizzas

Show Topping:       GET /api/toppings/:id
Show Pizza:         GET /api/pizzas/:id

Update Topping:     PUT /api/toppings/:id
Update Pizza:       PUT /api/pizzas/:id

Delete Topping:     DELETE /api/toppings/:id
Delete Pizza:       DELETE /api/toppings/:id
```

Figure 7.1   The actions for the PizzaToppings API need to support CRUD—create, read, update, and delete. At the list level, the only two actions are to create a new item and read the list. For an individual topping, you can read the item information, update the item, or delete a specific item.

For the purposes of my PizzaToppings API, these would be the use cases, or activities, you want to support:

- Creating new toppings
- Getting a list of all toppings, including matching a particular string
- Deleting and updating specific toppings
- Creating a named pizza; only one per user
- Listing pizzas
- Adding toppings to a pizza
- Viewing the pizza
- Deleting the pizza for the specific user

Note that this is an extension of the current functionality of the code in the repository.

7.2.2 API resource methods

As you may remember, four main HTTP methods are used for web APIs:

- GET—Retrieve the representation of the object or list
- PUT—Replace (update) the object
- POST—Create a new entry at the top level
- DELETE—Delete an object from the system

For the PizzaTopping example API, you'll want client developers to be able to work at the collection level. Obviously, you'll want them to be able to GET a list of the toppings or pizzas currently in the system. They need to be able to POST a new object to the list. But you don't want them to be able to PUT a new representation of the whole list; many people are using this list, and you want everyone's items to remain. Similarly, you don't want developers DELETE-ing your list; it ruins the fun of playing with the API. The resources /toppings and /pizzas will need to accept GET and POST only.

It's important to be able to GET the information about a single topping or pizza. If a topping needs to be updated, it makes sense to allow a user to PUT a new description. Using PUT on the /pizzas resource allows you to add new toppings to the pizza for the particular user. POST doesn't make sense at the item level; new items should be added to the top-level resource list. DELETE, though, is fine for both a topping and a pizza.

In summary, the resources and their methods will be as follows:

- /pizzas
  - GET—Get a list of pizzas (also accept a search string)
  - POST—Add a new pizza to the list
- /pizzas/{pizzaid}
  - GET—Get a representation of a pizza
  - PUT—Update an existing pizza
  - DELETE—Delete a pizza from the list
- /toppings
  - GET—Get a list of toppings
  - POST—Add a new topping to the list
- /toppings/{toppingid}
  - GET—Get a representation of a topping
  - PUT—Update an existing topping
  - DELETE—Delete a topping from the list

7.3   *RAML*

Now that you have the basics of a general schema, we'll look at the specifics of two of the main schema modeling frameworks, starting with RAML. The specification for RAML, from the working group guiding its path, is as follows:

> *The RESTful API Modeling Language (RAML) is a concise, expressive language for describing RESTful APIs. Built on broadly used standards such as YAML and JSON, RAML is a non-proprietary, vendor-neutral open spec.*

RAML was created around the notion of design-first development. Although all of the specification languages can be used this way, RAML was designed this way from the outset. It makes it easy to create a code development life cycle that supports the development of APIs that meet your business goals and use cases. The documentation makes it easy to get started, so let's begin with this example.

The RAML website (http://raml.org) has good documentation, including strategies, best practices, and practical instruction. You'll find a basic tutorial for the RAML language itself at http://raml.org/docs.html. This tutorial will guide you through using the API Designer to conceptualize your API and write the schema model in RAML. It assumes that you know the basics of how REST APIs work, which are covered in chapter 4. The markup language used by RAML is Markdown, which may look familiar. Markdown is the markup language used on GitHub in README files and other documentation. Using a Markdown document means that when the document is displayed in GitHub, the formatting is nice and clear. If you want to grab the model and follow along, it's available on GitHub at https://github.com/synedra/irresistible/blob/master/schema_models/raml/raml.md and you can import it into the editor by signing up for MuleSoft's Anypoint portal at https://anypoint.mulesoft.com/apiplatform/. Click Add an API and paste the Markdown information into the API Designer.

7.3.1 *Getting started*

To get started with the RAML API Designer, you'll first need to create a (free) account on the Anypoint system, where MuleSoft maintains its RAML specific tools:

- Sign up for Anypoint at https://anypoint.mulesoft.com/apiplatform/.
- From the API Administration board, select Add New API to open the screen in figure 7.2.

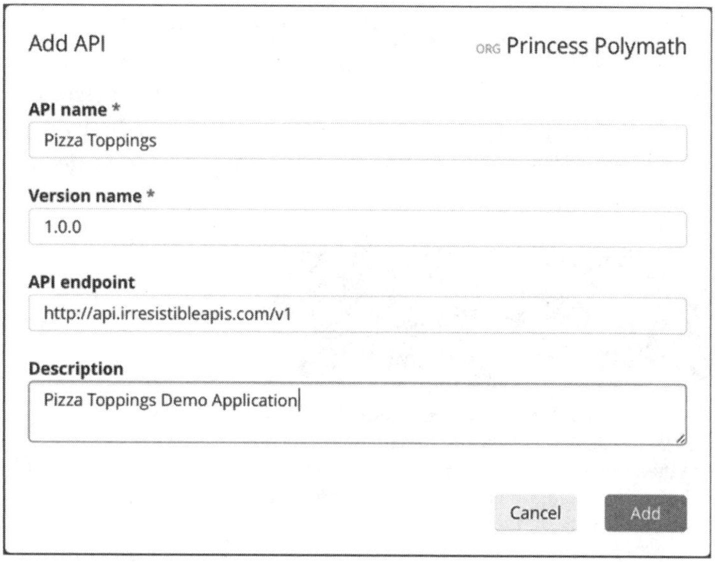

Figure 7.2 When you want to add a new API into Anypoint, the only required fields are the API name and Version name. The API endpoint is handy to have in your schema, and I suggest you make the description reasonably clear.

When you fill out the descriptions and fields, keep them the same as the ones in figure 7.2. These fields will be automatically populated when creating your RAML API schema model, so it's important that they match so you can follow along. Click Add and then click Define API in API Designer to see the beginnings of the API model you've created.

Figure 7.3 shows what the top of the RAML schema model looks like. Here are the included sections at the *root* of your document. The entire root section is described in the RAML specification's "Root of the Document" section at http://raml.org/spec.html. Refer to this specification with any questions you have as you move through building the document.

- *#%RAML 0.8 (required)*—The first line is required, and it indicates which markup language you will be using. Other modeling languages are compatible with RAML, and if you were to use one of them, you'd specify it here. Note that this is formatted as a comment, and any other comments in the document will start with the same #% markup.
- *Title (required)*—This tells a reader what the API is designed to do.
- *baseUri (required after implementation)*—This will be the base URL for each of your API calls, so be sure it makes sense for all of the endpoints that will be used by your API. For instance, if your API will have users and pages, you wouldn't want to create an API baseUri like http://users.api.com. The baseUri must be the same for all of the endpoints. This is required once you've implemented your API, so that wherever people encounter the schema model they'll know exactly where the API exists.
- *version (required when version is part of the baseUri)*—When the version is included as part of the baseUri, the specification is tied to the specified version on this line. If you haven't chosen to implement versioning, you don't need to include this in your model.

```
#%RAML 0.8
title: Pizza Toppings
version: 1.0.0
baseUri: http://api.irresistibleapis.com/v1
```

Figure 7.3   The information you put into the Add API form turns up at the top of your new specification. Note that you can change these values later. For instance, if you wanted to switch `v1` to `v1.1` at a future point, the only place you'd need to change it is here, in the schema.

This being the case, we need to have only two top-level resources: toppings and pizzas.

At the bottom of the editor is a section with hints as to what you want to add to the model (see figure 7.4).

Figure 7.4 The Anypoint RAML editor features a bottom toolbar for adding sections to the schema model. This toolbar is context-sensitive; it will only offer appropriate sections based on where you are currently in the schema.

7.3.2   Step 1: adding resources

The first things you want to add are resources. As mentioned earlier, in order to support the API use cases, you need four different resources, which you can add to the schema model using the New Resource selection in the toolbar. Note that there's nothing magical about adding items in this way, but it can help guide you through the process of creating your schema model. Figure 7.5 shows what these resources will look like.

```
1    #%RAML 0.8
2    title: Pizza Toppings
3    version: 1.0.0
4    baseUri: http://api.irresistibleapis.com/v1
5 ▼  /pizzas:
6      displayName: Pizza List
7      /{pizzaid}:
8        displayName: Individual Pizza
9 ▼  /toppings:
10     displayName: Topping List
11     /{toppingid}:
12       displayName: Individual Topping
```

Figure 7.5 At this point you've added all of the resources for this schema. They are listed with a `displayname`, but none of the requests or responses is represented yet. This is a skeleton of the schema model you're building.

7.3.3   Step 2: adding the methods

Now that you've defined the resources and where they'll be served, you're going to step up the model by indicating which methods will work on each of the endpoints. Don't be concerned if this seems confusing; the rest of the schema model will help you further refine the contract indicated by the schema model. Figure 7.6 shows how the different endpoints will be combined with actions to create the interface for the API.

```
5 ▼  /pizzas:
6      displayName: Pizza list
7      get:
8        description: Get a list of pizzas
9      post:
10       description: Add a pizza to a list
11 ▼    /{pizzaid}:
12       displayName: Individual pizza
13       get:
14         description: Show an individual pizza
15       put:
16         description: Update an existing pizza
17       delete:
18         description: Delete a pizza from the list
19 ▶  /toppings:◄
```

Figure 7.6 Because you know what actions will be available at each level, you can add the methods and their descriptions to the schema model. This matches with the information listed earlier; at the list level (`/toppings` and `/pizzas`) you can GET the list or POST a new item. At the individual item level (`/toppings/:id` or `/pizzas/:id`) you can GET the item, PUT an update, or DELETE the item entirely.

EXERCISE 1 For the `/toppings` and `/toppings/toppingid` resources, add the correct methods for the resource. Don't overthink this, and take the opportunity to become more comfortable moving around in the editor. When you're finished, there should be methods and descriptions for all four of the resources in the API. You now have a contract indicating what endpoints will be exposed in your API, and what methods those resources will accept. Great start!

7.3.4 Step 3: query parameters

I mentioned that one of the use cases is to limit the lists of toppings and pizzas by a string match. To do that, you need to add query parameter information to the specification to indicate that these options will be accepted for the associated method. Use the buttons at the bottom or the auto-complete in the editor to get your parameter ready to go. For brevity, you'll name this query parameter q, so

```
http://api.irresistibleapis.com/v1/pizzas?q=Maui
```

will return a list of all pizzas matching the string `"Maui"`.

Each of the query parameters needs to be defined so that the consumer knows what to pass and other information about the query string.

Next you need to add attributes for each of the query parameters. This is where you provide information about what the query parameter is intended for, so that readers of the specification or the eventual developers can understand what the parameter should do (see figure 7.7).

As you can see, the query parameters are quite straightforward. The query parameter isn't required because a bare request to the resource will return a list of all pizzas in the system, but if a user wants to narrow the search to a particular string, the API

```
1   #%RAML 0.8
2   title: Pizza Toppings
3   version: 1.0.0
4   baseUri: http://api.irresistibleapis.com/v1
5 ▾ /pizzas:
6     displayName: Pizza list
7 ▾   get:
8       description: Get a list of pizzas
9 ▾     queryParameters:
10 ▾       q:
11            description: String to match in the pizza name
12            displayName: Search string
13            type: string
14            example: Maui
15            required: false
```

Figure 7.7 Now that you've added the specific actions, it's time to break them out and add specifics on how the requests and responses will work for them. The GET for the lists is a little bit more complicated than the GETs for the individual items will be, because you're allowing the caller to search for a specific string.

will make this possible on the server side. Sometimes, this kind of behavior is expected to be handled on the client side, but this is a design decision that can be made while the schema model is being created—a big advantage of doing the modeling up front is to find and answer these questions.

> **EXERCISE 2** For the /toppings resource, add the query parameter and define the guidelines for its behavior. Use pepper as the example in the schema, which will match pepper, pepperocini, or pepperoni.

Now the specification for the API indicates that the lists for toppings and pizzas must allow the user to search for specific items containing the indicated string. It's great that you understand how the queries will work, but someone reading the specification will now understand exactly how those queries are expected to behave. Making the model complete is the best way to ensure that what you want is what's created, and customers who review the document understand exactly how the API will work.

7.3.5 *Step 4: adding mock data*

To complete this basic API specification, you need to add one more type of data, and this is a very important one: you need to add information showing what the request should have (for PUT and POST requests) and what the possible responses will look like from the server.

Although all of the schema modeling languages provide for a shortcut in these specifications—a way to define pieces of the requests and responses to be reused later—in this example you're going to do the exercise longhand so that the meaning of this section is easy to follow. The specification mentioned earlier has all the information you need to incorporate the shortcuts and references.

7.3.6 *Step 5: adding mock data—GET*

As in chapter 2, the requests and responses will be in JSON. To start, I'll show you how to represent the information for the /toppings list. The following extract demonstrates how to add the correct information for the GET at the top-level resource level (the lists of items). Additionally, a description is added to help set the context for what the endpoint is designed to do. You'll no doubt notice in these examples that I'm minimizing the sections you aren't currently working with to reduce the visual noise as you walk through the process.

Figure 7.8 looks similar to what was created in chapter 2 for the demo application, but now you can start to see a pattern, a method to the API schema. As you build the specification, it should become clearer how this will help you describe the purpose and behavior of your platform.

> **EXERCISE 3** Extend the /toppings resource to add the 200 response to /toppings. Remember that this is an array of toppings, not of pizzas.

```
/toppings:
    displayName: Topping list
    get:
        description: Get the list of toppings
        responses:
            200:
                body:
                    application/json:
                        example: |
                            { "toppings": [{
                                "id": "1",
                                "name": "pepperoni"
                            },
                            {
                                "id": "2",
                                "name": "pineapple"
                            },
                            {
                                "id": "3",
                                "name": "ham"
                            }],
                            "success": true,
                            "status": 200
                            }
```

Figure 7.8 The 200 (successful) response to the request for /toppings shows how the API will respond to a successful call. Because this is a JSON object, the top level is designated by curly braces, and the toppings item in the response is a list of the toppings in the system. The status pieces (success and status) reside outside of the list, as meta-information about the response.

As this is a sample API, there won't be any errors returned from the top-level list. They'll always return an array (even if it's completely empty). For a production API, you'd have error messages, which will be demonstrated in the POST section later.

7.3.7   Step 6: adding mock data—POST

To finish off the top-level resources, you need to add the POST responses. Included in that, you'll want to add information about what the body of a POST request should look like. Remember, this is the command to add a new item to the list, so you'll be sending the information needed to create a new item. Because we want to require the application to allow only a single pizza per user, the pizza id must be passed along with the rest of the definition of the pizza. Neither pizzas nor toppings allow for duplicates, so the API must check the name to make sure there isn't already an object of the same name.

The following example shows you how to create a response for a successful POST to add a pizza to the pizza list. The correct HTTP response code for a created object is 201, so that's what you'll use. A 201 response should always include information about where the resulting object can be found, and the specification will indicate this as location. Note that in the case where there's already a pizza with the same name or id, you'll use an HTTP status code of 409, which indicates that the request failed because of a conflict—in this case, the conflict is that there's already a pizza with the same name, or a pizza that shares the id. Again, so that you can keep our simple API simple, you're going to suggest that the API implementer expect an IP address as the id for a pizza (where toppings will get a new, unique number) so there's no chance of id collision.

```
42
43 ▼   post:
44       description: Add a pizza to a list
45 ▼     body:
46 ▼       application/json:
47 ▼         example: |
48 ▼           { "pizza" : {
49               "name": "Maui Wowie",
50               "id"  : "123.456.789.101"
51             },
52             "location" : "/pizzas/123.456.789.101"
53           }
54 ▼     responses:
55 ▼       201:
56           description: Pizza created
57
58 ▼       409:
59           body:
60 ▼         application/json:
61 ▼           example: |
62               { "message" : "Duplicate pizza name|id found" }
63
```

Figure 7.9 The `POST` method at the list level (in this case, `/pizzas`) is described here. Because this is a write action, a body is associated with the request, and an example of that is displayed under `example`. A successful creation will result in a 201 response, with no body, and the 409 response is given if there's already a pizza with the same `name` or `id`.

You'll also see the `POST` responses for the pizzas. Note that the use case is to allow only one pizza per user, so the application will need to pass an `id` with the pizza. Now, there are two different things that could cause a conflict, but the 409 HTTP response will be sent in both cases, so you'll update the message. The message example can be the same, and the API can return different messages when the `id` or `name` is duplicated, or you can return a single message indicating that one or the other is incorrect. In this case, you'll use a single message, but a comment line will indicate that the message could be `id` or `name`. Figure 7.9 shows what an entry looks like when the request will have content going with the request to the server.

Now you're done with the `GET` and `POST` requests and responses for pizzas. The `pizzas` resource is ready to rock! Now you need to get the toppings finished; then we can move on to the subresources.

EXERCISE 4 As you complete this exercise, remember that even though the topping list itself returns an array, the item being posted is a single object—the new topping to add to the list.

REQUESTS AND RESPONSES: SUBRESOURCES

Now that the top-level resources have been defined, including the responses for `GET` and `POST`, you need to define the responses and request bodies for the subresources. To start, you'll add the `GET` responses to the specification for both individual pizza and topping resources.

Lest you get lost in the details as we get lower down into the specification, remember that the type of URL you're calling might look like this:

```
http://api.irresistibleapis.com/v1/toppings/4
```

This would retrieve the topping with the `id` of 4 in the database. You can see that the return value of 200 for the status code is the same as the 200 response for the parent resource, but the subresource returns only one item, whereas the parent resource returned an array of resources.

In addition, you need to add in the error codes for the individual items, a single pizza or topping. What sort of things could cause an error for a GET? There's only one error condition we need to handle for this sample API when retrieving a single resource: if the resource doesn't exist. The top-level resources don't have this problem because the API doesn't allow a client to DELETE one of the lists, so they'll always exist in the system, even when they're empty. The HTTP status code for a missing page is a 404. You may have seen this error when browsing websites, when a page is missing or has been moved without leaving a forwarding address. This is exactly the same situation. The resource doesn't exist, so the API response, an HTTP response, uses the same status code as a web server does when a page isn't where you're looking.

7.3.8   *Step 7: GET response format*

The next step on the list is to describe the response format for the queries. To start with, you will update the document to add a GET response for pizzas. Figure 7.10 shows you how you would reference the entire list of pizzas, along with their names and the toppings on those pizzas.

```
/{pizzaid}:
  displayName: Individual pizza
  get:
    description: Show an individual pizza
    responses:
      200:
        body:
          application/json:
            example: |
              { "pizza" : {
                "name" : "Maui Zowie",
                "id"   : "123.234.345.123",
                "toppings" : ["1","2"]
              }}
      404:
        body:
          application/json:
            example: |
              { "message" : "Pizza not found" }
```

Figure 7.10   As you created an example request body for the POST section, you'll need to include an example response for GET requests. The information shown here is for the /pizzas/:id resource, which returns information for the single pizza being requested. Although a 404 response isn't necessary in a schema model (it always represents a missing item), it's included here for completeness.

7.3.9 *Step 8: PUT response format*

The PUT method is available for both the pizza and topping resources. Remember, though, this is only for the single items and not for the top-level lists. Note that the PUT responses run the whole gamut and include almost all the response codes you've seen already. The 204 status code for PUT means that the object was updated as requested and returns no other information. The 204 is appropriate for the PUT because the item will be exactly what was sent and the location is already known to the client—otherwise, the client wouldn't have had an address to send the PUT. This is illustrated in figure 7.11.

```
put:
  description: Update an existing pizza
  body:
    application/json:
      example: |
        { "pizza" : {
          "name": "Maui Wowie",
          "id"  : "123.456.789.101",
          "toppings": "1"
        }
  responses:
    204:
    400:
      body:
        application/json:
          example: |
            { "message" : "Missing id|name" }
    404:
      body:
        application/json:
          example: |
            { "message" : "pizza not found" }
    409:|
      body:
        application/json:
          example: |
            { "message" : "Duplicate pizza name" }
```

Figure 7.11 The PUT entry for an existing pizza (at `/pizzas/:id`) has an example request body and multiple potential responses. 204 indicates that the pizza was updated successfully, and the 4XX responses give descriptive error messages so that the caller knows what went wrong.

Wow, that's pretty cool, right? A reader can clearly see exactly what the object to be PUT should look like and exactly what all the response codes will look like.

7.3.10 *Step 9: DELETE*

Now that you've built up almost all the resource request and response items, it's time to deal with the final method the system will accept: DELETE. The two items that can be deleted are subresources:

- `/toppings/{toppingid}`—Delete a single topping from the system
- `/pizzas/{pizzaid}`—Delete a pizza from the system

For each, you'll add entries for DELETE to each subresource. DELETE is fairly simple; on success, it returns a 204 HTTP success code, indicating that there's no response body to send. The main failure this type of resource can encounter is a 404, indicating that the indicated resource doesn't exist (see figure 7.12).

```
 98 ▼      delete:
 99           description: Delete a pizza from the list
100 ▼         responses:
101             204:
102 ▼           404:
103 ▼             body:
104 ▼               application/json:
105 ▼                 example: |
106                     { "message" : "Pizza not found" }
```

Figure 7.12   The final method for the `/pizzas/:id` resource is a DELETE, to remove a specific pizza from the list. In this case, no body is required for the request or a successful response—either the pizza exists and is deleted, or it doesn't exist and a 404 response is sent.

There's a design decision to be made here. If a pizza has a topping, should the user be able to DELETE that topping? Let's consider three scenarios. This decision could be made at development time, but if you want the behavior to work a certain way, the specification is the place to indicate that. The potential paths to take are

- Go ahead and delete the topping from the system and remove it from any pizzas that contain it (unexpected behavior).
- Reject the request to delete the topping, listing the pizzas that have the topping (this requires that the client application make the calls to delete the topping from each pizza explicitly).
- Allow for a parameter to allow the client to have a "safe" or "all" mode for removing toppings. The safe mode would fail if a pizza has the topping. The all mode would remove the topping everywhere it exists (all).

The third option would be the friendliest one, but for the purposes of this demonstration you'll implement the second option. Delete the topping from the system only if it doesn't already exist on a pizza. If the topping does exist on pizzas, the system should return a helpful error message indicating that some number of pizzas contains the topping.

7.3.11 Step 10: searching

Because you'll be implementing this option, it's a good idea to provide a way for the client to search for a specific topping on a pizza. The example that follows adds a new query parameter to search the list of pizzas for any pizza containing the topping (see figure 7.13).

```
5 ▼    /pizzas:
6        displayName: Pizza list
7 ▼      get:
8          description: Get a list of pizzas
9 ▼        queryParameters:
10 ▼         q:
11             description: String to match in the pizza name
12             displayName: Search string
13             type: string
14             example: Maui
15             required: false
16 ▼         topping:
17             displayName: Topping ID
18             type: string
19             description: List of pizzas with a particular topping
20             example: 3
21             required: false
22
```

Figure 7.13 The `queryParameters` section allows you to add different optional (or required) parameters to the `GET` request. In this case, there's a q variable that indicates that the caller wants to search for a particular string in the pizza name (like `"Maui"`), and the `topping` variable requests a list of pizzas with a particular topping on them, using the topping `id` number rather than the name.

EXERCISE 4 In this exercise, take the information you changed about the pizza resource and bring it down into the topping API endpoint. Note that you don't need to change the query string to search for toppings on pizzas, because the toppings resource doesn't need that functionality.

You now have a complete specification for the next version of the PizzaTopping API. The complete file with all the changes can be found at https://github.com/synedra /irresistible/blob/master/schema_models/raml/raml.md.

7.3.12 Support tools for RAML

MuleSoft maintains some open source tools that can extend and improve your experience with a RAML specification. You used the API Designer that helps you design your schema from the ground up. An API Console graphical user interface is available that displays the structure and patterns and creates interactive documentation. The API Notebook provides a way to use JavaScript to test and explore APIs and create Markdown versions of the API to share on GitHub. You'll find hundreds of additional RAML tools at GitHub and on the raml.org website, which can help you create and leverage the schemas you build.

7.4 OpenAPI (previously Swagger)

Now that you've seen an API modeled in RAML, I'll walk you through the same example in the OpenAPI framework. OpenAPI was one of the earliest schema modeling frameworks available, and it has gone through a few revisions. Version 2.0 is the most recent one as of this writing. During the development of the various versions, they've incorporated many of the best practices uncovered by the other two languages, and OpenAPI remains one of the innovative frameworks available.

OpenAPI supports both JSON and YAML for its schema markup. (YAML stands for Yet Another Markup Language, and is a generic specification language.) You'll be using the Swagger Editor to create the OpenAPI version of the PizzaToppings API schema model.

The full model for this schema can be found at https://github.com/synedra/ irresistible/blob/master/schema_models/swagger/swagger.yaml on GitHub, if you'd prefer to follow along as I build it here. You can also import the YAML file from GitHub into the Swagger Editor and follow along in that way.

7.4.1 *Information about your API*

As with RAML, the first thing you'll need to do is open up the OpenAPI editor at http://editor.swagger.io. This editor is nice in that it builds a UI of the documentation on the right-hand side while you're creating the model on the left. The beginning of the file is, once again, the high-level metadata about the API you're designing. Figure 7.14 shows what the top of the file should look like.

```
 1  swagger: '2.0'
 2
 3  # basic metadata about our API
 4  info:
 5    title: PizzaToppings API
 6    version: 1.0.1
 7
 8  # the host to call to interact with this server
 9  host: api.irresistibleapis.com
10
11  # the basepath, which is appended to the host
12  basePath: /v1
13
14  # the schemes (http | https) to call with
15  schemes:
16    - http
17
18  # what default mediatype we consume for put, post methods
19  consumes:
20    - application/json
21
22  # what media type we produce
23  produces:
24    - application/json
25
26  paths:
27    /pizzas:
87    /pizzas/{pizzaid}:
150   /toppings/:
201   /toppings/{toppingid}:
247
```

Figure 7.14 For the OpenAPI (previously Swagger) model, the metadata is slightly different. More of the information can be added at the top of the model, such as the content-type for requests and responses, the base path (separate from the hostname), and what schemes it accepts (http or https, or both).

The root resource in OpenAPI requires some different information than I previously used. I've included information to make the two models similar in meaning. If you're curious about other items in the OpenAPI model, you can read the specification at http://swagger.io/specification/. Because I've already defined the use cases (in section 7.1.1), I'll use the same endpoints developed for the RAML specification. The specific pieces of the root section shown in figure 7.14 are as follows:

- swagger *(required)*—This is the version of OpenAPI you're using. Because I'm following the OpenAPI 2.0 specification, that's what's placed here.
- info *(required)*—A block of information related to the API description, with the following required fields:
  - title *(required)*—This represents the title of your API, which in this case will be PizzaToppings API.
  - version *(required)*—This is the version of your application (not the version of OpenAPI you're using).
- host *(optional)*—The host only, not the scheme (http://) or a path. If the host isn't included, the system hosting the documentation is implied.
- basepath *(optional)*—The base path for all API endpoints. This should start with a /. If not included, it will be expected that the API is served directly under the host's root.
- schemes *(optional)*—The scheme (such as http://) that describes how the API can be accessed. If not included, it will be set to the same scheme used to access the documentation.
- consumes/produces *(optional)*—These parameters indicate the content-type sent for responses and accepted in requests. Placing these at the top level means that it's not necessary to list them for each resource.
- paths *(required)*—This is a list of the paths that will be served by the API. This is a part of the main OpenAPI object, and the methods, parameters, and behaviors for these paths will be included in the objects for each endpoint. Because you already know what these endpoints are from the previous section, I've included them here to start out.

The steps for the OpenAPI standard are slightly different than in RAML, and I'll cover this process at a much faster pace because you've already seen the sections in action in this chapter. For this reason, the steps will be different in the OpenAPI example.

7.4.2 Step 1: API top-level resource methods—GET

The paths for the endpoints have already been defined, so the next item on the list is to describe the methods for each of the objects. In OpenAPI, a great number of items can be included in this section, but I'll constrain the definitions to what was specified in the earlier RAML document. The first method to add is GET for the first resource, pizzas/ (see figure 7.15).

```
27 ▾   /pizzas:
28 ▾     get:
29         description: Retrieves a list of pizzas in the system
30 ▾       parameters:
31 ▾         - description: String to match in the pizza name
32           in: query
33           name: nameString
34           required: false
35           type: string
36 ▾       responses:
37 ▾         '200':
38           description: Pizza list
39 ▾         schema:
40             type: array
41 ▾           items:
42             type: object
43 ▾           properties:
44 ▾             id:
45               type: string
46 ▾             name:
47               type: string
48 ▾             toppings:
49               type: array
50 ▾             items:
51               type: integer
52 ▾         examples:
53           application/json: [{"id":1,"name":"Maui Wowie","toppings":[2,3]},{"id":2,"name"
                :"Kirsten's Pizza","toppings":[1]}]
```

Figure 7.15   The formatting for the GET behavior is different than in the RAML document, but comparing them side by side you can see that the included information is the same. The structure is called out more explicitly (defining where there are arrays, objects, or strings), and this more explicit model is preferred by many people.

As you can see, all the information needed for the 200 HTTP status response is still nested within the `resources` object, under the `pizzas/` resource. The Markdown shown earlier is similar to the RAML version, but it's articulated in a very different way.

As you build the model, the documentation is built in the right-hand window. This can help you make sure that your schema is being presented exactly the way you want it to. Figure 7.16 shows what that window looks like for the GET call to the `pizzas/` resource.

EXERCISE 5   For the `toppings/` resource, add the GET response based on the previous example and the RAML examples from earlier in the chapter. Remember that the topping only has `name` and `id`; there are no toppings on a topping! If you want to see the full example, check it out on GitHub at https://github .com/synedra/irresistible/blob/master/schema_models/swagger/swagger.yaml.

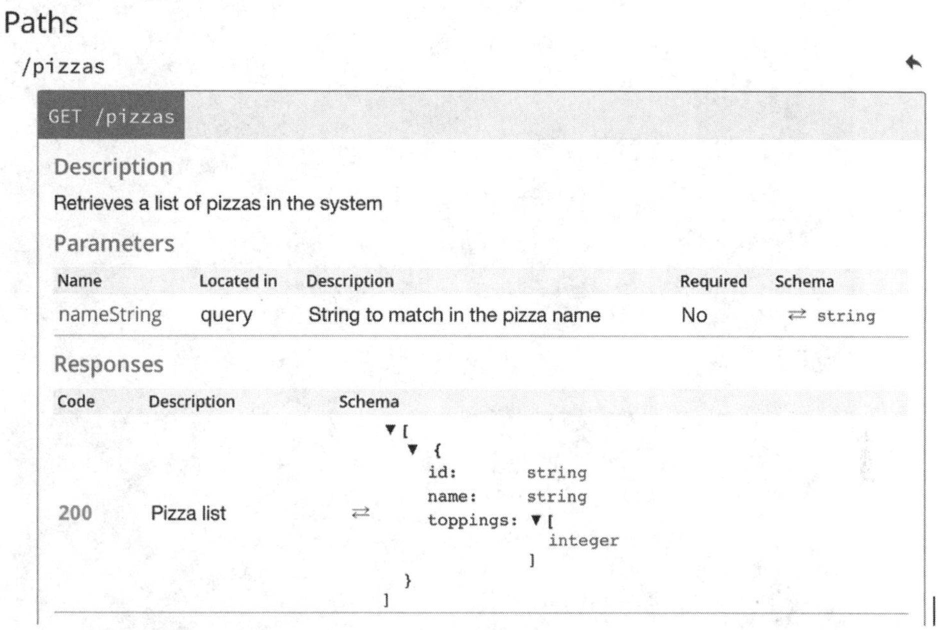

Paths

/pizzas

GET /pizzas

Description

Retrieves a list of pizzas in the system

Parameters

Name	Located in	Description	Required	Schema
nameString	query	String to match in the pizza name	No	⇄ string

Responses

Code	Description	Schema
200	Pizza list	⇄

```
▼ [
  ▼ {
      id:       string
      name:     string
      toppings: ▼ [
                    integer
                ]
  }
]
```

Figure 7.16 As you build the schema model in the Swagger Editor, the documentation will auto-generate on the right-hand side of the page. Again, the description and output are at a higher level than a specific example, so it's easier to understand the structure. But you lose the ease of reading that comes with an explicit example.

7.4.3 Step 2: API top-level resource methods—POST

The next task will be to add a POST request/response to the top-level resources (pizzas/ and toppings/). As you saw earlier, this is the method for adding a new subresource to the lists represented by these top-level resources: adding a new pizza to the list of pizzas, or adding a new topping to its associated list. Figure 7.17 demonstrates what the POST request and response should look like. Note that although this editor doesn't provide helper tags as in the MuleSoft API Designer, there is autocompletion, and the auto-generated documentation makes it easy to see if you're on the right track.

```
54 ▾    post:
55         description: Adds a new pizza to the list
56 ▾       parameters:
57 ▾         - description: ID for the pizza (only one per user)
58           in: body
59           name: pizza
60           required: true
61 ▾         schema:
62             type: object
63 ▾           required:
64               - id
65 |             - name
66 ▾           properties:
67 ▾             id:
68                 type: string
69 ▾             name:
70                 type: string
71 ▾             toppings:
72                 type: array
73 ▾               items:
74                   type: integer
75 ▾     responses:
76 ▾       '201':
77           description: Pizza created
78 ▾         schema:
79             type: object
80 ▾           properties:
81 ▾             id:
82                 type: string
83 ▾             name:
84                 type: string
85 ▾             toppings:
86                 type: array
87 ▾               items:
88                   type: integer
89 ▾             location:
90                 type: string
91 ▾         examples:
92             application/json: {"id":1,"location":"/pizzas/1.2.3.4","name":"Maui Wowie","toppings"
                :[2,3]}
93 ▾       '409':
94           description: Duplicate pizza name or ID found
95 ▾         schema:
96             type: object
97 ▾           properties:
98 ▾             message:
99                 type: string
00 ▾         examples:
01             application/json: { message: Duplicate pizza ID found }
```

Figure 7.17 The POST request, with all of the definitions for the pieces, ends up being much more verbose than the RAML example. Still, the request and responses reflect exactly the same information, so whichever one feels easier for you is likely to be the best choice for your schema models.

Again, as you're building the schema you can see the documentation for the POST method being built in the right-hand column. Figure 7.18 shows the specific documentation for the POST method on /pizzas.

The POST section, as with GET, has the responses nested underneath the information needed to make the call. As you follow along, think about how much information you're gleaning about the API from this model, and how you could use it to describe the functionality.

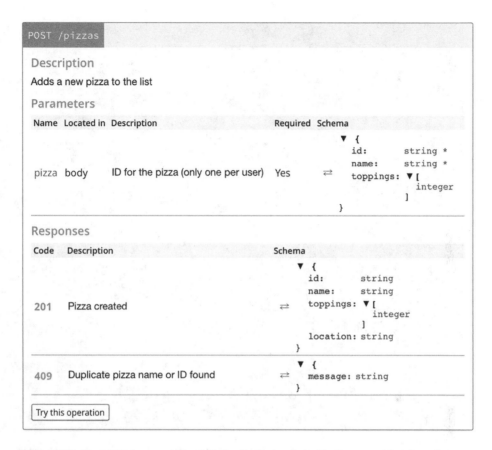

Figure 7.18   The POST documentation includes the body required in the request (again, only PUT and POST require bodies in the request). Under the responses you can see the successful Pizza Created response as well as the error (duplicate pizza name or id found).

> **EXERCISE 6**   For the `toppings/` resource, add the `POST` response based on the previous example and the RAML examples from earlier in the chapter. If you want to see the full example, check it out on GitHub at https://github .com/synedra/irresistible/blob/master/schema_models/swagger/swagger.yaml.

7.4.4   *Step 3: API subresource methods—GET, PUT, DELETE*

Reviewing the methods needed for the individual `toppings/{toppingid}` and `pizzas /{pizzaid}` resources, these endpoints will accept `GET` to obtain information about a single subresource, `PUT` to update a particular item, and `DELETE` to remove the topping or pizza.

As demonstrated in figure 7.19, subresource responses for a `GET` are almost identical to the responses for the top-level resources. An error can occur, though, if the requested pizza ID doesn't exist. This resource would look similar to this as a URL:

```
http://api.irresistibleapis.com/pizzas/2
```

```
102 ▾    /pizzas/{pizzaid}:
103 ▾      get:
104          description: Retrieves an individual pizza
105 ▾        parameters:
106 ▾          - description: ID for the pizza
107              in: path
108              name: pizzaid
109              required: true
110              type: string
111 ▾        responses:
112 ▾          '200':
113              description: 'Pizza '
114 ▾            examples:
115                application/json: {"id":1,"name":"Maui Wowie","toppings":[2,3]}
116 ▾            schema:
117                type: object
118 ▾              properties:
119 ▾                id:
120                    type: string
121 ▾                name:
122                    type: string
123 ▾                toppings:
124                    type: array
125 ▾                  items:
126                      type: integer
127 ▾          '404':
128              description: Pizza not found
129 ▾            examples:
130                application/json: { message: No pizza with that ID found }
131 ▾            schema:
132                type: object
133 ▾              properties:
134 ▾                message:
135                    type: string
```

Figure 7.19   The subresource GET description is also more verbose in the OpenAPI format, though it more explicitly documents the types and names of each of the values within the object.

Following the same pattern as before, the next thing to add is the write operation, shown in figure 7.20. In this case, again you'll use PUT. Because you're accessing a single resource, it's not appropriate to POST a new item to a single item. Instead, PUT will be used to update the resource itself, perhaps adding a new topping or changing the name.

Again, for PUT you're returning a 204 when the system is successful in updating the item, and a 404 if there's no item at that location.

```
136    put:
137       description: Pizza update
138       parameters:
139         - description: ID for the pizza
140           in: path
141           name: pizzaid
142           required: true
143           type: string
144         - description: ID for the pizza (only one per user)
145           in: body
146           name: pizza
147           required: true
148           schema:
149               type: object
150               required:
151                 - id
152                 - name
153               properties:
154                 id:
155                     type: string
156                 name:
157                     type: string
158                 toppings:
159                     type: array
160                     items:
161                         type: integer
162       responses:
163         '204':
164           description: Pizza updated
165         '404':
166           description: Pizza not found
167           examples:
168             application/json:
169               message: No pizza with that ID found
170           schema:
171               type: string
```

Figure 7.20 Note that the OpenAPI description includes `pizzaid` as a parameter, even though it's part of the path (`/pizzas/:pizzaid`). This is one of the differences between this framework and RAML; having it as a specific parameter means that it can be explicitly defined as a string that is required. There's no functional difference, but you may prefer one over the other when reading through the schema.

The next task is adding the DELETE response for a particular resource (see figure 7.21). Again, the resource being requested has a specific ID, so it's possible that a DELETE would encounter a missing item. The responses necessary here are 204 with no body to indicate success and a 404 to indicate that the item wasn't found.

Okay, that's pretty awesome. The responses for the DELETE are almost identical to the PUT request. Next you have one more exercise:

EXERCISE 7 For the `toppings/` resource, add the POST response based on the previous example and the RAML examples from earlier in the chapter. If you want to see the full example, check it out on GitHub at https://github.com/synedra /irresistible/blob/master/schema_models/swagger/swagger.yaml.

```
172 ▾      delete:
173          description: Deletes an individual pizza
174 ▾        parameters:
175 ▾          - description: ID for the pizza
176              in: path
177              name: pizzaid
178              required: true
179              type: string
180 ▾        responses:
181 ▾          '204':
182              description: Pizza deleted
183 ▾          '404':
184              description: Pizza not found
185 ▾            examples:
186 ▾              application/json:
187                  message: No pizza with that ID found
188 ▾              schema:
189                  type: string
```

Figure 7.21 DELETE is quite simple: it can be even more streamlined, as the 204 and 404 responses are the standard responses for a DELETE. It's all right to assume standard responses, and include the responses that are different from the norm, or have specific error messages included.

At this point, your Open API schema model is complete. The final document can be found at https://github.com/synedra/irresistible/blob/master/schema_models /swagger/swagger.yaml.

7.4.5   *OpenAPI tools and resources*

As with RAML, OpenAPI has many tools and resources available for your use with Swagger schema models. The OpenAPI framework is supported by SmartBear, an API testing company. This being the case, many of the tools provided focus on testing, consistency, and the ability to create starter code (stubs, which expose the endpoints for the API, giving the developer the opportunity to work on the back-end functionality with the exposed endpoints already defined).

7.5   *Summary*

In this chapter, I've covered two of the most common schema modeling languages. Whichever you pick, remember that any schema model is one of the most powerful tools you can have in guiding the development of your API to meet the use cases you've identified. Both of the models have excellent editing toolsets, as well as a comprehensive ecosystem of open source tools.

- OpenAPI has a very strong schema modeling language for defining exactly what's expected of the system—very useful for testing and creating coding stubs for a set of APIs.
- RAML is designed to support a design-first development flow and focuses on consistency.

Each of the schema modeling languages can be used for any of the use cases listed here. I suggest that you take the time to explore the editor and toolsets for these languages to determine which one works best for you. Remember that your goal is to create a contract between the development team and its customers, including other teams, customers, and project managers.

The next chapter talks about using a schema model to drive design-driven development. It covers the code stubs that can be created by the schema modeling toolsets and how to make sure that the contract is being met by the resulting API.

Design-driven development

With a schema model and a good sense of the use cases you want to support, you're finally ready to go through the process of developing the API. The development of the API requires that you continue to leverage the work done in the previous chapters so that the API you create emerges as a solid product.

After reading this chapter, you'll have an entire system for the development of your API, with several checkpoints throughout to help you make sure you're still on track to building the API you've envisioned.

8.1 Development strategies for your API

Several kinds of code development strategies exist out in the wild today, each providing a new mind-set for creating success for your software. This applies equally to API development strategies as well. In fact, because APIs need to be flexible and adapt to the needs of customers, it's even more important to pick the right kind of development strategy for your API. Long-term API development projects without checkpoints are likely to drift from the needs of the customers rather than react in a meaningful way to new use cases or requirements.

Note that these approaches aren't identical in scope. They're presented here less as hard-and-fast rule sets, and more as a buffet of options, where you can pick the pieces that make the most sense for your needs. A blended model is often a great choice, as long as you identify the outcomes that you're most concerned with.

8.1.1　*Waterfall development*

Before the emergence of the newer models, software development was generally done by writing a complete functional specification (usually focused on functionality rather than usability), and each piece was built—hopefully with some unit tests, followed by human testing of the specified functionality. When the entire monolith was ready to be deployed, it was released to the world. This process is known in the industry as the *waterfall* model (figure 8.1). With the waterfall method, any given project or product can take months or even years to see the light of day. This type of project management doesn't focus on iterative improvement or checkpoints or dividing the work into functional chunks. Few opportunities arise for asking whether the project is on the right track or for adjusting the vision during the process.

There are a few downsides to this approach. The tests are written after the code, which makes them much more likely to miss edge cases or validate functionality that isn't right. Writing a test after you write the code generally turns into an examination of the code, figuring out what the hooks are into the code, and making sure that it behaves exactly as it already does. This is okay for future regression testing (did I

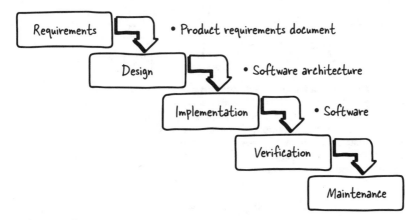

Figure 8.1　In the waterfall development methodology, each step in the process is completely finished before the next section begins. The entire cycle from start to finish can take months, or even years, without any built-in review or reflection in the system. This doesn't mean that waterfall development never has this kind of adjustment, but it isn't inherent in the system.

break something that used to work?) but not good for identifying places where the engineer hasn't implemented the functionality properly. The lack of intermediate customer checkpoints to validate the implementation of specific modules or features almost invariably leads to required changes at the end of the road. At the present time, there are several other development methodologies that address the downsides of this more historical approach.

8.1.2   *Agile/test-first development*

The first leap forward in development strategies was the introduction of test-first development, which became popular during the 1990s when the industry experienced the emergence of agile as a new overall product methodology (see figure 8.2).

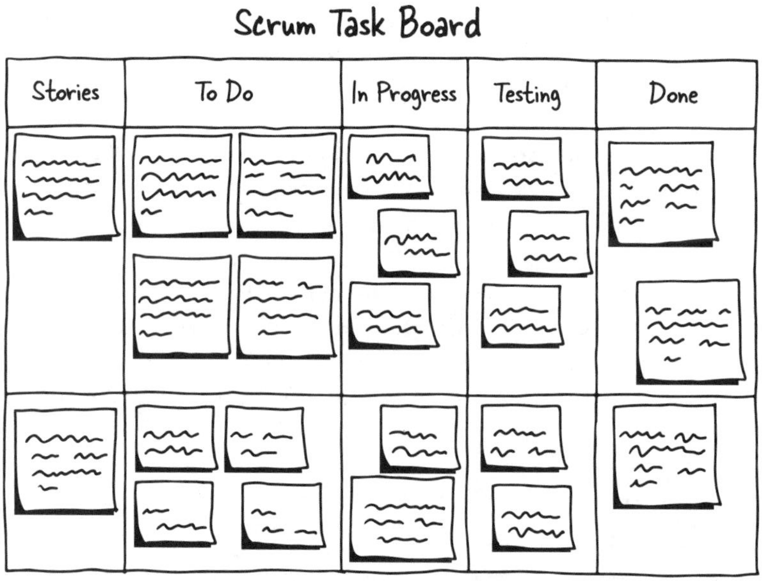

Scrum Task Board

Figure 8.2   **The agile scrum board looks fairly arbitrary and temporary by design. A sticky note or small pinned paper can easily be moved around, from the Stories waiting for attention, into the To Do column, through the additional columns, to Done. There's nothing keeping a task from moving backward when the situation demands it, from Testing back to In Progress, because something didn't work correctly, or from To Do back to Stories when other priorities emerge. This agility is at the base of the "agile" project management method.**

One common method of implementing agile development integrates scrum and kanban:

- The term *scrum* refers to the agile methods of sprints, including planning, task assignment, daily standups, and review/retrospective.
- Kanban is a complementary idea, which, in an agile context, describes how to place those tasks on a board (frequently with sticky notes) for moving through

various stages of completeness for tasks: Backlog, To Do, In Progress, Verification, and Done.

- At the beginning of any development, the team and customers create user stories, which are use cases. A fully fleshed-out story would be "As a user, I want to be able to list my contacts, so I can find my friends," and would ideally contain hard requirements for what Done means. These requirements are termed *acceptance criteria.*

- As a scrum practice the team has daily standups, designed to be 15 minutes or less, to facilitate collaboration throughout the team.

- Using scrum, development is done in sprints. A *sprint* is a relatively short period of time—sometimes a week or two, but no more than a month. When kanban is implemented, the team uses a kanban board with tasks, stories, and swim lanes, designed to help visualize the productivity of the team (figure 8.3).

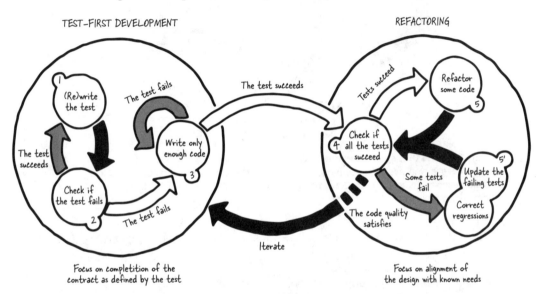

Figure 8.3 **When tests are written before the code is written, the expected behavior is expressed before an implementation can emerge, and the resulting code is much more likely to behave as expected. Tests are a great way for a team to communicate what they expect the functions to do within the system. For each test, only enough code is written to make the test pass, and then the entire test suite is run to make sure that everything still works as expected. This is repeated until all the tests succeed and the programming work for the project is done.**

If you're interested in the agile methodology, you can find many books and websites devoted to the topic, including http://agilemethodology.org, which points to various other resources. The concepts of agile are relatively easy to understand at a high level, but they can be challenging to implement. I recommend you do some research if you're interested in the topic, so you can hit the ground running with the process with minimal hiccups.

8.1.3   *Behavior-driven development*

Behavior-driven development (BDD) is an extension of test-driven development (TDD). In BDD (figure 8.4), additional software tests represent the acceptance criteria, so the developer now has two sets of tests to work against, and the overall use case is much clearer for any given subset of the code. For each acceptance test, there must be a workflow, which is tested based on the story itself.

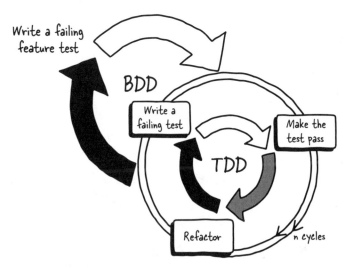

Figure 8.4   The BDD cycle incorporates TDD into a larger cycle of behavior-driven, or use case–driven, tests. These integration tests express what the system as a whole needs to do, which helps keep holes from developing between individual units of the product.

With BDD, the overarching focus is on making the acceptance criteria real and helping developers to keep track of the main goal for the software in question.

8.1.4   *Design-driven development*

Design-driven development (DDD) adds a design layer on top of the test-first development and BDD stack for the goal of designing consistent interfaces, whether from other software sections or for the users' use. The design layer is covered by the process outlined in this book. After defining the use cases, the schema model (in the case of a web API) is outlined, which makes it easy to create test cases based on the design goals. In fact, many open source testing frameworks can import a schema model and create appropriate tests for the software.

To learn more about these testing frameworks, take a look at the following post by Kin Lane, "the API Evangelist," covering automatic client code generators. The post can be found at http://apievangelist.com/2015/06/06/comparison-of-automatic-code-generation-tools-for-swagger/. Here's the list of client code generators for OpenAPI:

- Swagger.io is the official host for the open source Swagger CodeGen project.
- REST United uses a customized version of the Swagger CodeGen project and performs better than the official branch.
- Restlet Studio uses Swagger CodeGen for Objective-C but has its own CodeGen engine for Android and Java.
- APIMATIC has its own CodeGen engine for all languages.

A client designed to hit each of the endpoints as specified in the schema can perform valuable tests to make sure that your design is being implemented exactly as described in the schema model. Unfortunately, the current client code generators still need some work in creating foolproof code that compiles each time. When you're using the generators, regardless of the language you're using, it's best to expect that you'll need to spend a small amount of time getting it ready for prime-time.

Using these code generators is one advantage to design-driven development. The overarching goal of this type of project management is to make sure that the design of your API happens first and is the driving vision used to guide development. Like test-first development and behavior-driven development, design-first development carries a mind-set where the code is created to match a specific, defined specification—in this case, the schema model.

8.1.5 Code-first development

For completeness, I'm going to give you an idea what code-first development looks like. Note that many APIs that have already been created have been done in this way— developers are told to create a (single) API or set of endpoints, and they add code on top of the back-end system to meet this deliverable.

The problem with this approach should be obvious—because the API isn't considered to be a complete, first-class citizen in the product ecosystem for your organization, it's developed backward. No specification is needed to create an API, and the technical challenge is minimal. But when APIs are created in this way, they tend to be inconsistent with the main product and among the endpoints, and frequently the code needs to be rewritten later to meet the goals of the customers. Worse yet, a poorly planned API rollout means that there is an API that customers are using that can't easily be deprecated in the future.

A web API isn't a subproduct for the main product, and the action of adding new functionality, endpoints, and features requires the same amount of planning as teams commit to planning other software projects.

8.1.6 Why does project management matter?

Project management is a critical aspect to the success of any software engineering endeavor—indeed, for any product, whether software or something more tangible. In 2009, a software statistical company called the Standish Group, found at www.standishgroup.com/news/index, did a study on software project outcomes in the United States. This was before the upsurge in popularity for agile development models. In this study, 24% of the projects failed outright, and 44% were challenged, either falling behind or meeting unexpected challenges. Thirty-two percent of the projects succeeded. Although there was no direct mapping of project methodologies, this kind of outcome exposes the issues we were having with project management at the time. The waterfall method created too many opportunities for failure, and without regular iterations and check-ins, those failures could snowball into something untenable before the issue was discovered.

When developing APIs, you must be able to meet new requirements, work with your clients during development, and verify that development is creating the right APIs. When you're creating a system for which you own the entire stack, some assumptions can be made about what the system will do. But a web API is an interface to your system for different organizations to use, not merely your own, and as such it's subject to many different opinions and requirements. For this reason, the project management methodology you choose is critically important.

8.2   Project management for APIs

To achieve the best possible result with the process outlined in this book, you'll find a design-driven methodology makes the most sense. Using agile methodologies where they work for you is a fantastic idea, but it's not required. In the design-driven methodology (figure 8.5), the steps are in a slightly different order than with the waterfall method.

First, you'll create your functional specification document. In parallel or shortly after, the schema model is created with use cases. Before developing, you create acceptance criteria for developers to work against along with the unit tests. Only then do you start with development. Instead of developing the entire system at once, you can parallelize and have different engineers working on different use cases so that they can deploy the API. In this section, I break out each of these actions so you can see how they flow together into a strong deployment process.

8.2.1   Functional specification

We haven't discussed the functional specification explicitly yet, but your organization likely has a functional specification standard for software projects. If you don't, your product managers need to create a document that, at the least, answers the following questions:

1 What problem is the project solving?
2 What is the business value?
3 What are the metrics and use cases?
4 What resources are needed or available?
5 What does "done" look like?
6 What could go wrong?

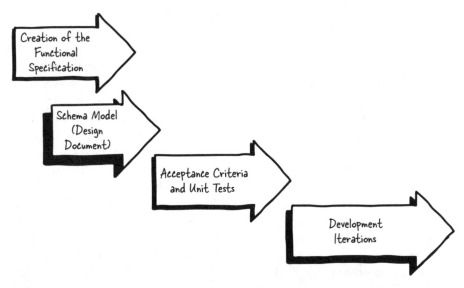

Figure 8.5 Ideally, API project management includes the development of a functional specification in parallel with the schema model. Only once these two documents have been completed should the acceptance criteria be written and unit tests developed. After all of this infrastructure is in place, the development iterations can begin. Although this seems like a huge amount of work up front, it reduces the amount of development time significantly—and more importantly, it reduces the chances of incorrect work that would need to be redone.

Obviously, a more complete functional specification will be a more powerful design and vision document, but a basic document covering these points will help the developers and other stakeholders understand the goals of the project. This may seem obvious, but so many people have created their APIs as side-coding features rather than unique products that this part of the process—the functional specification—is frequently skipped entirely.

Most of these factors probably look similar to the concepts described previously in the book, so I won't belabor the points other than pointing out that this is the right place and time to figure out those factors. I'll cover the others in more detail so they make sense in context.

First, what problem is the project solving? In plain English, describe exactly what's happening that needs to be addressed. Keeping this information with the functional specification helps to avoid the "drift" that tends to happen once the project is under way and folks start focusing on implementation details. Help to make sure that every time the functional specification is referenced, the overriding goal of the project is front and center.

What does "done" look like? This question is quite important: What things will be true when the work is done? In development projects far and wide, there are situations where developers don't understand what's required in order to be finished with a project, and the features creep in during development. This is bad for the productivity of your development resources, and it also makes it difficult to follow strong coding practices while creating the product. If there's a moving target, people are more likely to patch in changes rather than do the feature holistically from the beginning. Make sure that the acceptance criteria—the things that are necessary for the product to complete—are described completely and correctly, and that all stakeholders on both sides (product team and customers) are in agreement about what those criteria are.

What could go wrong? This is one concept that's frequently missed in feature specifications, but one that I strongly suggest you adopt. You won't be able to identify every possible challenge that the project may encounter, but if you're relying on another team for some functionality, then you have a requirement that's outside your control. Identifying this on the functional specification helps in two ways: it shines a light on this requirement, and it also gives you the ability to include that team in communication about the needed functionality, when you need it, and why it's important to your project.

Every time you're planning a project, it's tempting to bound the specification as closely as possible to the ideal path, without taking the time to consider what issues could delay or sidetrack the project. The real world is messier than this. As you find new challenges, or meet new goals—or as your customers add new features to the requirements, as they'll almost certainly do—update that functional specification so that it remains the one true narrative description of what the finished project will do.

Take caution when making functional specifications that are focused too heavily on architecture. The architecture of an API is less interesting than the developer experience expressed by the interaction model, resource schema, and workflows that are made possible via the project.

8.2.2   Schema model

I've talked a great deal about how to create a schema model. To sum up the information from chapter 7, a *schema model* helps your team ensure that the API is consistent across all the endpoints and can be used as an artifact or design document to spark discussion with internal and external team members before the coding is done. A schema model, like a functional specification, should be kept up to date if changes occur to the implementation, requirements, or acceptance tests.

Which format you choose for your schema modeling is up to you. All the versions I've covered, along with any new upcoming modeling languages, will work for any API. The schema is for your benefit, so whichever of the languages works best for you is the right one to use.

Once you've created both the schema model and the functional specification, it should be quite easy for anyone reviewing those documents to understand the purpose, goals, and plan for the project itself.

8.3   *Road-testing your API*

Before you kick off development, it's a great idea to create a mock server using the schema model to help you validate your plan with your customers, whether internal or external. Whether you review the server with your customers before you start coding or in parallel with the development activity, having the opportunity to have those conversations to validate your model and functional specification with your customers can save you a lot of time and resources as you avoid direction changes nearer to completion. Depending on the development methodology you choose, you may have checkpoints throughout the development cycle where the direction can be tweaked or the vision revisited. Don't miss out on this valuable chance to gain insight on the validity of your API plan. If changes need to occur, those changes should be prioritized in the context of other requirements for the project. The customer can then determine whether the change is needed in the context of the project as a whole.

8.3.1   *Creating a mock server API*

Creating a mock server is easy with any of the schema modeling languages. Each of the companies that owns or maintains a particular schema modeling system provides open source tools designed to help create a mock server. If your enterprise IT department doesn't support external servers, you can always use one of the lightweight cloud hosting providers, such as Heroku or DigitalOcean, to bring up a mock server that your customers can access from outside of your network. After discussing the basic principles of creating and working with mock servers, I'll add an exercise for folks who want to set up à mock server visible in the cloud.

The easiest place to observe this difference is on the main irresistibleapis.com website. The "live" version of the demo is the interface you worked with in chapter 2. It's a basic API that doesn't have the pizza functionality, only toppings.

The link to that original view is at http://irresistibleapis.com/demo. The API is running right underneath the functionality, and you can still add new toppings, remove them, and rename them, all using the fundamental API I described first.

OpenAPI makes it relatively easy to create a mock server. I've implemented it on the same server at http://irresistibleapis.com:8080/docs. This is the documentation section of the mock server. As you can see, it appears that all the endpoints are working correctly, and they are, insofar as you're expecting the canned response from the mock server. Before I give you the tools you need to get this mock server running on your own, I'll show you how to tell the difference between the two. Figure 8.6 shows the /toppings endpoint within the extra context of Chrome Developer Tools.

As you work with the page demonstrated here, changes you make will change things within the system. This is a live API and changes to the data are kept. This is a direct HTTP call to the toppings API:

```
http://irresistibleapis.com/api/v1.0/toppings
```

Figure 8.6   The original toppings from chapter 2. As you probably recall, the page itself is making a call back to the `/toppings` endpoint and processing the returned JSON to create this user interface. To see this in practice, use the Chrome browser and watch the network traffic to see how the JSON relates to the resulting HTML page.

If you work with the live server interface—the "All Toppings Active API" page in figure 8.7—changes will happen to the toppings as you create them, rename them, and delete them.

Figure 8.7   This live server response represents what you'll see in the Chrome Network tab when the initial user interface page in figure 8.10 is generated. The CSS and HTML pages are used to create the single-page application based on the back-end API response.

Figure 8.8 This looks exactly the same as the live response, but it's the OpenAPI mock server responding with the information from the schema model. Responses from a mock server won't change (so if you delete a topping it will still appear). Nonetheless, these servers are an excellent way to create a prototype or demo application to test and make sure the schema will support your use cases.

With a mock server you'll get a similar API interface to the system, but your interfaces with the system won't change values within the system. The mock server is designed to help you look at how the endpoints will work such that you can create sample clients to test against the eventual live API. Figure 8.8 shows how this mock server behaves, similarly to a live call to the API itself.

A mock server is a service that contains static data and provides endpoints for you to work with. A mock service can be challenging to understand compared to a simple API, but having one helps a great deal when validating the model you've created. Using OpenAPI gives a couple of pieces of functionality for exploring the Mock API. First, you can get to the /api-docs endpoint, which will show the JSON version of the schema model (see figure 8.9).

Besides this simple view into the schema model, there's an excellent way to browse through the Mock API. On the same server you'll find http://irresistibleapis.com :8080/docs, an interactive method for exploring the API endpoints represented on the system.

```
{
  "swagger": "2.0",
  "info": {
    "title": "PizzaToppings API",
    "description": "This is a sample server Petstore server.\n\n\n[Learn about Swagger](http://swagger.io) or join the IRC channel
`#swagger` on irc.freenode.net.\n\n\nFor this sample, you can use the api key `special-key` to test the authorization filters",
    "version": "1.0.0"
  },
  "produces": [
    "application/json"
  ],
  "host": "localhost:8080",
  "basePath": "/v1",
  "paths": {
    "/toppings/": {
      "get": {
        "summary": "",
        "description": "Retrieves a list of toppings in the system",
        "x-swagger-router-controller": "Default",
        "tags": [
          "Default"
        ],
        "operationId": "toppingsGet",
        "parameters": [
          {
            "name": "nameString",
            "in": "query",
            "description": "String to match in the topping name",
            "required": false,
            "type": "string"
          }
        ],
        "responses": {
          "200": {
            "description": "Topping list",
            "schema": {
              "type": "array",
              "items": {
                "type": "object",
                "properties": {
                  "name": {
                    "type": "string"
                  },
                  "id": {
                    "type": "string"
```

Display a menu

Figure 8.9   In this case, the mock server is running on port 8080 on the localhost, as you can see from the host entry. The schema model here is the same one created in chapter 7 and should in fact meet all the use cases identified in that chapter.

Although discussing the API with your customers before bringing the development resources online (or while they're working) is a great idea, you also get another fantastic advantage to having a mock server. Armed with your use cases, you can create all the needed workflows to support those stories and write client code that implements each of the use cases to ensure that the use cases you started with will be easy and straightforward (see figure 8.10).

As a quick exercise, go ahead and click GET for the /toppings/ resource. Note what the values are; they'll always be the same in this mock server. Figure 8.11 shows exactly what the mock server will return.

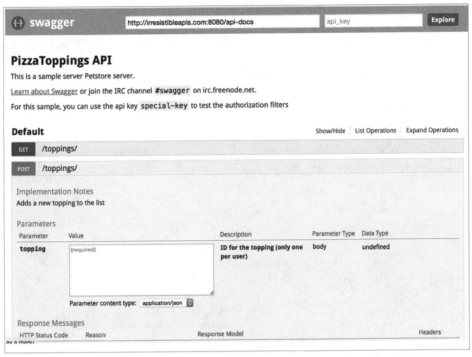

Figure 8.10 When running a mock server using the OpenAPI tools, you also get an interactive console to explore the endpoints and see how they work. This functionality is also available for the live server when it's created. When you're sharing the schema model with other developers or customers, sometimes it's helpful to give them a visual way to explore the platform.

```
[
  {
    "id": "1",
    "name": "pepperoni"
  },
  {
    "id": "2",
    "name": "ham"
  },
  {
    "id": "3",
    "name": "pineapple"
  }
]
```

Figure 8.11 This call to http://irresistibleapis.com:8080/v1/toppings/ is accessing the mock server and is returning exactly what the schema model indicates. Again, if you make a call to add a new topping, update a topping, or delete one, this call won't change, because there's no live service on the back end but only a static model.

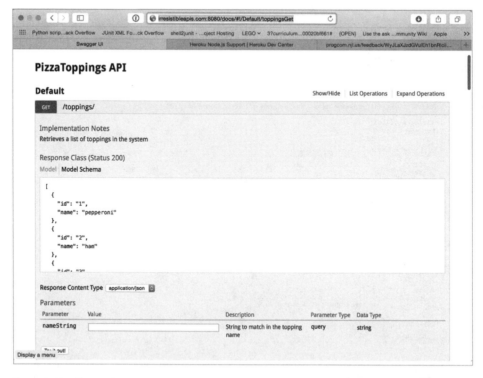

Figure 8.12   Along with the interactive console for exploring the APIs, there's also interactive documentation created by the OpenAPI system. This is the same documentation you'll be able to provide to your users when the API itself is live—which is one of the reasons to make sure that the API itself stays in sync with the schema model.

You can see this exact call in a much nicer format at http://irresistibleapis .com:8080/docs/#!/Default/toppingsGet. Figure 8.12 demonstrates this view.

This interactive documentation browser allows you to see quite clearly how the HTTP interactions work with the system. Although write interactions won't change values in the system, understanding how the requests and responses work is quite powerful. Moving down the page to the POST for toppings, you can get a better idea of what I mean about the mock server. POSTing a new topping or DELETE-ing a topping will have no effect on the values the GET responses provide.

ADVANCED

The previous section certainly demonstrates the differences between a live API server and a mocked-up one. But I'm going to take a little time here to walk through the process of getting your own mock server visible from the public cloud, so you can use it to work with your customers and hone your eventual API into perfection.

```
● ● ●        swagger_irresistible_mock — root@mfpb-gxqy: /home/synedra/irresistible/webapp — bash — 114×50

sjc-mpl23:mockswagger khunter$ heroku login
Enter your Heroku credentials.
Email: synedra@gmail.com
Password (typing will be hidden):
Logged in as synedra@gmail.com
sjc-mpl23:mockswagger khunter$ git clone http://github.com/synedra/swagger_irresistible_mock
Cloning into 'swagger_irresistible_mock'...
remote: Counting objects: 2174, done.
remote: Compressing objects: 100% (1666/1666), done.
remote: Total 2174 (delta 346), reused 2174 (delta 346), pack-reused 0
Receiving objects: 100% (2174/2174), 3.56 MiB | 2.10 MiB/s, done.
Resolving deltas: 100% (346/346), done.
Checking connectivity... done.
sjc-mpl23:mockswagger khunter$ cd swagger_irresistible_mock
sjc-mpl23:swagger_irresistible_mock khunter$ heroku create
Creating infinite-basin-6068... done, stack is cedar-14
https://infinite-basin-6068.herokuapp.com/ | https://git.heroku.com/infinite-basin-6068.git
Git remote heroku added
sjc-mpl23:swagger_irresistible_mock khunter$ git push heroku master
Counting objects: 2174, done.
Delta compression using up to 4 threads.
Compressing objects: 100% (1666/1666), done.
Writing objects: 100% (2174/2174), 3.56 MiB | 531.00 KiB/s, done.
Total 2174 (delta 346), reused 2174 (delta 346)
remote: Compressing source files... done.
remote: Building source:
remote:
remote: -----> Node.js app detected
remote:
remote: -----> Creating runtime environment
remote:
remote:
remote: -----> Caching build
remote:        Clearing previous node cache
remote:        Saving 2 cacheDirectories (default):
remote:        - node_modules
remote:        - bower_components (nothing to cache)
remote:
remote: -----> Build succeeded!
remote:        ├── connect@3.4.0
remote:        └── swagger-tools@0.8.7
remote:
remote: -----> Discovering process types
remote:        Procfile declares types -> web
remote:
remote: -----> Compressing... done, 15.1MB
remote: -----> Launching... done, v3
remote:        https://infinite-basin-6068.herokuapp.com/ deployed to Heroku
remote:
remote: Verifying deploy... done.
To https://git.heroku.com/infinite-basin-6068.git
```

Figure 8.13 The process for pushing your model and server to Heroku is relatively straightforward, and it gets easier after the first time. All you'll need to do is edit the files and push them back out to Heroku. In this case, the server infinite-basin-6068.herokuapp.com was created, and now the documentation and mock server are available on the internet to share with other people.

HOSTING PROVIDER: HEROKU

I've chosen Heroku as the best server for this strategy because the interaction with the system is quite simple, and you get some bonus adorable haiku names for your services. The code you need to work with is already in the code you've pulled down before, but I'll start the process anew to make sure everyone has the same experience (see figure 8.13).

1 Get a Heroku login. The most basic level of use, which is what you'll be using, is free.
2 Install the Heroku toolbelt from https://toolbelt.heroku.com.

3 At the command line, type your Heroku login followed by this:

```
git clone http://github.com/synedra/swagger_irresistible_mock
cd swagger_irresistible_mock
heroku create
git push heroku master
```

The Procfile at the base of the repository clone tells the Heroku server what to do when the code is pushed up:

```
web: node index.js
```

At this point, you'll have a new service, available from anywhere, where you can demonstrate the API via the mocked-up version. Whether you run this locally or separately, it will be an excellent tool for your use in moving forward with development. Heroku provides you with a `haiku-server-name`, which is unique for your use. The process in the command line works fairly simply.

In this example, if you want to view the interactive documentation, do so by accessing https://infinite-basin-6068.herokuapp.com/docs/.

8.3.2   *Acceptance tests and use cases*

When discussing testing, many developers consider *unit tests*—tests that determine a specific module or code set is working as written. Unit tests are important to ensure that the cogs in the wheel are working correctly. But unit tests don't cover all the testing that you need to do for your API. Acceptance criteria are critical to verify that you're making the use cases as easy as designed and not getting off track.

I mentioned acceptance criteria earlier, and now I'll walk through the process of creating acceptance criteria, what the goals are, and how to implement them. I'll use the standard agile methodology in building up these tests.

A *user story* in agile methodology is a description of one of the things that needs to be enabled by the project. These stories are generally created to follow this template:

- As a <type of user>
- . . . I want to be able to <perform an action>
- . . . so that I can <create an outcome>.

Figure 8.14 shows an example of a user story for the pizza toppings API.

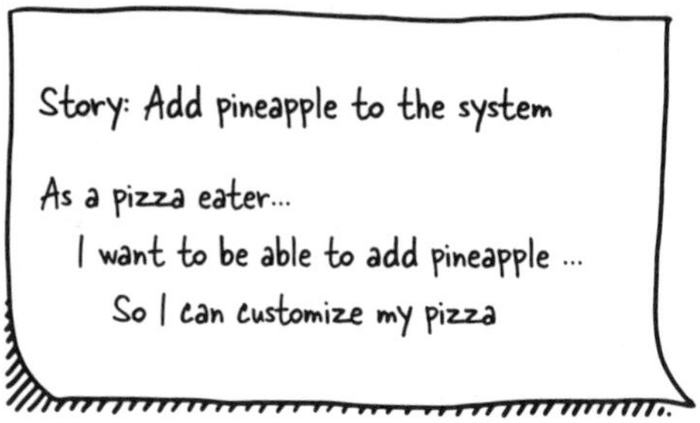

Story: Add pineapple to the system

As a pizza eater...
   I want to be able to add pineapple ...
      So I can customize my pizza

Figure 8.14   The standard agile storyboard format is easier to understand with an example. It can often feel forced, but having all three sections of the story makes it much easier to ensure that the requirement is well defined, and there's a shared understanding of what needs to happen in order for the story to be done.

Once the user story is created, you can turn it into a testing scenario—the second step on the way to creating a good code test to make sure you've got the right behavior. The difference between the user story and the testing scenario is that the latter will describe specific actions and their outcomes, to solidify exactly what's needed to validate that the code covers the user story.

In this case, there are a couple of pieces of information you'll want to include. First, a new topping needs to be added to the system, to make it available to be subsequently added to a pizza. The steps are listed, including the action taken by the user and the subsequent test to make sure that it happened correctly.

Scenario: Add pineapple to the system

- Given the pizza topping doesn't exist
- And I add a new topping to the system
- The list of toppings should include the new topping

This is a different way to express the goals from earlier, in a measurable and precise manner. Some user stories might end up with multiple scenarios. Don't feel constrained to create one scenario per user story, but each one should have at least a single scenario.

From here, you can create an acceptance test case. An *acceptance test case* is different from a unit test case in that the behavior and workflow of the user case is tested, rather than the exact behavior of specific functions within the code. This is not to say that there's no place for unit tests, but as you can see from the workflow listed in figure 8.14, the acceptance tests that we're creating live outside of the realm of the unit tests. They're an overarching test to make sure that the set of functionality that was created—which should also meet the goals of the unit tests—combine to meet the needs of the user story being considered here.

The acceptance test will look similar to the following scenario:

Acceptance test case: Add pineapple to the system

- Get a list of pizza toppings in the system
- Verify that the new topping doesn't exist
- Add a new topping to the system
- Get the list of pizza toppings
- Verify that the new topping has been added

I realize this seems simplistic, but remember that tests aren't supposed to be complicated or difficult; they need to verify that the use case you've selected is easy, straightforward, and functional when the user tries to do it. It may be that you want to verify that the previous case works when the topping exists in the system already, so you'd create an acceptance test case similar to the case where there's a specific topping (in this case pineapple) already in your toppings list:

Acceptance test case: Add pineapple to the pizza

- Get a list of pizza toppings in the system
- Verify that the new topping does add a new topping to the system
- Verify that an error is returned with a developer-friendly message

The goal of the acceptance tests is to follow the workflow that developers will use to interact with your system, to make it simple for them to be able to do the things you expect and want them to do. When you have these acceptance tests, you can use them as the basis of tutorials you can include in your documentation to help guide developers through the workflow as you expect it to happen. This helps reduce frustration in your customer developers, but even more, it helps you to avoid the case where your developers try to find other ways to create the same result. It's best to do everything you can to keep your customer developers on the same page as you are when they're implementing the use cases you've identified, and the easiest way to do that is to make sure that you've communicated clearly how you expect specific actions to be implemented.

8.4 *Planning development*

Once you've decided on your development model, you can move on to planning how your development will proceed. For this book, I'll encourage you to use a behavior-driven development model, enhanced to add design-driven development. For API development, where third-party and external users will be interacting with your system, it's critical that you do everything you can to make sure that you've covered the use cases you want to support, and that the interface is as intuitive and complete as possible. This being the case, you likely want to break down the user stories into what you need for a minimum viable product and work from there.

For the system I'm describing here, it may be that you want to support a few use cases to start. Perhaps you only want to have full functionality for the toppings, similar to the beginning API described in chapter 2. This could be your initial release, and that would be fine. Different endpoints or sets of endpoints can be released at different times, and as long as you have an overarching design for your API, it's reasonable to release different parts of the system.

Here's the list of use cases described in chapter 7 while I was building all the schema models:

- Creating new toppings
- Getting a list of all toppings, including matching a particular string
- Deleting and updating specific toppings
- Creating a named pizza—only one per user
- Listing pizzas
- Adding toppings to a pizza
- Viewing the pizza
- Deleting the pizza for the specific user

For development planning, perhaps the toppings functionality is sufficient for the first release. You may not want to release it externally, but for this case perhaps you want to front-load the list of toppings so that when the pizza functionality is available there will be lots of toppings to choose from. Similarly, you want to make sure that the functionality works well for your internal and external customers. If you create a subset of your minimum viable product as a subset of endpoints, you can always allow some customers to interact with it and make sure that the interaction methodology that you've selected is easy for them to use and the API works well from their point of view. Targeting a subset of endpoints also makes it possible for you to split the team into two subteams, one working on each set of endpoints. Knowing that you have a schema model can give you confidence that the two teams won't diverge while creating the API. This may not seem super critical for an API that's as simple as this one, but imagine much more complicated APIs and you'll start to see the advantages. For this API you may want to develop in serial—toppings, then pizzas—and release them as a single customer

Think of Twitter, for example. Twitter has APIs for user information, for a user's feed and lists, searches, and live streams. It adds new functionality regularly based on what users are looking for, making it possible for their own products and third-party clients to keep up with customer demand. It'd be quite difficult for them to keep up with the various use cases in a waterfall manner, with a monolith—they need to be agile and adapt to the social media requirements, so they can break down releases into subsets and create and integrate the new functionality as soon as it's ready. The only time they've needed to make a large and overarching release is when they changed the underlying system for their APIs—and this will be true for nearly any API vendor. If it turns out you need to streamline the overall system, you may have to make a large release and it may frustrate your developers. Keep up that constant communication and work with them to make it as easy as possible.

8.5 Development sprints

Returning to the scrum section of the agile project management philosophy, the development is done in *sprints*. Each sprint can be whatever length makes sense for your team. Common sprint lengths are one to two weeks. These time lengths are ideal for many development goals because a week or two is long enough to address several user stories and come back together at the end to make sure that the overall development is on track.

PLANNING

The first task during an agile sprint is the planning session (see figure 8.15).

During this time, most teams work with a board like figure 8.15—the scrum task planning board. The stories are selected from the left-hand (backlog) column and are placed into the swim lanes (the horizontal rows across the board). Each swim lane may be a particular type of task (development, documentation, or QA), and each will start in the To Do section of the board to start the sprint.

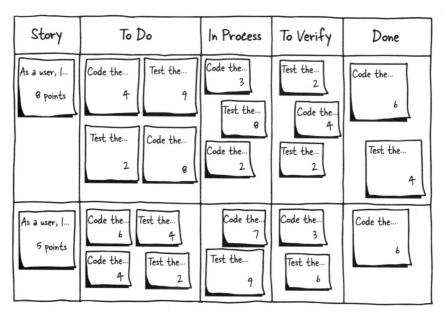

Figure 8.15 A scrum planning board generally has the same columns: a Story column for backlogged stories and tasks in the To Do column. As tasks get assigned or selected by team members, they're put into the In Process state. Once they're ready, they're Verified by a different team member, and finally they're moved to Done.

Determining how many of the tasks will make it into the sprint is done by an estimation system. With agile development, I've seen many different ways to do estimation, but most commonly I've seen teams choose to work with increments of half a day. It might take three days to write the listing function for the toppings, whereas implementing the delete functionality may only take a half day or so. One of the things I admire about most agile teams is that the process of estimation is much more reasonable than what happens with waterfall planning, because things are viewed in a manageable timeframe and it's easier to see where expectations are unreasonable. Engineers are expected to be doing other things throughout the week, and the amount of time they have for active development is drawn from what's left (for instance, an engineer might have meetings to attend, support tasks to attend to, or a large volume of email to respond to). The goal of the estimates is not to "race" or force people to extend themselves to achieve heroic ends; the goal of the estimates is to honestly determine what things can happen in the correct amount of time so that the team can meet deadlines appropriately and be aware when a delivery has been overpromised.

One other strategy that can be quite helpful when estimating is to aim to make sure that no task is more than a day long. If a task is longer than one day, it can likely be broken down into smaller subtasks, which may allow for more parallelization, or at least quicker movement into the verification stage.

STANDUPS

As the development progresses through the sprint, the team meets, ideally daily, in a short meeting called a stand-up. You may have heard about stand-ups in the past, and in fact they're one of the things many people truly hate about the agile process, so I'm going to go back to the original intent of these meetings. First of all, the reason it's called a stand-up is that everyone, whether the team is local or remote, should be physically standing up during the meeting. This helps retain the sense of a quick session to touch base on the project. The goal of the stand-up is to verify that everyone is on track with his or her tasks and to make sure there are no blockers. It's not an overall status meeting, and it should take no longer than 15 minutes, even for a large team. Any blockers that are identified should be taken to smaller meetings outside of the stand-up, and the entire process should be less interruptive to the developer's day than a conversation around a water cooler. One way to understand the general communication is to consider 3 P's: progress, plans, and problems. What did I do yesterday? What am I planning to do today? What might go wrong?

KANBAN "SWIM LANES"

During the development of the product, each task, which has a clearly defined definition of Done, starts in the To Do column before it's assigned to an engineer or pair of engineers, at which point it is In Process. Once the developer(s) believe that the functionality is complete, the task moves to To Verify, at which point, ideally, another engineer or engineers verifies that the functionality works as expected and the task moves into the Done column. Note that depending on the requirements your team has for completion, this may indicate that the code is done, the tests are done, and/or the documentation is done. These requirements need to be clear and measurable, so that the handoff is clean and developers can move to the next task without having to come back to polish up their work. This is accomplished by having clear "definitions of done" at each step as well as for the final product. In the case of the behavior-driven development process I'm discussing, making sure that the acceptance tests pass, to the best of the developer's ability, is part of making sure things are ready for testing.

The testing phase is generally done by a separate engineer, who should take the unit tests and acceptance tests and verify that the code, documentation, and tests as written are correct when compared to the original goals of the story in question.

As engineers are freed up throughout the sprint, they take new items from the To Do column and start working on them until the sprint finishes. If one of their completed tasks fails verification, the task moves back to To Do and an engineer (likely the same one) is responsible for fixing the issues and moving it back to the testing phase. In the extremely unlikely event that some extra time rears its head, the developer can bring it up during the stand-up so the team can pull in another story from the backlog.

RETROSPECTIVE

The *retrospective* is one of the things that many engineering teams try to skip over. It's uncomfortable thinking of something that feels like it might be a blame-fest. But the goal of the retrospective in an agile team is not to blame people for failures, but to identify areas for improvement in the process. Are your estimates less accurate than you'd hoped? Why? Are you getting held up by dependencies on other teams? How can you manage these issues better in the future? An ideal agile sprint would finish exactly the right amount of work in the expected time, but that almost never happens. The retrospective is one of the most valuable exercises in the agile toolkit, so it's important to move past the discomfort and see it for what it is: an opportunity for the team as a whole to see where the planning and expectations matched—or didn't— with the outcome of the sprint. Ideally your retrospective should take place before the planning session for the next sprint so you can see what needs adjusting and put it into practice right away, before it fades back out of your memory.

This is also the ideal time to discuss items that didn't meet the customer's expectations when they were released, and determine how to better express those expectations going forward. Don't fear the retrospective; the goal is to reduce the anxiety and uncertainty of the team going forward, so that work doesn't need to be redone and engineers are given the necessary amount of time to get their work done. Additionally, the retrospective is an opportunity for the team to congratulate each other for the work that was done well.

8.6   *Summary*

This chapter covered various elements of software development methodologies, with an eye toward making sure that your API is successful as soon as you're ready to deploy it. The chapter explored the following topics:

- Different project-management strategies include waterfall, agile, design-driven development, and behavior-driven development. Waterfall is the "old way" of doing development and can be generally understood as a system where you define an entire project and then move through the sections of the product without significant refactoring, pivoting, or other adjustments to your workflow. Agile is a newer method in which the work is broken down into smaller sprints, and the progress toward the higher-level project is reviewed and discussed regularly throughout the development phase. Both design-driven and behavior-driven development add to this agile process by adding use cases and strong tests to validate that the project is moving in the right direction to end up with the right product to meet the requirements.

- Road-testing your API via a sprint review involves checking in with customers, shareholders, product managers, and client developers to make sure that the API being developed will meet the needs as described by the product's specification and schema model.

- Planning development sprints using use cases to determine which parts of your API should be created helps you design and deploy valuable sections of your API as quickly as possible.

- With development sprints, when you focus on short iterations for your development execution, you can identify issues or make adjustments quickly, reducing the need for refactoring your code at a later time.

9

Empowering your developers

This chapter covers

- Pillars of developer experience
- Clear communication
- Documentation
- Building blocks
- Support

Once your API is ready to be released into the wild, you may think you're in the home stretch. But the success or failure of your API will hinge much more on the developer experience you provide than on any specific technical choice you've made. Developer support sometimes takes a back seat to new development projects, but in the case of an API, where you're working with developers outside of your team, it's critical that you create an experience that truly shines.

After reading this chapter, you'll have an entire system for the development of your API, with several checkpoints throughout to help you make sure you're still on track to building the API you've envisioned.

9.1   *Pillars of developer experience*

When your team thinks about developer experience, it may be tempting to pay less attention to internal APIs that other employees are required to use than you would to an external API for use by external developers. This is a fallacy: anyone who's going to use your API needs excellent support. I'll help you understand the value of spending time and resources getting this most important piece perfect. Providing the right experience for your developers works for you in multiple ways. The trade-off always comes down to cost and speed for your team as opposed to goodwill among your customers. Figure 9.1 shows the pillars of API support required to create a great customer experience. I cover these in more detail throughout the chapter; this quick overview is to help you understand how the pieces fit together to create a fantastic developer experience for all of your client developers.

For external APIs, it's clear that you need to make sure your developer customers understand the API, can use it successfully, and don't get stuck. You want to ensure that they understand how the API should be used through use cases and comprehend the guidelines for working with the APIs. Guiding your customers through an excellent developer experience—outlined in this chapter—will create happy and successful developer customers. But that's not the only advantage to your team. Those customers will help other customers to be successful. They'll be able to get started and extend their applications with minimal help. Seeing that the developer experience is a priority will encourage new developers to give the system a try.

For internal developers, who may be required to use your system, it is *still* critical to provide a fantastic user experience. If developers are forced to use a system they

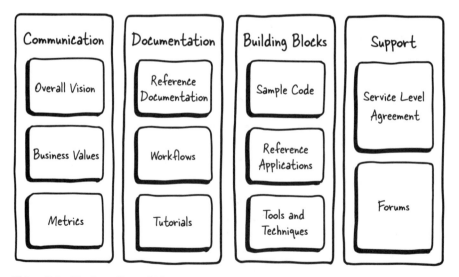

Figure 9.1   The four pillars of API support are communication, documentation, building blocks, and support. Every one of these pillars improves your client developers' understanding of the platform, and with that understanding comes engagement and integration.

struggle with, they may try to work around it, implement inefficient and unsupported workflows, and generally create a support burden for your team.

This chapter covers the steps required to create a phenomenal developer experience. It may be tempting to cut corners or skip some of the pieces. I strongly encourage you to reconsider the costs this can create in extra support and developer confusion. Some of these items align more closely with an internal or external API, but in reality they're all important in both cases.

9.2 Communicating with your developers

In general, companies and organizations want to keep their vision and strategy close to the chest. Revealing this sort of information outside of your development organization feels like a vulnerable choice, but it's critical for a new platform, or an existing platform, to provide as much context around the API program as possible. I'm not talking about reference documentation, tutorials, and example code. For this high-level communication I'm referring to things like the overall vision, business values, and metrics.

9.2.1 Failures of communication

I've worked at two different companies, Netflix and LinkedIn, where information about the business goals for the API weren't shared. Additionally, I've spent a great deal of time studying the trials and successes of Twitter. In the first two cases, poor communication, combined with a lack of overall vision for the platform, contributed to the eventual demise of, or serious deadening of, the API program. Twitter was more successful because the reach of its API was so strong it could weather the storms it encountered.

NETFLIX

At Netflix, there was no real understood business value. The company wanted to have an API because it was the new path to integration with applications, and put out the API hoping for the best. The information shared with developers was sanitized and designed to present a friendly, nonthreatening face. Part of this was designed to "let a thousand flowers bloom," the thought being that with little guidance on how the API was designed to be used, the developers would stretch and create new and unexpected uses for the API, and revenue would sprout fully formed from the uses of the platform. But what happened over time was that these thousand flowers didn't bloom. The company decided that the third-party developers using the API weren't providing value to the company. The company did discover, as I mentioned earlier, that the API was extremely valuable in the world of device integration, so the API didn't go away.

But the third-party developers weren't creating revenue for the company, so the decision was made to phase out the API. This decision made sense from a business standpoint, and it was certainly the right decision. Netflix even went through the trouble to phase out the open API gradually. This was not communicated to the developer community, though. The support was pulled back drastically, the forums lay fallow, and no answers were given. The developers who were relying on the platform to power their applications didn't have any way to know about the new direction. Few missives were sent out to help developers plan for the eventual sunset of the platform. As a result, a number of developers got short shrift, and Netflix got a poor reputation among third-party developers.

LinkedIn

LinkedIn was another company without a strong plan for the API going in. Although the developers working on the platform were talented and motivated and created an excellent platform, there were many detractors within the company. The sales team believed strongly that the API was being used to scrape the company's database and didn't want to have a search API available for developers. The API was maintained with all the functionality, including search, but without strong executive support. After a couple of years the platform was put on hold, and the engineers were distributed to the other engineering teams. None of this information was given to third-party developers using the API, who were left to deal with a slowly contracting set of APIs available to them. Business partners with close contractual ties to LinkedIn were given access to the original APIs, but this excluded third-party developers, an action that fomented a lot of discontent among the developer community.

Twitter

Twitter started out without a great plan for its API. It began with a single page to input the 140-character messages and soon after had an API available for third parties to use. Third-party applications flourished as this simple social network blossomed. There were some serious hiccups as the company pivoted to address different use cases, and even, in some cases, copied new functionality from the third-party developers to add into its platform. This was a great example of how the terms of use need to be strong and firm in order for there to be a shared understanding between the company and the developers. Twitter hadn't necessarily originally planned to copy functionality from the developers, but it also hadn't explicitly expressed it as a possibility in the terms of use (it wasn't against the terms of use but wasn't included in them either).

Twitter didn't do a good job of keeping developers informed about the changes in its strategy, leaving a plethora of dissatisfied developers. Their developer base is incredibly strong and so Twitter weathered the problems. Twitter has become much better recently at sharing their company direction, with blog posts and press releases and presentations at their conferences.

9.2.2 *Strong communication*

Whenever you have an open platform, communicating openly with your developers is critical to the success of your APIs as a whole. Although sometimes the message may be unpopular, your customers—the developers using your platform—are likely to trust you to give them notice when something significant is going to change.

Google is a great example of this kind of communication. It has a multitude of APIs, which cover everything from mapping to calendar functionality. Some products in this pipeline don't succeed, and Google makes the decision to sunset the APIs in order to place its resources on other, more promising products. Developers who work with Google APIs can have confidence that they'll be informed via email, blog posts, and documentation updates as soon as the priority for the API changes within Google. Google has met with a great deal of animosity over the choices it's made in retiring old APIs, but treating its developers like adults who can understand business decisions gives Google a good reputation as a strong communicator in the API industry.

9.2.3 Advantages to strong and consistent communication

To provide your developers with good information about your platform, you need to fully understand your business value and metrics. It may seem odd to share your organization's vision information with developers, but the truth is, many of them do care deeply about why your company has an API, what you're trying to accomplish, and whether it's a high priority for your company. There aren't a lot of companies who have nailed this piece of the developer experience puzzle, but in my 10 years of working with APIs, I've found that the more clearly the company communicates with the developers, the more the developers become strong advocates for, and successful users of, the platform.

For example, imagine that you have a social network application. Your application runs on a platform—because you've decided to go with API First as a strategy—and you're looking to drive usage of your existing users and attract new users to your system. Your goal is to increase the amount of interaction with the system by 20 % over two years. You plan to measure the success of the platform using a few different metrics:

- Number of users reading or writing via the API
- Usage through the API versus through the main product
- Number of applications interacting via the API
- Number of new users coming through via third-party applications

To communicate this with your customer developers, the information has to be clearly available for them to read. The wording must be clear and approachable and make it easy for the developers to understand why you have the API and what you're hoping to accomplish with your platform. When putting together the message, try to avoid flat and generic text, or "sales-speak," which talks abstractly about the platform without specific examples and goals:

> *We have an API because we want to increase integration with our system for third-party applications. We have made it possible to access the users, messages, and contacts.*

This message has a lot of eye-glazing information without a good feel for the meat of the message. The first sentence can be said of every platform created, ever. APIs are always created in order to increase integration with the system. Additionally, all the access methods for the API are given equal importance, and there's no feel for what it is that the company wants to accomplish with the platform. No examples are given about what the API could be used for. If developers don't already know what they want to do with your platform, they won't suddenly have a flash of inspiration from the given phrase.

A more effective message would have a strong message about what the API was created to do, and what the company wants to accomplish with it. This is that 10-second elevator pitch discussed earlier, where you have a limited amount of time to express to the reader exactly why you have an API. Here are some examples you could use as a starting place for describing the purpose of your API:

- We created a platform so developers could find more ways for users to interact with our application. We're measuring our success by enumerating the applications with consistent, heavy usage of the type we desire—whether that's reading or writing. Our main goal with this API is to allow users to interact in whatever way makes the most sense for them.
- Our API was designed to help extend the reach of our application into other online activities. Along with the REST API, we're creating widgets to enable "sharing" or "liking" of online content.
- This web API was developed to increase the amount of content created by our users in our system. Our goal is to have unique content be 20% API-driven by the end of the year. We'll be watching the write performance of the API compared to the growth of the system in order to check its success.

Obviously the wording you use will be different, and the information will be more extensive. Feel free to take the time to expand on the information and make it more compelling and engaging. Avoid sales-speak at the abstract level and instead tell developers why you've created the system. Think of them as partners, because that's what they are: partner developers. The more they know about the point of your API, the more likely they are to create applications that dovetail nicely into your ecosystem, creating the user experiences you're trying to provide.

Once you've established *why* you have an API, you need to talk about what the API can *do*—but not in a flat, reference documentation way. Although reference documentation is indeed important, your documentation can't stop there, because developers outside your organization may not have enough context to understand how they can use these APIs to good effect. Describe a couple of use cases and what the workflow would look like. This description doesn't need to be as detailed as a tutorial would be (although these examples will likely also be in the tutorials you provide later). You need to explain what the use cases are and provide a high-level description of how tasks would be accomplished using the APIs you're providing.

Here are a couple of examples of the kind of information that should be included on the page describing your overall API strategy:

- We're looking forward to seeing developers create innovative interfaces into the system so that there are numerous ways for users to interact with the platform. Here are some examples:
  - Using the "user" API, you can get customized information about users, such as their full name and photo, in order to provide a personalized interface. Pulling the most popular shared information from their personal network, you could then allow them to share the information, comment on it, or save it to a favorites list.
  - If your system has actions associated with it—such as fitness goals, blog posts, calendar events, or game results—you can post this information to the user's timeline using the status API.
  - When the user is interacting with different content throughout your application, you can integrate related information from the timeline—or write new information to the timeline based on what users discover via your application.
- We've created several widgets and REST endpoints to enable developers to make it possible for users to share content they've found elsewhere with their personal network on the system. Here are a few ways this could be used:
  - The simple widget can be placed on any web page anywhere on the internet with a simple copy-paste of the JavaScript code. Alternately, the code can be generated with the page in order to automate adding share buttons to the pages. These widgets are updated frequently to add more functionality, such as tagging, grouping, and commenting on the content. The widgets can be set up to show how many users have shared the information.
  - While users are reading through a different interface for data, such as a magazine or news highlight application, that application can use one of the REST endpoints to allow for sharing an originating page to their network, friends, or to the larger network.
  - You can create a custom widget for sharing information that shows which of your users' friends have shared the information, what comments they've made on the content, or even which friends might be most interested in seeing a particular page.

These types of examples, on the landing page or close to it, make it far more interesting for developers to interact with your system. When you can engage them quickly and get their creative juices flowing, you'll have bought yourself some time to help them get up and running with the system. If you're able to show small example applications performing the tasks you list in the overall API system, so much the better.

9.3   *Documenting your API*

The second pillar of developer experience is documentation (see figure 9.2). Documentation covers a wide range of different methods to help developers understand the platform, work with it, and succeed in integrating the API into their own system.

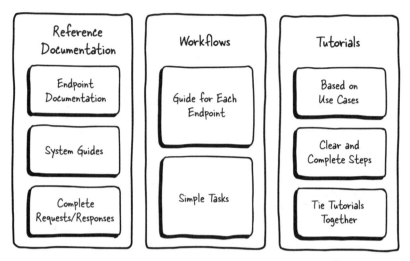

Figure 9.2   Documentation takes many forms, and it's critical to understand that reference documentation—what each endpoint does, and what the requests/responses look like—is only the beginning. Developers need to understand workflows for complicated chains of requests, and tutorials and guides are also critical to helping them understand the entire system more clearly.

The types of documentation you need to have are as follows:

- *Reference documentation*—"What does it do?" This is the documentation you're probably expecting to need. You'll be answering more specific questions such as "What does each endpoint of the platform do?" "How does a developer call it?" and "What is the expected response to a call?"
- *Workflows*—"How do I do something with the platform?" This type of documentation tells a developer how to achieve specific tasks using the platform.
- *Tutorials*—"How can I get started?" These tutorials should take your specific targeted use cases and create step-by-step guides for developers to follow in order to get started using the system, or achieve common, simple tasks. Usually the tutorials you should include are the most important items from the workflow list.

9.3.1   Reference documentation

Reference documentation is the "standard" documentation you've likely seen for APIs: a list or other way to see each of the endpoints for the platform along with a basic description of what each endpoint does. This documentation is frequently done poorly, with only a skeletal description that's difficult for outsiders to understand. Even though the reference documentation isn't going to cover all your needs, doing a great job on it is vital. When developers can't figure out how to interact with an endpoint, or with the system itself, they get frustrated quickly and your support load increases dramatically.

This section explores how you can create effective reference documentation and the advantages of each approach.

BARE MINIMUM

At a bare minimum, reference documentation must have the following:

- A catalog of endpoints to find the resource a developer is seeking
- Clear instructions on interacting with the system itself:
  - Header information
  - Authentication
  - Error codes
  - Any other general information a developer will need to make a successful call
- For each endpoint, the following is required:
  - The exact endpoint for the call
  - How to make a successful request
  - What a response will look like

Building this kind of documentation takes more time compared to much of the API documentation out in the world, but without all these items, you're leaving out information that's needed in order to figure out how to use the system. Honestly, it's frequently difficult to impose a requirement on developers to create excellent documentation. To provide this bare minimum of documentation, you can help your developers or technical writers by creating templates so that they can see exactly what's expected and required for each endpoint. It doesn't matter how you create this documentation or how you present it as long as it's understandable without any additional context.

PROVIDING OPPORTUNITIES TO EXPLORE THE API

Once your reference documentation has the basic necessities, strongly consider providing a method for exploring the API. This can be done in various ways:

- All the major schema modeling frameworks provide documentation that includes all the bare minimum requirements listed earlier along with the ability to interactively explore the endpoints without writing code and making live calls. For reference, the schema modeling frameworks I covered earlier were RAML and OpenAPI.
- There are some independent systems, like I/O Docs, that allow you to document your API and provide interactive exploration without using a formal modeling system.
- Companies like Apigee include an interactive exploration console as part of their API management offerings. The console provided by Apigee allows for simple authentication and makes live calls against the database for the user.
- If you choose to use hypermedia, you can provide a simple tool that uses those references to find related information, creating a different method for exploring the API.

Whatever path you choose, providing this kind of exploration tool will

- Help your developers answer questions about which endpoint they want to use
- Show them what a successful call looks like to a particular endpoint
- Build a strong mental model of what your overall platform looks like

When your basic reference documentation implements an exploration tool for your customer developers, it improves your developers' experience immeasurably and reduces your support burden.

All platform providers have to have some basic reference documentation available, and frequently their documentation doesn't even reach my bare minimum requirements. Keep in mind that you want your API to stand out for positive reasons: you want it to be easy for people to figure out which endpoint to use for a particular purpose, and you want developers to have confidence that they can use other endpoints, knowing that the documentation will give them a solid understanding.

9.3.2 *Workflows*

Now that we've covered the question of what each endpoint does and how the developer should work with it, it's time to answer the question of "How do I do something with your platform?" This question is rarely answered with a single endpoint; most endpoints need to be used together to create a meaningful integration into the platform. Enter workflows, the best way to answer this question for your developers.

A *workflow* describes, briefly, the steps needed to use a particular endpoint to retrieve information (see figure 9.3). It's frequently the case that one endpoint isn't usable without first calling other APIs to retrieve parameters to pass to that endpoint.

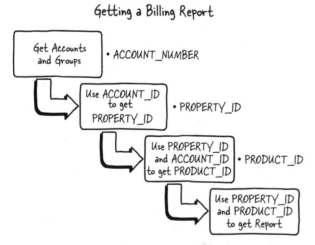

Getting a Billing Report

Get Accounts and Groups → • ACCOUNT_NUMBER

Use ACCOUNT_ID to get PROPERTY_ID → • PROPERTY_ID

Use PROPERTY_ID and ACCOUNT_ID to get PRODUCT_ID → • PRODUCT_ID

Use PROPERTY_ID and PRODUCT_ID to get Report

Figure 9.3 Getting an Akamai Billing Usage report from scratch can be somewhat daunting. You need to call three different API endpoints to get specific information in order to make the final call. Creating sample code or documenting workflows can help users get past this type of challenge with minimal frustration.

Here's an example of a workflow similar to many instances I've seen in the past:

Goal: Get a billing usage file for all products for an account

- Call one endpoint to retrieve the ACCOUNT_NUMBER.
- Using the ACCOUNT_NUMBER, call another endpoint to retrieve the PROPERTY_ID.
- Using both of these parameters, call a third endpoint to find out which PRODUCTs were active during a particular time period.
- Finally, call the billing endpoint using all of the previous pieces of information.

This workflow isn't particularly complicated. It's flowchart information describing how to use the API to retrieve information, but without this kind of additional information, it can be extremely confusing for customers who aren't sure where they should be getting these required parameters from.

Note that there's a goal at the top. Each of your workflows should describe, in narrative form, exactly what the goal is for the workflow you're including. It may, and probably will, seem painfully obvious to you and silly to include this information, but include it anyway. Your developers will thank you for the ability to scan through the workflows and find exactly the one they want, using the goals at the top of your examples.

Although your tutorials can be focused on the main use cases for the API, you need workflows for every set of endpoints to make sure that developers don't flounder around looking for the information they need. Even if the information they need isn't in the API, tell them that. It's never a bad idea to add more helpful documentation for someone who's trying to use your system.

Workflows are the cornerstone of your platform, demonstrating the various ways users can interact with the system. These workflows must be easy, straightforward, and understandable. This is a good time to talk about usability testing. As an industry, we've done an increasingly good job of testing the usability of systems we create. But the same can't be said for API developer interfaces. When you're pretty sure that you've got the workflows covered, it's a great idea to get people outside your group to try to work with each of the APIs you have, following the reference documentation and workflows that you've provided.

9.3.3 Tutorials

When my current company wanted to redo its developer portal, we reached out to the current developers and asked them what they'd like to see on the site. The overwhelming majority of the respondents replied that the thing they needed most was a Getting Started section to work through. Creating and adding this tutorial to the system increased the number of developers working with our system significantly, and we spent far less time answering simple questions from new developers.

Tutorials are one of the best ways to help developers ramp up on knowledge about your platform. In addition, creating these tutorials based on your most important use cases gives you an opportunity to help your developers understand how you want them to interact with the API.

Before I demonstrate how to write an excellent tutorial, here are some guidelines for creating these guides:

- Do not assume any specific level of knowledge for the readers.
- Have someone with excellent writing skills write the steps if at all possible. The tutorial will need to be more narrative than the reference documentation or workflows.
- If you choose to provide the tutorial in both text and video form, make sure that both stand alone as excellent narratives. Don't slight one in favor of the other; developers learn in different ways and you want to make sure the experience is great either way.
- Break down the steps into separate pages. Give each step a beginning (goal), middle (technical content), and end.
- Provide sample code that follows the tutorial so that developers can follow along without cutting/pasting or retyping code, allowing them to move more quickly and focus on understanding what's happening in the step. In terms of language to use, it's great if you can provide different programming languages, but if not, be considerate of students who might not be familiar with the programming language you choose.
- At the end of each step, give the student a virtual high five for having accomplished the task.
- Tie related tutorials together in a Choose Your Own Adventure presentation to encourage developers to work through multiple tutorials in a row and get a good, deep understanding of the system.

When creating a Getting Started tutorial it's quite important to realize that this tutorial aims at developers who are not at all familiar with your system. Everything you can do to make this more accessible for your readers is helpful. My experience with the tutorial we've made, which is now quite well received and meets most developers' needs, was this:

- I started out with a simple Python code sample (shown later in this chapter), and we made step-by-step instructions for how to implement it.
- The authentication steps turned out to be difficult for developers to follow, so I added a new script to simplify the integration of authentication information into their system for use by the sample code.
- We discovered that on Windows boxes, the SSL implementation in Python doesn't work in versuib 2.7 (except in Cygwin), or in Python 3.3, so I had to come up with another way for Windows users to work through the Getting Started tutorial.
- I created a Docker container (as I did for this book) so that the developers could pull the container onto their system and follow along with the examples, and also use the other sample code in the repository.

The acceptance tests created in chapter 8 are a great place to get outlines for your tutorials. One of the examples from that chapter was as follows:

Acceptance test case: Add new pizza topping

- Get a list of pizza toppings in the system
- Verify that the new topping doesn't exist
- Add a new topping to the system
- Get the list of pizza toppings
- Verify that the new topping has been added

GETTING STARTED: INTRODUCTION

To get started on a tutorial, you'll want to write a short introduction to it. Restating the acceptance test in this section is an excellent idea, because it gives the developer the opportunity to know which steps are included. Start out with a summary of what task the tutorial is modeling for the student.

> *In this tutorial, you will be adding a new pizza topping to the system. To do this, it's critical that the system is checked to verify that the topping isn't already there. Additionally, you will check the topping list after adding it to make sure that the topping has been added correctly. The samples will be created in Python, but the code is quite well commented and runs as written. Rather than focus on the code itself, focus on the concepts in the tutorial.*

This simple introduction helps to add context for developers. They'll understand what they'll be doing, and it should make it quite simple to follow the instructions.

INDIVIDUAL STEPS

Each step should be presented on its own page, although you can combine two related steps into a single step that's slightly more complicated. For this example, I'll merge "Get a list of toppings" and "Check to make sure that the topping doesn't exist." This example will be in Python, but I'll comment the code clearly. The reason I use Python for my example code and tutorials is that it's the easiest language to read if you don't know the language yourself. It reads similarly to English, and when you're creating code samples for tutorials or other learning, you can increase the readability with code comments and clearly defined variable names.

Sample tutorial step one: get a list of toppings

For the first step, you'll be getting a list of current toppings from the system. To retrieve this list, you need to send a GET request to the toppings (linked to the reference documentation) endpoint:

```
GET /api/v1.0/toppings
```

This code will return a JSON array of toppings that you can work with:

```
{u'toppings':
    [
        {u'id': 1, u'title': u'pepperoni'},
        {u'id': 2, u'title': u'peppers'}
    ]
}
```

(continued)

Once you have the list, you can check to make sure that the topping in question doesn't yet exist. The following Python code can be found at http://toppings .com/code_samples. The code works with Python 2.7. Minor changes are needed for Python 3.3, and that code is available in the repository as well.

```python
#! /usr/bin/python

# Create a variable to hold the topping name
topping_to_check = "Sun-dried Tomatoes"
topping_in_list = False

import urlparse as parse
import requests

# Create an HTTP session for making requests
session = requests.Session()

# Make the HTTP request to the toppings endpoint
toppings_result =
    session.get("http://www.irresistibleapis.com/api/v1.0/toppings")

# Transform the result from JSON into an object for the "toppings" item
toppings_list = toppings_result.json()["toppings"]

# Iterate over the topping list to check for the specific topping
for topping in toppings_list:
    if topping["title"] == topping_to_check:
        topping_in_list = False

if topping_in_list:
    print "In List"
else:
    print "Not in List"
```

In this example:

- I gave an exact example for what comes back from an API call.
- The code sample is simple and straightforward.
- I didn't use any fancy functions or abstract concepts, and I added a healthy number of code comments.

At the end of each step, congratulate the student for having accomplished the task in question. And after all the steps, summarize the task again and how it was accomplished. Then point students to other tutorials they might want to move forward with to continue their exploration of the system.

9.4   *Building blocks*

As I've mentioned, marketing to developers is not like marketing to other people. As developers, we like to see examples of things and be given building blocks to work with. Most developers I've met would rather stick a fork in their own eye than read through a PowerPoint presentation or sit through an abstract "Buzzword Bingo" meeting without any hands-on content. You can choose among several different ways to provide a coder with pieces to build from, or show them how something works from the code side rather than showing pictures to describe the overall effect. Detailed, hands-on toys that allow developers to build working models are the best way to reach them.

9.4.1 Sample code

One of the first things that developers will seek out once they've learned what they want to do with your system, or even while they're exploring, is sample code that lets them get started using the system right away. It's important to provide an easy way for them to learn about the authentication system for your platform, but it's equally important to give them some building blocks to start working directly with the system as quickly and efficiently as possible.

AUTHENTICATION LIBRARIES

When a developer starts working with your system, the number one difficulty encountered is generally related to authentication and authorization. Providing supported libraries in as many programming libraries as possible is critical to making sure that clients written for your platform use the authentication mechanism in a reasonable way. Most authentication systems require knowledge of both encryption and the HTTP protocol. Cryptographic signing algorithms are complicated to create, and it's easy to make mistakes when creating a signing library. Leaving this task to your developers, who aren't likely experts in this field, creates unnecessary work for them, as well as a strong likelihood that there are some incorrect assumptions in their code.

When providing a signing library, you also need to include a great README file to help your developers implement the code—code guidance that makes it simple to integrate the code into their client. The Akamai platform has many signing libraries available in the GitHub repository that follow these guidelines at www.github.com /akamai-open.

Besides this requirement, it's quite helpful to provide sample code for most, if not all, of the endpoints in your platform. The next section discusses how to create useful sample code and provide it in a form and location that's useful for your customer developers.

REFERENCE IMPLEMENTATIONS AND CODE SAMPLES

Working examples for the endpoints, workflows, and integration possibilities make it quick and easy for a developer to see how to interact with different endpoints. Even if you don't have code for each endpoint, the more code you have available, the better. You can run reports on your API to see which APIs are called the most by your customers and be guided by that knowledge when making your sample code. Additionally, when meeting with or training your customers, be sure to make a note of the functions the customers are most excited about. Even if they're asking for something a bit more complicated, providing sample code for that use case helps you serve that customer as well as other customers.

Great sample code does the following:

- Demonstrates one of the workflows you included in the documentation
- Avoids any tricky mapping or abstract functions
- Provides debugging output so that the user can see what the conversation between server and client includes
- Is consistent across all the examples in terms of error handling, debugging, and verbose output

An example of good sample code is found in the following listing, which is used by Akamai as part of the Getting Started tutorials. It includes the use of an authentication mechanism and an example set of calls to the diagnostic tools endpoint. The code itself does something simple—calling the standard network utility `dig`, but even this makes for a great Getting Started guide, as most engineers are familiar with this utility, so the only thing they're focused on is the interaction with the system.

Listing 9.1 Basic API sample code

```
#! /usr/bin/env python
# Very basic script demonstrating diagnostic tools functionality
#
import requests, logging, json, sys
from http_calls import EdgeGridHttpCaller
from random import randint
from akamai.edgegrid import EdgeGridAuth
from config import EdgeGridConfig
import urllib
session = requests.Session()
debug = False
verbose = False
section_name = "default"

# If all parameters are set already, use them. Otherwise
# use the configuration from the ~/.edgerc file
config = EdgeGridConfig({},section_name)

# Allow for command line or configuration file inclusion
# of "verbose" and "debug"
if hasattr(config, "debug") and config.debug:
    debug = True

if hasattr(config, "verbose") and config.verbose:
    verbose = True


# Set the config options
# This is the standard method for all of our signing
# libraries in every language - set the authentication
# for a standard HTTP library using the client_token,
# client_secret and access_token
session.auth = EdgeGridAuth(
    client_token=config.client_token,
    client_secret=config.client_secret,
    access_token=config.access_token
)
```

```
if hasattr(config, 'headers'):
    session.headers.update(config.headers)

# Set the baseurl based on the 'host' information in the
# configuration file
baseurl = '%s://%s/' % ('https', config.host)
httpCaller = EdgeGridHttpCaller(session, debug,verbose, baseurl)

# Request locations that support the diagnostic-tools
print
print ("Requesting locations that support the diagnostic-tools API.\n")

location_result = httpCaller.getResult('/diagnostic-tools/v1/locations')

# Choose the first location for the diagnostic_tools call
location = location_result['locations'][0]
print ("We will make our call from " + location + "\n")

# Request the dig information for {OPEN} Developer Site
dig_parameters = { "hostname":"developer.akamai.com.", "location":location,
    "queryType":"A" }

dig_result = httpCaller.getResult("/diagnostic-tools/v1/dig",dig_parameters)

# Display the results from dig
print (dig_result['dig']['result'])
```

This example demonstrates several useful patterns. It's clearly demonstrating a fairly simple workflow:

- Request the locations from the platform
- Select a location from the list
- Make a `dig` call using this location

Without sample code and a workflow example, developers were getting confused about where to get the location information in order to make the `dig` request. There are two requests to the system:

```
GET /diagnostic-tools/v1/locations
GET /diagnostic-tools/v1/dig?\
hostname=developer.akamai.com&queryType=A&location=Schiphol%2C+Netherlands
```

In this case, the example shows how to make a call with and without extra parameters, in the code language being used.

Note that in the case of Akamai, we've created the `diagnostic-tools` script in six different languages, and we have a goal of including all the languages we have libraries for. The more examples you can provide that are meaningful to the most customers, the more success they'll have without needing direct handholding from you.

9.4.2 *Reference applications*

Sample code is generally about a simple workflow—figuring out how to get specific information from an API endpoint. To create a meaningful application, many of these will need to be combined together. Providing a couple of sample applications that are more functional is a great way to help developers see how to work with complicated data from the API. If you check the GitHub repository for Akamai, you'll find a few application examples using Node.js. In fact, one of the examples was documented in seven separate blog posts on the forum so that users could work through the example from start to finish and run it on their own system to browse through the information it provided.

9.4.3 *Tools and techniques*

An excellent teaching/guiding set of tools and techniques should be available to help your developers learn about the whole set of APIs provided by your team. As different people learn in different ways, so too do different people like to explore and understand topics in their own direction. Provide tools and techniques that help each user learn about your system in the way that makes the most sense to that individual.

USING API CONSOLES TO UNDERSTAND CALLS

Earlier, in section 9.3.1, I provided a short description of API consoles. For an example, take a look at figure 9.4, a screenshot of the Apigee console for the Twitter API. This is a great example of using a console to look inside a successful request to the API. I've set up the tool to use OAuth authentication, which represents synedra on twitter—hence, synedra-twitter. Any calls I make to the system will happen on behalf of this user. Below that section is an area where you can pick out which API you want to call using the console.

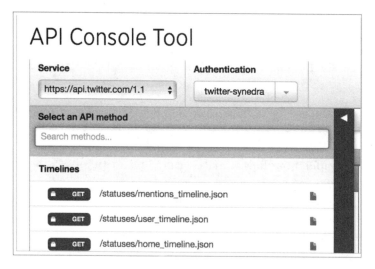

Figure 9.4   The Apigee console for exploring the Twitter API lists the most common endpoints in the Twitter API, making it easy to understand the breadth of information available via the platform. The authentication can be activated to use your Twitter identity, using OAuth, so that the API responses are exactly what you see when accessing Twitter directly.

As an example, I'll select the `/statuses/home_timeline.json` option. Figure 9.5 shows the result of this query. The screenshot doesn't show the response headers (although if you scroll up they're there), nor does it show the entirety of a request. I encourage you to play with this console yourself at https://dev.twitter.com/rest/tools/console.

The Apigee console is available on its website. You can build your own Apigee-to-go console to embed in your developer documentation. A generic console is also offered at https://apigee.com/console/others.

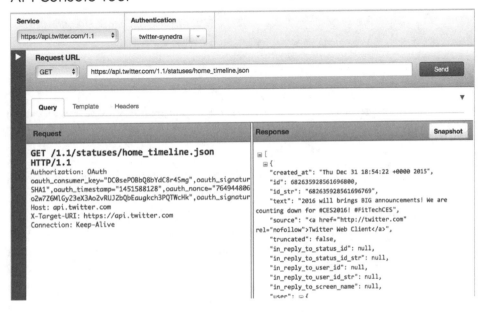

Figure 9.5 For the Twitter API, there are example calls for the majority of the Twitter endpoints. Selecting one of these demonstrates what the request and authentication look like, and how the response is formatted.

Figure 9.6 demonstrates how the Apigee generic console can be used to access the Irresistible API. As you can see, if it's a simple enough API, it's easy to fit everything in one screenshot.

A couple of other consoles available—in fact, all the schema modeling languages I discussed—make it simple to create mini-consoles for all the calls. The difference between a schema model–based example call and a console call is that the console is making the request directly to the API, whereas the schema model will only return exactly what appears in the document. Both are valuable, but it's worth considering whether you should add the console to the toolboxes of your users in order to provide that extra dose of confidence live calls make. In addition, providing examples of

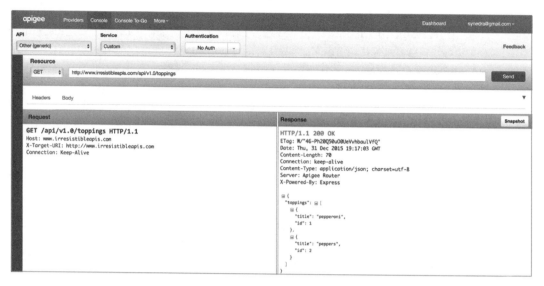

Figure 9.6 The Apigee generic console can be used to call the `/toppings` resource from irresistibleapis.com, making it possible to see all of the request and response information in an easy-to-read format. This enables you, or your users, to easily explore and understand the various endpoints.

successful calls can help developers debug their calls themselves, by showing what the exact request path, body, and headers should be to get the desired response.

COMMAND-LINE UTILITIES

Consoles are great, but the utility is pretty much bounded in the web page. It's not possible to interact with the input/output without copying and pasting. If a developer can successfully make the call from the command line, it becomes much easier to grab the result and stick it in a file or process it with a local script. There are two main command-line utilities for making HTTP calls:

- curl—The curl command is the old standby. Most developers and system administrators are familiar with the curl command as a way to request web pages. It can, and does, get used to scrape web pages and is quite useful for grabbing HTML files in order to process them. But it's not tuned for API use, and the output formatting makes it difficult to visually parse the response for a request to a JSON-formatted REST API call. Additionally, creating a custom authorization module is not straightforward, and so companies frequently "wrap" curl to include the authentication in the calls (which means the credentials are likely to be passed on the command line).

- HTTPie—HTTPie was recently written as a command-line alternative, and it's strongly tied to API calls. JSON responses are formatted well, with color coding and indentation. Writing an authentication plug-in is relatively easy, and because of this several HTTPie authentication plug-ins are available. It's open source, free, and definitely worth including in the documentation as an easy way to interact with the API from the command line.

OTHER TOOLS

Several places in the book have pointed to different tools and techniques you might well want to share with your developers. Remember, the more information you provide to them about ways to interact with the system, the more likely they are to become engaged, productive members of your community.

- *HTTP sniffers*—These tools make it possible to watch the traffic as it flows to and from your personal device. They are great, but some of these tools (such as HTTPScoop) can only view HTTP traffic, which locks out any debugging of traffic. Those that do provide a proxy answer to sniffing HTTPS (Charles, Fiddler) are sometimes still not able to see the traffic if the API engine has been set up to disallow proxy calls.
- *Code debugging*—Teach your developers how to inject error handling and HTTP debugging into their code. All your code samples should support this by default. More information is almost always better, and it means that your developers will ask more meaningful questions.
- *Building clients from schema models*—Each of the schema modeling systems I've discussed have open source tools available to allow your developers to bootstrap a simple client so they can work from there to build exactly what they want. When you don't have sample code for a particular endpoint, make it easy for your developers to leverage the base API design document to get where they're going as easily as possible.

There's no specific list of tools you should provide guides for or make available to your developers. Listen to your partner developers to understand where their pain points are in getting started, working with your simple APIs, or integrating your more complex APIs. Then find ways—even odd, unconventional ways—to help the developers succeed at what they're trying to achieve.

9.5   *Developer support*

The final pillar of developer experience is developer support. As with the other pillars, I'm going to tell you that it's critically important to the success of your API. It's arguably the most important piece because your developers will only need help of this type when they're stuck and frustrated. If you don't provide excellent support, you can encounter various challenges:

- Developers could get frustrated and give up on using the API. They may come up with different, inefficient, or unsupported answers to their problems.
- Although slighting any facet of the developer experience can make developers grumpy, failing to respond to a specific blocker can create a great deal of loud, negative sentiment for your team among the developers.
- Taking the time to listen to the challenges that your users have can help you improve the experience for future developers by making answers excellent and making sure they're findable within your portal.

In short, it's extremely important to have a plan for how you're going to actively support your developers *before* your API gets deployed.

Some companies have the resources to provide support around the clock—and APIs that need that level of attention. But most APIs, in particular when they start out, can get by on much less support. The better you've done with the earlier items in this chapter—with communication, documentation, and tools and techniques—the less support you'll need to do.

What is important, though, is that your developers know what kind of turnaround they can expect for questions they ask. It's best to try to get back to developers with questions within a business day. Your developer portal needs to be organized well so that the information they're seeking is easy to find.

There are two different areas of support to consider. The first is interactive support, such as a forum, help desk, or email alias, where developers can ask specific questions and receive answers from your team. Based on the interactions you have, you can, over time, build up a noninteractive repository of blog or forum posts, or create a FAQ, to help future developers find the answers they need quickly.

9.5.1 *Interactive*

Interactive support is generally the mainstay of your developer support program. This is the system you implement in order to handle the questions from developers and the answers you provide.

SUPPORT MODELS

You can use many different mechanisms to handle this type of support, and each has its advantages and disadvantages:

- *Email alias*—This is the most common support methodology that companies implement, and it's a tempting proposition. It's free, customers know how to use it, and it doesn't take any time to set up. But an email support queue has several problems:
  - There's no archive but individual email archives.
  - You aren't building a knowledge base out of the interactions you have with your customers.
  - If someone leaves the company, all the interactions that person had will evaporate.
  - There's no way to find similar questions/answers to add more appropriate assistance.
- *Help desk application*—This is a great option for many companies that want to give users a personalized feel while building up a knowledge base, but the system is somewhat closed to visitors and won't necessarily help them find information that they need.
- *Forum*—This is the most time-intensive, but it creates a knowledge base as it goes along, so that customers and visitors can type a question into the search box and find appropriate previous threads. Additionally, this system supports

posts with tutorials or overarching posts about the system, allowing you to cover frequently asked questions in a deliberate way.

Selecting the correct model for you will take time, and you may go through a few different options before you land on the one that works best for you.

EFFICIENT INTERACTION

As you run through different interactions, you'll probably encounter many developers who don't ask questions efficiently. It's critical to set context when providing documentation, and it's important for developers to give you the right context when they're asking for help. The experience when the context isn't set looks a lot like this:

> *Q:* This is broken. Help.
>
> *A:* What is broken?
>
> *Q:* The cookbook endpoint.
>
> *A:* What happened?
>
> *Q:* It didn't return all the books.
>
> *A:* What were you doing at the time?
>
> *Q:* Trying to get a list of 1999 cookbooks.
>
> *A:* What did you expect to get?
>
> *Q:* A list of all of the 1999 and later cookbooks.
>
> *A:* That's not how it works.

Okay, that's a little drawn out, but I've seen so many conversations that go through these cycles, and seriously, there's little that's more frustrating for any human than having to keep iterating on a problem that's not working. Teach your developers to ask questions well. If they don't, give them the pattern so they get it on the second iteration. It looks like this:

- I did X.
- I expected Y to happen.
- To my dismay, Z happened instead.

You may argue that the second section isn't needed, but trust me, it is. So many "broken" things are "broken expectations." Note that this is still a bug in your product, but it's a documentation bug. You set their expectations incorrectly. To illuminate the types of problems you might see, here's an example:

- I jumped off a cliff.
- I expected to sprout wings and fly.
- To my dismay, I plunged to my death instead.

See there? It's not a bug in gravity. The problem was with the expectation. If they'd said, "I jumped off a cliff and plunged to my death!" you'd be hard-pressed to understand why this was an unexpected result. Help your customers to give you good, complete questions so that you can answer their question and quell their frustration with one or two interactions instead of dragging both of you through the mud.

9.5.2 *Noninteractive*

As you answer questions that users have, you'll likely experience clumps of questions related to particular issues, which is your signal that it's time to create some noninteractive information. Yes, when a conversation happens in your forum (or other system), there's an archive of that information, but sometimes you need to start at a higher level and walk people through the solution step by step. In those cases you'll want to create static content so that when people search on a particular topic, they find a fully fleshed-out answer to the question.

Here are some examples of topics that I've written blog posts to clarify:

- *Purge*—Several different APIs at Akamai allow customers to purge the content from the edge (cache) systems. But how they interact, which one is current, and how to plan for the future is not at all clear. I wrote a post clarifying what a new integration should do and how.
- *Tutorial*—We created a set of seven blog posts within the forum system explaining how to create a sample application around one of our more complicated API systems.
- *Context*—We wrote a few different posts explaining how our system worked and what users should expect when working with it.

9.6 *Summary*

This chapter explored the following:

- *Pillars of developer experience*—You learned the essential factors for ensuring that your developers achieve success easily and quickly.
- *Clear communication and a discussion of the various types of information to share with your developers*—Consistent, clear, and transparent messages about your business value, metrics, and expected use cases are critical to creating a great developer experience.
- *Documentation*—Although reference documentation is vital, it's not the only type of documentation needed for your API clients to thrive. Even more essential is information on what can be done with your API and tutorials to guide developers through the process of accomplishing those tasks.
- *Building blocks*—Developers respond enthusiastically to sample code and applications—examples to help them get started quickly and effectively. Additionally, libraries to abstract difficult tasks such as authentication can smooth out the trickier tasks on your platform.
- *Support*—Providing a consistent method of asking questions, finding answers, and learning new information about the system is equally important to the other pillars. Whichever method you choose, whether it be a forum, email, or some other mechanism, the most important piece of support is making sure that your customers understand where to get help and what kind of response time to expect.

index

RELATED MANNING TITLES

Amazon Web Services in Action
by Michael Wittig and Andreas Wittig

ISBN: 9781617292880
424 pages, $49.99
September 2015

Secrets of the JavaScript Ninja,
Second Edition
by John Resig, Bear Bibeault, and Josip Maras

ISBN: 9781617292859
464 pages, $44.99
August 2016

Elastic Leadership
Growing self-organizing teams
by Roy Osherove

ISBN: 9781617293085
325 pages, $39.99
October 2016

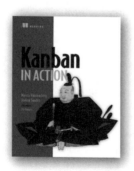

Kanban in Action
by Marcus Hammarberg and Joakim Sundén

ISBN: 9781617291050
360 pages, $44.99
February 2014

For ordering information go to www.manning.com